SECULARIZATION WITHOUT END

The Yusko Ward-Phillips Lectures
in English Language and Literature

SECULARIZATION WITHOUT END

■ BECKETT, MANN, COETZEE ■

Vincent P. Pecora

University of Notre Dame Press
Notre Dame, Indiana

Library of Congress Cataloging-in-Publication Data

Pecora, Vincent P., 1953–
Secularization Without End : Beckett, Mann, Coetzee / Vincent P. Pecora.
pages   cm. — (The Yusko Ward-Phillips Lectures in
English Language and Literature)
Includes bibliographical references and index.
ISBN 978-0-268-03899-1 (pbk. : alk. paper)
ISBN 0-268-03899-6 (pbk. : alk. paper)
1. Fiction—20th century—History and criticism.
2. Secularism in literature. 3. Religion and literature.
4. Secularization (Theology)—History—20th century.   I. Title.
PN3351.P43   2015
809'.93382—dc23
2014047516

For

OLIVIA AND AVA

When man has been taught that no good thing remains in his power,

and that he is hedged about on all sides by most miserable necessity,

in spite of this he should nevertheless be instructed to aspire

to a good of which he is empty, to a freedom of which he has been deprived.

—JOHN CALVIN

■ CONTENTS ■

■ A C K N O W L E D G M E N T S ■

This book began with an invitation to give the Ward-Phillips Lectures for 2013, hosted by the English Department at the University of Notre Dame. I am deeply grateful for the opportunity to deliver the lectures that became this volume. I owe special thanks to Elliott Visconsi, who conveyed the invitation and patiently worked through possible topics with me; to David Wayne Thomas, who was a splendid host during my time at Notre Dame; to Henry Weinfield, who proved to be an astute and indefatigable interlocutor, and who forced me to sharpen my argument; and to the many faculty members and graduate students who generously offered comments on my presentations. I benefitted from the chance to deliver a nascent version of the chapter on Samuel Beckett to the English Department at the University of California, Los Angeles, for which I must thank Ali Behdad; I am also grateful to Michael North, who offered insightful queries about my approach to Beckett's work, and to Debora Shuger, whose long support for my engagement with questions of religion and secularization is something I hold dear. Jon Snyder kindly invited me to present an even earlier and less developed version of the project to the Department of Italian and French and the Department of Religious Studies at the University of California, Santa Barbara. I am especially indebted to Jon and Lucia Re, whose hospitality is second to none, and to Enda Duffy, who convinced me (perhaps inadvertently) that J. M. Coetzee needed to be part of what I was trying to say. Kathryn Stelmach Artuso gave me the opportunity to present the introduction and key parts of later chapters to the Western Regional Conference on Christianity and Literature at Westmont College, where the response was astute, challenging, and very enjoyable, and where I benefitted especially from Kevin Seidel's provocative questions. Nancy Ruttenberg invited me to take part in a conference at the Center for the Study of the Novel at Stanford University, where I presented an early draft of my introduction, and where Franco Moretti graciously responded with a simple question that forced me to think more deliberately about how to approach the nature of religious belief in the novel. This conference also allowed me to learn much from conversations with Derek Attridge, whose work has been of singular importance to the study of Coetzee. Robert Hudson invited me to give a lecture at the Generative Anthropology Summer Conference at Westminster College, where I presented another very early version of my first chapter and benefitted from the give-and-take with Eric Gans and many others. Bruce Robbins invited me to join a panel at a meeting of the Society for Novel Studies. His comments, along with those of fellow panelist Simon During, were very helpful in rethinking my general approach. Nancy Armstrong's support at this time was also very welcome. Finally, I must thank Susan Hegeman, who asked me for an entry on the topic of religion for *The Encyclopedia of the Novel* (Blackwell, 2010), an entry that became the intellectual seed for the introduction to this book.

The entire manuscript received superb readings from the two reviewers for Notre Dame Press, Thomas Pfau and Russell Berman. Their careful attention to the details of my argument, and especially their learned advice concerning the chapter on Thomas Mann, improved the manuscript immeasurably. Scott Black, a colleague in the University of Utah English Department, offered important advice on my treatment of Cervantes. I must also thank Stephen Little, acquisitions editor at Notre Dame Press, for his enormous help in guiding the project through the early stages; Kellie M. Hultgren, whose remarkable attention to the text in the copy-editing phase—and in several languages—has saved me from much embarrassment; Wendy McMillen, whose intelligence and patience in working out the design of the book are greatly appreciated; and Rebecca R. DeBoer, the managing editor for the project.

Not least, I want to thank my students in two classes at the University of Utah—an undergraduate senior seminar on Samuel Beckett and J. M. Coetzee, and a graduate seminar on the idea of political theology and allegory that concluded with Coetzee's *The Childhood of Jesus*—for their contributions to this book. They asked questions I had not considered, pointed to telling details that I very much needed to address, and generally demonstrated a level of engagement with the novels of Beckett and Coetzee that challenged me to be clearer and more precise, but also told me that there might be even more going on in the novels than I had initially imagined. After all this help, the flaws that remain in the book are entirely of my own devising.

Finally, I must thank the University of Utah, which generously provided me with a year's sabbatical during the book's composition.

Introduction

Secularization and the History of the Novel

When future generations of scholars look back at the last half of the twentieth century, they may conclude that it was less an era when formalism, Marxism, psychoanalysis, deconstruction, and new historicism competed with one another for intellectual credibility than an age in which the secular criticism of literary texts rose to dominance. They may also conclude that this secular approach to literature accounts in large part for the emergence of the novel as *the* most salient and significant object of literary interpretation in the academy. For surely, during this period, no literary genre came to exemplify the advent of secular society and culture more fully than did the novel, and no elaboration of the meaning of secular society and culture was complete without careful consideration of the novel. It would be no exaggeration to say that if the last half of the twentieth century began with Ian Watt's claim, in *The Rise of the Novel*, that the novel was one of the most important products of secular society, we have now arrived at the far more remarkable claim that modern secular society is itself the product of the novel. In *Love's Knowledge*, Martha Nussbaum reads the genre primarily as an elaboration of secular moral philosophy.[1] And in the first chapter of *Inventing Human Rights*, Lynn Hunt locates the beginnings of human empathy itself— somewhat surprisingly for anyone familiar with the great world religions—in books such as Samuel Richardson's *Clarissa* (1747–48).[2] Given so Eurocentric an approach, one can only wonder how the Arabs, the Indians, and the Chinese survived for so long without empathy while they waited for a translation of *Clarissa* to be smuggled across the borders. The result is what David Foster Wallace, when not writing about the Jesuit substitute teacher for the Advanced Tax course at DePaul University who describes the analytical concentration needed for "real-world accounting" as nothing short of "heroism," might have called "the teeming wormball of data and rule and exception and contingency" that makes modern interpretation of the novel something akin to the interpretation of modernity itself.[3]

This book is instead about what I would call the afterlife of the novel, the word *afterlife* here meaning (a) the novel's current belatedness as a secular, realistic literary form (it lost the ability to compete in terms of realism with cinema in the 1930s and television in the 1950s, and newer electronic media, including electronic literatures, have made the genre seem all the more quaint) and (b) the lively reemergence within the novel of certain, supposedly forgotten, religious discourses that become legible by means of—indeed, I will claim because of—the secular trajectory of the prose that is its vehicle. Such an afterlife is not a neatly circumscribable period of literary history; it has no obvious beginning point. If one must identify a progenitor, Franz Kafka will do. But the authors found at the heart of this book are all exemplary manifestations of a profound and almost inhuman shame at the fate of being human, and as I hope to show, this shame is given new force after 1945 even as it draws upon some of the most disturbing yet consequential motifs—the inescapable corruption of the human spirit and the helplessness invoked by divine election—in all of Christian theology.[4]

▪   ▪   ▪

Watt published *The Rise of the Novel* in 1957 and in many ways set the tone for the next fifty years' identification of the novelistic and the secular. He certainly does not ignore the Puritan inheritance in Defoe or in English literature as a whole, but the secularization narrative that Watt borrows largely from Max Weber eventually nullifies this heritage as so much ideology. That neither Chaucer's nor Shakespeare's characters really fit Watt's claim that pre-eighteenth-century individuals had little moral autonomy and "depended on divine persons" for their meaning—tell that to the Wife of Bath or to Macbeth— we will simply excuse as a function of Watt's youthful irrational exuberance.[5] But it was precisely Watt's cavalier way of summing up entire epochs that allowed the novel to take on the function that would come to be most often assigned to it, that of the leading cultural instrument of Weber's rising bourgeoisie. Members of that class, having been instructed by Luther that a worldly calling was every bit as pleasing to God as a religious one, and finding intolerable the depressing isolation into which Calvin's ideas about predestination threw them, began to look for the signs of their possible salvation in terms of worldly, secular, and capitalist success.

Those who followed in Watt's steps—and they are legion— fleshed out the Weberian narrative he started, none more fully than Michael McKeon. While, like Watt before him, McKeon claims to be skeptical of Weber's logic—he stresses instead the "absolutism" of a Pietism that paradoxically reforms "absolutely" enough to overturn the old religious order—it is Weber who again finally rules this new version of the novel's rise.[6] By the time we get to Franco Moretti's two-volume (four in Italian!) *summa romanorum*, it would have been quite a shock *not* to find Jack Goody writing, in the opening pages, the following remarkably unremarkable lines. "The modern novel, after Daniel Defoe, was essentially a secular tale, a feature that is comprised within the meaning of 'realistic.' The hand of God may appear, but it does so through 'natural' sequences, not through miracles or mirabilia. Earlier narrative structures often displayed such intervention, which, in a world suffused by the supernatural, was present everywhere."[7] When I first read Goody's sweeping dictum, I wondered whether Goody had simply confused Protestantism with secularism—both of which eschew miracles. And then I wondered whether that rakehell Christopher Marlowe or any of his less savory friends actually ever imagined a world "suffused by the supernatural," or whether Shakespeare—whose Cassius, alluding to what was once

thought to be Sallust's advice to Caesar "that every man is the architect of his own fortune," tells Brutus that "men at some time are
masters of their fates"—ever really believed (as Goody maintains)
that divine intervention was "present everywhere."[8] To contemporary
critical discourse, Moretti himself contributes the wonderful term *fillers*: that is, the expansion of mundane passages of conversation or
description in the realistic novel in which nothing seems to happen.
Honoré de Balzac's *Illusions perdues* (1837–43), George Eliot's *Middlemarch* (1871–72), and Thomas Mann's *Buddenbrooks* (1901) are
apparently full of them. Moretti's explanation for fillers is Weberian
routinization in a nutshell, as applied to the novel: "Fillers are an attempt at *rationalizing the novelistic universe*: turning it into a world
of few surprises, fewer adventures, and no miracles at all."[9] By this
measure, we could say that all of Henry James is one long filler—
though on closer inspection we might say it is a peculiarly Puritan
and confessional sort of filler. People still go to church in Henry
Fielding; Laurence Sterne comically adapted his own sermons for
Tristram Shandy. But the thesis of the secularizing novel pays little
attention to such topical embellishments, for it assumes from the start
that the novel is the aesthetic exemplification of the deists' universe,
with its *deus absconditus* and Weberian social rationalization.

That we have now reached the point, with Nussbaum and Hunt,
at which the history of the novel has actually come to supplant the
history of religion as the basis of our moral sensibility—indeed, of
human empathy itself—might for some raise the possibility that the
secularization represented, and perhaps inaugurated, by the novel
might not be as straightforward an affair as it sometimes appears to be
in Watt or McKeon or Goody. If for many of its early readers the
novel was in fact a secular substitute for diminishing religious feeling,
then we might do well to consider Hans Blumenberg's sense that Enlightenment rationality was often pressed into service as a "formal
reoccupation" of now "vacant" theological "answer positions."[10] In
this light, the Weberian interpretation of the genre always seems to
be haunted by that of Weber's Hegelian and then Marxian student,
Georg Lukács. In the view of the early Lukács, the novel was the
supreme expression of nostalgia for the "immanence" of meaning

once supplied by religion and the epic. Lukács's novel is a secularized epic, and he specifies the "answer position" the novel has come to reoccupy: "The novel is the epic of a world that has been abandoned by God."[11] The novelist's irony, "with intuitive double vision, can see where God is to be found in a world abandoned by God" (Lukács, *Theory*, 92). Lukács subtly reworks the perspective of Hegel, who elaborates the novel (most obviously the genre of bildungsroman initiated by Goethe's *Wilhelm Meisters Lehrjahre* [1795–96] and its sequels) as exemplifying the unfortunate way irony dominates modern culture. What was fatally missing in the novel, Hegel claimed, was *earnestness*, which means that the novel lacked all capacity for epic achievement and forms of understanding that transcend the quotidian pursuits of everyday life—which is what fillers represent. Lukács turned Hegel's criticism of the novel's formal failing into a brilliant, melancholy commentary on its spiritual homelessness. "The novel is the form of the epoch of absolute sinfulness," Lukács wrote in starkly Augustinian-Calvinist terms, borrowing his phrase from J. G. Fichte, and the novel's irony negatively illuminated culture's profound longing for a world redeemed from its sublunary bad faith and emptiness (Lukács, *Theory*, 152). I like to think that the novel Lukács had most in mind here is Stendhal's *Le Rouge et le Noir* (1830), for it is Stendhal with his liberal, Jansenist (that is, pseudo-Calvinist) sensibility who writes that Julien Sorel (in many ways a distorted version of Stendhal himself), awaiting his execution, realizes that there is no "natural law," as his prosecutors have alleged, indeed nothing "natural" at all beyond force and want, so that honorable men are no more than "rogues" who have not been caught red-handed.[12] Contemplating his fate, he "began laughing like Mephistopheles," but at the same time as one who "sees clearly into his own heart" for the first time (Stendhal, *Scarlet*, 503). Absolute sinfulness is not far off the mark, however much sympathy Stendhal may have felt for Julien, whose sins and subsequent disgrace are the whole point of the novel.

Lukács famously abandoned all this metaphysical handwringing for the clearer (if somewhat bloodier) certainties of Stalinism. But the underlying idea that the novel's manifest secularism was at the same time a mode of ironic mourning, even melancholia, for a narrative immanence and wholeness it could not recover never really disappears from either the novel or our accounts of the novel's secularity. Odysseus, we recall, just wants to get home. When he does, he never asks, and does not need to ask, "But what have I done with my life?" as Virginia Woolf's Mrs. Ramsay does in *To the Lighthouse*.[13] About a decade before Watt's game-changing intervention, Erich Auerbach produced his *Mimesis*, a still-unparalleled history of the novel's career as the genre in which secularization in a Lukácsian rather than Weberian sense predominates. Over time, the formal alterations to the genre delineated by Auerbach transcend the "absolute sinfulness" of Lukácsian despair in what is, finally, a full-throated German, Lutheran, Hegelian *Beruf*—a call to earnest, nonmiraculous, democratic Reformation Christianity, despite all of Hitler's grotesque efforts to derail that story. Auerbach's focus is narrative form broadly conceived, including drama and verse. But it is the novel that occupies most of his attention after Cervantes' *Don Quixote* (1605), and it is the novel that becomes the robust telos of Auerbach's primary thesis. Yet this thesis depends on a notion of secularization more evident in Lukács (and throughout Hegel's work) than in the later criticism of Watt, McKeon, Moretti, and others. Auerbach's sympathetic, nonsystematic perspective is the final product of the long development of Christian humanism in Europe, beginning in what Auerbach discerns as the mixture of styles and the imaginative sympathy granting tragic sublimity to the lowest social orders in the Gospel of Mark (a sympathy absent in Homer, Tacitus, and Petronius, and generally available in antiquity only via the Horatian decorum that demanded comedy when representing the plebian social orders). Auerbach rooted this stylistic confusion in the story of Christ's human incarnation amid the humblest of circumstances and in the earlier Jewish idea of universal history in which the sublime and everyday could be united (as in the story of Abraham and Isaac). For Auerbach, the nineteenth-century novel's "revolution against the classical doctrine of levels of style" was simply one revolt among many in Western literary history.[14] Auerbach made clear "when and how this first break with the classical theory had come about. It was the story of Christ, with its ruthless mixture of everyday reality and the highest and most sublime tragedy, which had conquered the classical rule of styles" (Auerbach, *Mimesis*, 555). The demise of the stylistically hierarchic thus accompanies—or, rather, generically records and compels—the demise of the spiritually hieratic. As has been the paradoxical case for numerous historians and sociologists of religion, the story of secularization that becomes the story of the European novel actually begins for Auerbach with the story of Christ.

I certainly do not mean to imply that the secular narrative Watt outlined has had no competitors beyond Lukács and Auerbach. Alternatives to Watt's narrative have long existed. G. A. Starr and J. Paul Hunter emphasized, to a far greater extent than Watt or McKeon, the religious sources of *Robinson Crusoe*—the first in broadly Christian terms, the second as Puritan (Bunyanesque) guide—in which spiritual quest, pilgrim allegory, and typological thinking predominate.[15] Though neither Starr nor Hunter places romance at the novel's rise, they do highlight characteristics of *Robinson Crusoe*, the work they too consider the founding model for the realistic novel, that reflect the techniques of romance writing. And this is an important choice, for it is precisely the earlier dominance of romance that allows Goody to describe the subsequent novel as a distinctively secular form, and that allows Moretti to emphasize the vectorless routines of its fillers. A genre with classical origins and the mythic motifs of quest, ritual, archetype, symbol, and allegory, romance becomes for others the template that rivals Lukács's epic. Northrop Frye's use of romance illustrates elements in the modern (post-Defoe) novel that remain anchored in religious tradition.[16] Margaret Anne Doody emphasizes not only the generic continuity of classical and medieval romance (from Heliodorus to Rabelais) with the novel after Cervantes, as well as the contributions of African and Asian sources to romances of the Roman Empire, but also the self-serving nature of the generic distinction itself within English novels and criticism.[17]

It is this last point—the degree to which national/religious traditions may be playing a role in this discussion of the nature of the novel—that deserves further scrutiny. It is not trivial that the English novel, putatively spawned by worldly travel and the quotidian entertainment of the *news*, would appear to diverge from the older

European tradition of the *roman*. To me it seems fairly obvious that the classical tradition of romance fed far more seamlessly (despite later French claims to realism after Stendhal) into Roman Catholic (and often Neoplatonic) traditions of European romance in medieval and Renaissance literature than it did into post-Reformation English literature. One need only compare Dante's *Commedia* to Milton's *Paradise Lost* to begin counting the differences. Even when he confronts the grotesque satire of Christian idealism in Rabelais, Auerbach is careful to point out that Rabelais's stylistic olio is an imitation of late medieval sermons (quite unlike Sterne's), which were "at once popular in the crudest way, creaturely realistic, and learned and edifying in their figural Biblical interpretation," as well as a product of Rabelais's experience with the earthy, mendicant life-world of the Franciscans (Auerbach, *Mimesis*, 271). (Auerbach's point reminds us of that terribly Rabelaisian Catholic James Joyce, whose sermon in *A Portrait of the Artist as a Young Man* [1916], lifted with scrupulous meanness from an actual Catholic sermon manual, is a later version of what we observe in Rabelais.)

The contrast with English Reformation—and, later, American Puritan—narratives could not be more impressive. For what emerged instead in England and America was a sober anti-Platonism, a rejection of Dante's vivid imagery and medieval Catholic cosmology, and the tailoring of the spiritual-amorous quest (filigreed with remarkably colorful symbolism in a verse romance such as the *Roman de la Rose*) to fit the more spare and direct allegory of *Pilgrim's Progress*. As one can see in Defoe's affinity with Bunyan, a nationally underwritten Protestantism bequeathed to the English novel a form of ethical earnestness while it routinized (as implied by Watt, McKeon, and Moretti) any overtly religious sensibility to the point of banality. Even when it is bitterly satirized, religious feeling is often elaborated by the French novel in striking, exotic, and intimate detail, in ways that suggest the degree to which Lukács's description of the novel as the epic of "absolute sinfulness" often makes far more sense in French than it does in English. (Indeed, the contrast between social climbing and its consequences in Stendhal and Thackeray, the latter being a writer for whom religion had become a more or less invisible element of a national sensibility, is obvious.) Nothing in Jane Austen, Charles Dickens, or George Eliot—despite the latter's Dorothea Brooke, in whom, unlike her uncle, "the hereditary strain of Puritan energy . . . glowed alike through faults and virtues"—remotely approaches the religion haunting Flaubert's Emma Bovary.[18] And nothing in the English novel would allow a reader to understand what Flaubert does with religion in *Trois contes* (1877), *Salammbô* (1862), and most of all in his dramatic novel, *La tentation de Saint Antoine* (1874), on which Flaubert labored throughout his life in the face of his friends' unsparing ridicule, a closet drama that he nevertheless appears to have considered his finest work.

We should then not be surprised, I suppose, to find that the two-thousand-page English version of Moretti's *The Novel* devotes only trivial, passing remarks to the greatest religious novel yet written—Dostoevsky's *Brat'ia Karamazovy* (1880), of which "The Grand Inquisitor" chapter is likely the single most important literary reflection on religion in modernity, a text equal to (and perhaps influencing) the last writings of Nietzsche. Moretti's choice here too follows directly from Watt, for whom Dostoevsky's novels "in no sense depend for their verisimilitude or their significance on his religious views" (Watt, *Rise*, 84)—though one wonders what sort of interpretation of Dostoevsky Watt was able to produce, given such self-imposed constraints. To read in this fashion is to read while only half-awake, even if one is a thoroughgoing materialist. Dostoevsky's engagement with Russian Orthodoxy is very different from Flaubert's with Roman Catholicism, but one cannot discount the singular roles of these two writers in creating the formal and thematic foundations of the twentieth-century novel. Lukács in fact pointed beyond the bitter disillusionment of Tolstoy's secular realism toward the future impact of Dostoevsky, who, he claimed, "did not write novels" and promised an escape from the "age of absolute sinfulness" (Lukács, *Theory*, 152–53).

Lukács's anticipatory comments about Dostoevsky imply, however, that we may be dealing with something like a historical shift at the end of the nineteenth century and not merely opposing national or religious traditions. George Eliot is in this regard a wonderful transitional figure, filled as she is with the ambivalences fostered by her reading and translation of Friedrich Strauss and Ludwig Feuer-bach. (Still, like others before me, I wonder why it is that Daniel Deronda never noticed that he had been circumcised, which he must have been, given his orthodox origins; perhaps Mary Ann Evans's famed research was not quite as extensive as we generally assume.) But after Eliot the religious floodgates open wide, quite despite a half century or so of critical commentary that often refused to acknowl-edge the event. Apart from vexed questions about the persistence of romance, the European, English, and American novel alike after (or despite, or perhaps because of) the flowering of naturalism in the nineteenth century, and the concomitant rise of a deeply Platonic symbolism in French poetry (as Edmund Wilson long ago argued in *Axel's Castle*), recovered much that was central to religious sentiment and its mythic, archetypal, symbolic, and allegorical machinery: J.-K. Huysmans's *À rebours* (1884), which was stimulated into existence by Flaubert's religious exoticism, only to be called fatal to naturalism by Émile Zola; Oscar Wilde's *The Picture of Dorian Gray* (1890); Thomas Hardy's *Tess of the D'Urbervilles* (1891) and *Jude the Ob-scure* (1896)—in which many more people talk about religion than ever did in Dickens; André Gide's *L'immoraliste* (1902), which Gide traced to Dostoevsky, about whom he wrote at length, and *La sym-phonie pastorale* (1919); James Joyce's *A Portrait of the Artist*, *Ulysses* (1922), and *Finnegans Wake* (1939), in all three of which there is, as far as I can tell, both a fair amount of religious anxiety and a rather stunning absence of fillers; D. H. Lawrence's *The Rainbow* (1915), a novel complete with biblical floods and far too much begetting; E. M. Forster's *A Passage to India* (1924), which is perhaps the most signifi-cant English novel of the early twentieth century about religion (it is far more about religion than empire, in my view, and far more "reli-gious" than "political" in its perspective); William Faulkner's *Light in August* (1932) and *Absalom, Absalom!* (1936); Ernest Hemingway's *The Old Man and the Sea* (1952), along with the great host of his biblically inflected, if generally too trite, titles; Thomas Mann's *Der Tod in Venedig* (1913), *Der Zauberberg* (1924)—where the conversa-tions between Naphta and Settembrini alone rival those in Dosto-evsky's "Grand Inquisitor"—*Joseph und seine Brüder* (a reworking of the origins of monotheism, written between 1926 and 1943, and perhaps the work Mann thought his most significant), *Doktor Faustus* (1947), which is clearly the apotheosis of the modern religious novel, and finally *Der Erwählte* (1951); Albert Camus's religious allegories *L'etranger* (1942), *La peste* (1948), and *La chute* (1957); and most perplexingly yet deeply religious of all, the entire blessed corpus of Franz Kafka (1883–1924). In praising *Das Schloss* (1926), Mann called Kafka "a religious humorist."[19] I believe we could attach the phrase broadly to many of the novelists of Kafka's era. By the same token, we should perhaps also refer to this development in the history of the novel as the revenge—or better, the Heideggerian *Verwindung*, the spiritually distorted return—of religious romance, and I will elaborate this point in more detail in my first chapter. It may yet turn out that the quotidian, rationalized, and apparently secular novel that began with Defoe came to a halt with Zola, and that the *novel* as so many continue to see it will soon be understood as no more than a two-century aberration in literary history.

▪   ▪   ▪

As subsequent chapters will make clear, I believe the early Lukács was right, at least in part, about the larger effects of Dostoevsky's fiction on the history of the novel, though perhaps for the wrong reasons. The novel imagined as the epic of "absolute sinfulness"—that is, the realist novel between Richardson and Zola—was not, in the end, a sustainable project, as Lukács intuited, but the consequences of this observation were not at all what Lukács anticipated in his early years. In particular, the potential for something epic, heroic, and finally redemptive to arise, via Dostoevsky, from the ashes of realism and naturalism would never be realized in Lukácsian terms, as he later acknowledged. While the twentieth century did in fact produce both the heroic epic of socialist realism and the heroic epic of *Blut und Boden* National Socialism, these perfectly dismal results were almost enough to kill off the genre entirely, even without competition from cinema and television.

What Lukács missed completely, largely because of his later Stalinism, was the fact that the denouement of the novel's era of "absolute sinfulness" led not to the emergence of a new, redemptive literature, but instead to a literature of absolute, even primordial, shame. Franz Kafka is the great progenitor of this version of novelistic writing. His novella *Die Verwandlung*, first published in German in 1935, is the epitome of fiction that is motivated and consumed by pure shame, shame that in its most extreme elaborations begins, however perversely, to take on the garb of religious allegory. This is, I think, what Mann meant by calling Kafka a "religious humorist," which is to say one who finds an unstable, disturbing, but also oddly consoling dark humor in the utter shamefulness, the utter disgrace, of human existence as it might be judged (even if it is not) by a divinity, and it is a shame that is also explored in the existentialist parables of Albert Camus. In his later years, Lukács overlooked the possibility of this path in the novel's trajectory—in fact, he rejected Kafka explicitly and for the most part uncomprehendingly—because of what Theodor Adorno quite rightly called his acceptance of "extorted reconciliation": his politically intransigent demand that social reconciliation, redemption of a sort, be produced, in his lifetime and however artificially, through a sufficient expenditure of critical analysis aimed at a comprehension of the totality of social life.[20] Instead, what Kafka's work suggests is that the novel's most engaging afterlife might not lie in the direction of redemption at all, but rather in the much more ambivalent and difficult path of shame, disgrace, and the complete disavowal of redemption of any sort—though it is a disavowal, as I wish to demonstrate, with a certain religious and hence hardly straightforward pedigree.

In the chapters that follow—on Samuel Beckett, Thomas Mann, and J. M. Coetzee—I trace out some of the implications of this onerous disavowal of redemption in the post-1945 period. My objective is not at all to claim that these three figures are somehow representative of the entire postwar era. All of them, and not by accident, are white men of relative privilege, situated within Europe's dominant and Protestant aesthetic, political, and religious traditions (even Mann, whose mother was Catholic), from which they borrow with great enthusiasm. Nevertheless, the confluence of several important intellectual currents in these writers is especially noteworthy. First, there is a recognition that the surviving, if highly self-conscious, inwardly turned "realism" of so much modern narrative (whether of Proust or Joyce or Faulkner or the early Mann) would no longer suffice formally, since the kinds of rational, secular comprehension it implied could no longer be sustained (as Kafka demonstrated) in any seriousness. Second, there is an acknowledgment that the age of great imperial hubris, which had eventuated in two horribly destructive wars in the first half of the century, followed by an even longer period of violent decolonization in their wake, yielded only a kind of unimaginable disgrace and humiliation in response, at least for white men of a certain privilege and culture. And third, there is the deeper intuition that the kind of narratives that were still possible, profoundly godless and secular in their overt commitments, nevertheless wound up producing varieties of religious doctrine native to Augustinian and Calvinist understandings of irreducible, ineradicable guilt and shame, which then also prompted an even deeper and more humbling appreciation of the unfathomable nature of redemption—which is to say, the abyss of divine election itself.[21]

This last rubric is the focus of my approach to Beckett, Mann, and Coetzee. The somewhat unexpected development in Western fiction exemplified by all three is the fact that the secularization both reflected and enabled by the novel as a genre is a secularization without end, a secularization that has in the most artfully imaginative ways possible resisted the seemingly inevitable historical plot that Watt, McKeon, Goody, Moretti, and so many others have constructed for the novel. Whether that narrative resistance is a sign of new intellectual, moral, and political vigor or nothing more than a remnant, a meaningless and trivial afterlife, is a much more perplexing issue to raise, though I will nevertheless try to address it in my conclusion.

▪   ▪   ▪

In one of the most cryptic essays of a career filled with cryptic essays, Walter Benjamin wrote in his characteristically gnomic fashion of the archaic powers of mimicry—the tendency of human beings both to recognize similarities in nature and to produce similarities, to behave "mimetically."

> Nature produces similarities; one need only think of mimicry. The highest capacity for producing similarities, however, is man's. His gift for seeing similarity is nothing but a rudiment of the once powerful compulsion to become similar and to behave mimetically. . . . We must assume that in the remote past the processes considered imitable included those in the sky. In dance, on other cultic occasions, such imitation could be produced, such similarity dealt with. . . . Allusion to the astrological sphere may supply a first reference point for an understanding of the concept of nonsensuous similarity. True, our existence no longer includes what once made it possible to speak of this kind of similarity: above all, the ability to produce it. Nevertheless we, too, possess a canon according to which the meaning of nonsensuous similarity can be at least partly clarified. And this canon is language.[22]

I believe that one compelling way of understanding what Benjamin means here by "mimetic" behavior, which we no longer have the ability to recognize or produce, is religion. And I mean religion in the widest sense possible, not unlike the way it would be used by any number of anthropologists, that is, referring to what we would now call magic, superstition, the occult, astrology, haruspication, reading tea leaves, Neoplatonism, spiritualism, theosophy, animism, totemism, gnosticism, and kabbalah, as well as the multitude of Hindu, Buddhist, Sikh, Zoroastrian, Taoist, and Shinto beliefs and practices (and many others far too numerous even to list), and including those Abrahamic religions "of the book" called Judaism, Christianity, and Islam. Benjamin writes here, I think, in terms of what he considers the most primitive, the most "archaic" representations of all such religions, and that is "mimetic behavior."

In the course of his brief essay, Benjamin outlines a quasi-evolutionary (or quasi-Hegelian) process by which the "occult practices" of reading "what was never written"—as embodied in the immediate presence of what Lukács, at the beginning of *The Theory of the Novel*, called the starry "map of all possible paths" that were available to those ages fortunate enough not to need "philosophy," and hence embodied also in astrology and haruspication—give way to a "mediating link of a new kind of reading" based on runes and hieroglyphs, which is in turn overcome by modern phonetic writing, that is, the "semiotic aspect" of language by which verbal signifiers (both written and spoken) are tied by seemingly arbitrary convention to their conceptual signifieds (Benjamin, "Mimetic Faculty," 721–22).[23] I believe that the opposition Benjamin draws here between archaic mimetic behavior and modern writing is at the same time an opposition between the religious and the secular. In both cases, an evolutionary process is at work. Just as we might refer to the secularization of religious ideation and ritual, we could just as easily refer to the secularization of mimetic behavior by writing. And just as, in certain versions of the "secularization thesis," religion is not simply abandoned, overcome, or forgotten, but rather persists via constant transformation into newly coded remnants of earlier concepts, remnants that then become routinized and unremarkable elements of our modern secular universe (anthropologists, following E. B. Tylor, call these remnants "survivals"), so too, for Benjamin, the residues of mimetic behavior survive, however unrecognized, encoded within the routinized, secular, mechanical, and seemingly transparent practices of phonetic language and writing.[24]

Yet Benjamin also claims that the forgotten elements of mimetic behavior lying hidden and dormant within modern, purposive phonetic language may at times manifest themselves "like a flame": "the nexus of meaning of words or sentences is the bearer through which, like a flash, similarity appears . . . it flits past" (Benjamin, "Mimetic Faculty," 2:722). Orthodox readings of the Torah have long assumed that the letters of the Hebrew alphabet, precisely because it is the language of Yahweh, do not merely function as arbitrary (secular) elements of a phonetic language with instrumental purposes, but rather become mimetic glyphs in and of themselves—individual letters are, as divine effects, "mimetic" of Yahweh's presence and guidance—and it is hard not to assume that Benjamin is drawing heavily on Rabbinic interpretation of the Torah in his essay. The big difference for Benjamin in this sudden, modern reappearance of mimetic behavior is that, in its latest incarnation as a lightning flash of similarity within the arbitrary conventions of reading and writing, mimetic behavior is no longer linked in any way to the ideas and rituals of archaic magic or religion. Rather, once it has been secularized by the fallen yet prophylactic medium of purely instrumental language, mimetic behavior appears to have "liquidated" the power of magic and religion. It is as if, as I will discuss in chapter 1, what Jürgen Habermas calls the "semantic potential" of archaic beliefs—their core rational, philosophical, and finally secular significance, one might say—has been modernized, so that such core significance no longer requires the artificial and irrational trappings of magic or religion to function for us. It is as if, when we read Shakespeare's exemplary dictum of secular society—"The fault, dear Brutus, is not in our stars, / But in ourselves, that we are underlings" (Shakespeare, *Julius Caesar*, 1.2.140–41)—we are given a glimpse of precisely what the text itself seems to deny: the secular magic of Shakespeare's language enchants us, quite apart from its overt, rational claim, in a way that cannot help but recall, however fondly or nostalgically, the lost magic of astrological thinking. We may now agree rationally, morally, and politically with Shakespeare's—or at least Cassius's—eminently secular point: we are responsible for our own actions, our own fates, even if this is why some are "underlings." And yet the entirety of our secular literature, both before and after Shakespeare, never stops questioning his dictum, and it is always the most aesthetically engaging formulations of the questioning that work their magic best. Tolstoy's demolition of the idea that we can control our fates, Proust's rather thorough undoing of our pretension to understand the past in conscious, rational ways—none of these would work for us had they not been so well expressed. As readers we are, in short, always subject to the mimetic power of the language we read.

In what follows, I want to apply Benjamin's curious account of mimesis in a way that reminds us that the use of modern, secular language does not—perhaps cannot—liquidate the powers of magic and religion as Benjamin claims they can. Throughout the novels I discuss, the supposedly liquidated force of religion is not only once again legible in the secular language of the prose, but also flashes up on almost every page and with a kind of insistence that I find remarkable in the literature of so secular an age. And that is for me a very good reason to think that the novel's bag of tricks may not be quite as empty as we might otherwise assume.

Martin Heidegger, John Calvin, and Samuel Beckett

In a lecture he delivered in 2001, Jürgen Habermas proposed bridging the cultural gap that opened anew on September 11, 2001, when "the tension between secular society and religion exploded" in an entirely new way, by recourse to "the civilizing role of democratically enlightened common sense."[1] This recourse to "common sense" itself depends on Habermas's often-stated axiom that all participants in democratic political debate, from the militantly fundamentalist to the radically materialist, must first recognize that "the ideologically neutral state does not prejudice its political decisions in any way toward either side of the conflict between the rival claims of science and religious faith." Yet it is obvious that Habermas's presumption of the liberal state's ideological neutrality is precisely what so many have come to question, especially outside the West. Republicanism of both the French and American varieties has long assumed that, in the final analysis, the needs of the secular state must always trump matters of faith. What "common sense" actually means for Habermas, however, includes what he tends to call a *translation* of religious positions— almost exclusively Judaic and Christian positions—into (for example) Kantian, or postmetaphysical, ethics.[2] This way of understanding the relation of a secular, philosophical future to a religious, theological past is the essence of the secularization thesis itself in one of its most prominent historical guises, as I have tried to demonstrate elsewhere.[3]

19

Whether we return to Kant's dualistic *Religion within the Limits of Reason* or to Hegel's more organic and monistic *Philosophy of Religion*, the historical translation of religious into nonsectarian "philosophical" truth has been one of the main paths of secularization. The argument I outline in what follows is that the "common sense" secular ideal represented by Habermas's resolution of the conflict between faith and knowledge is in all likelihood an impossible and perhaps, in some ways, even undesirable goal.

Habermas's idea of gradually translating, via "communicative action," the truths of religion into secular ethics runs throughout his philosophical project. As he writes in "Transcendence from Within, Transcendence in this World" (citing himself from *Nachmetaphysisches Denken*), "As long as religious language bears with itself inspiring, indeed, unrelinquishable semantic contents which elude (for the moment?) the expressive power of a philosophical language and still await translation into a discourse that gives reasons for its positions, philosophy, even in its postmetaphysical form, will neither be able to replace nor to repress religion."[4] Habermas voiced similar sentiments in his earlier essay, "Walter Benjamin: Consciousness Raising or Rescuing Critique?," and he has returned to them whenever asked to speak about religion and reason.[5] It is the core of what Hegel meant by dialectical *Aufhebung*, which is to say that for Hegel and for many who followed him, especially in European philosophy, it is what has come to be understood by the term *secularization*. Hans Blumenberg lays it out in more sophisticated terms, and Habermas develops his own account of the process, but it is one version of what we talk about when we talk about secularization.[6] The other primary version of secularization, as seen, for example, in Jonathan Israel's notion of a "radical Enlightenment," assumes that the scientific revolution marked a fundamental rupture with the past and bequeathed to modernity a new, rational, and materialist mode of understanding owing little or nothing to prior religious thought.[7] Blumenberg tries to negotiate between these two versions of secularization, even if an idea of fundamental rupture is basic to his defense of modernity's legitimacy. Indeed, most historians tend to switch back and forth between the two versions without warning—it is what we have always done, at least since Hegel (on one side) and figures such as Herbert Spencer and Thomas Huxley (on the other).

To find a way past the antinomy posed by these competing accounts of secularization, one would have to reject not only the all-at-once break with the religious past demanded by contemporary materialists, such as Christopher Hitchens, Richard Dawkins, and Sam Harris, among many others, but also the Hegelian approach by which the rationally or ethically "unrelinquishable" core of the religious past is gradually translated, in good democratic fashion, into rational discourse that "gives reasons" for its positions.[8] But if we reject both the all-at-once and the slow-translation versions of secularization, what remains of the idea? How should we approach the contemporary global paradoxes and contradictions of secularization, which some have seen as good reasons for trashing the standard "secularization thesis" altogether, and which have been emphasized with such scholarly energy over the past two decades or so?

I want to reconsider a path once suggested by Martin Heidegger— the refusal of, or the "step back" away from, the entire history of Being in the Platonic–Christian–Enlightenment model of progressive reason—though in decidedly non-Heideggerian terms. Heidegger's notion of *Verwindung*—the distortion that also opens up a space for a new approach to Being, one that allows us to "get over" the inherited Western narrative—is the very opposite of Hegel's self-consuming *Aufhebung*.[9] But Heidegger's notion of curative distortion may also, and in ways surely unintended by Heidegger, suggest new ways for thinking about secularization, that is, secularization not so much as an inevitable, one-way street to either sudden materialist transformation or slow Hegelian translation (however "non-synchronous" either of these may be geographically), but rather as a process in which even "strong religion," if I can borrow the term, will periodically recur. And religion will recur, in various guises, for a variety of reasons quite apart from fear and ignorance and material underdevelopment. It will return as a form of resistance to the seemingly inexorable, even mythical, imperatives of rationality (as in the arguments of the

Frankfurt School); as an escape from certain forms of perverse political expediency (as implied by Max Weber's charismatic counterweight to bureaucracy); and, perhaps most of all, as the imagination's spontaneous overflow of powerful emotion, tranquilly recollected or not, that we once naively thought could be safely contained by "the aesthetic." Though on one level I share Habermas's desire (fond hope?) for a truly thoroughgoing democratic, dialogic, and universal postmetaphysical secular ethics and politics, I doubt finally whether it is possible to get there from here and at times wonder if we would like it entirely when we did. In the end, I claim that culture should be understood historically neither as an inexorable progression from zealotry to indifference, from enchantment to disenchantment, or from magic to science, nor as a sudden rupture with a benighted past, but rather as in part a peripeteia—a wandering, errant process that often folds back on itself, producing not only the return in distorted form of something perhaps hastily repressed (and, as in Kemalist Turkey or the Shah's Iran or Mubarak's Egypt, often coercively repressed), but also a host of unintended consequences (political, social, and cultural) that we have only begun to understand.

In his English translation of Gianni Vattimo's Italian translation of Heidegger's German, Jon Snyder renders the notion of *Verwindung* as "secularization."[10] (If we take "distortion" as one of the meanings of Heidegger's concept, then it would be fair to say that my appropriation of this concept is itself the consequence of one long chain of distortions!) The German verb *verwinden* refers to our ability "to get over" something—perhaps physically, as a barrier, but more likely in psychological terms, as in getting over some mistake, or some illness, or some traumatic event of the past. In handicrafts and engineering, the verb more literally means "to twist," "to distort," or "to contort," and this is true of the gerund *Verwindung* as well, which thus denotes "contortion" or "distortion," or more generally "transformation." Heidegger no doubt liked the superimposition of the two meanings, one psychological and one mechanical, especially since one of them was rooted in that technological shaping of material reality he tended to treat as both fetish and threat, that is, a threat to be transformed or gotten past. Getting over or past something psychologically or epistemologically is then also a way of twisting it, of distorting its nature in some way. Heidegger's use of the term occurs in a lecture he delivered in 1957 on "Der Satz der Indentität," or "The Principle of Identity," which was published along with another lecture ("On the Onto-theo-logical Constitution of Metaphysics") in *Identität und Differenz*. In his lecture, Heidegger speaks of the technologically dominated "framework" of the "atomic age," the culmination of what he elsewhere and more carefully calls the "age of the world-picture," a framework in which Being and man are forced to confront one another, and are delivered over to one another, by means of a strange ownership and appropriation (Heidegger, *Identity*, 33, 35).

Heidegger had referred in a 1938 lecture to "the world-picture [*Weltbild*] of modernity" and in a subsequent essay to "the age of the world-picture," by which phrase he meant primarily the era of Western technology since the Renaissance, which had so powerfully objectified and situated the world while establishing the centrality of the representing subject. In this context, he also referred to the more contemporary appearance of the media and especially to radio.[11] Heidegger's point is to address how we might move from this mere prelude to the appropriation of Being and man toward the *singulare tantum* of the "event of appropriation," where "the possibility arises that it may overcome the mere dominance of the frame to turn it into a more original act of appropriation. Such a transformation [and "transformation" is Stambaugh's translation of *Verwindung*] of the frame into the event of appropriation, by virtue of the event, would bring the appropriate recovery—appropriate, hence never to be produced by man alone—of the world of technology from its dominance back to servitude in the realm by which man reaches more truly into the event of appropriation" (Heidegger, *Identity*, 36–37).

Heidegger thus proposes a step back, away from our apparent forgetting of all philosophical problems of ontology in the age of the world-picture, in order to comprehend the history of Being in Western thought from the outside, as it were. He saw an entire epoch of forgetting that was closing with the singular event, or *Ereignis*, of atomic warfare, which had revealed humankind's capacity to end human being, *Dasein*, altogether. This "event" was also then an opportunity to rethink everything about the nature of Being that we had previously, supposedly, overcome. Heidegger's most obvious target here, I think, is Hegel: where Hegel's quite progressive Über-windung once was, there Heidegger's epochal *Verwindung*—the transforming, but also distorting and recuperating, process that represents our "getting over" the forgetting, or false overcoming, of the question of Being—shall be. One can see, I think, how clever Vattimo was in reducing to the concept of secularization all this abstruse talk about getting over the forgetting of the question of Being, however much Heidegger himself would surely have objected.

That is, it may be possible to rethink the process of secularization that has become one of the most powerful narratives regulating the production of knowledge in our academies so that rather than being satisfied only with the ironies and unintended consequences by which religious thought produces rationalizing and secularizing motivations from within itself, as Max Weber so brilliantly understood, we also pay attention to the manifold ways secularization manages to stimulate, often from within its own machinery, religious thinking in return. Here, it is important to take note of Odo Marquard's claims about the "troubles" or "problems" (*Schwierigkeiten*) of the philosophy of history. For Marquard, the secularization effected by critical idealism (*Idealismuskritik*), which is to say the tradition from Kant, Fichte, Schelling, Schleiermacher, and Hegel, through its reformulation by Kierkegaard and into the twentieth century with figures such as Karl Barth, Emil Brunner, Franz Rosenzweig, and Martin Buber (this is finally a very ecumenical "reform, catholic, orthodox, and Jewish" tradition), is not only "inspired" by theology merely as something to be surpassed.[12] In Marquard's view, such secularization paradoxically produces a more rational or refined sense of religious theodicy than had existed before, and does so by means of a kind of "preventative" theology (Marquard, *Schwierigkeiten*, 65). By emphasizing human autonomy and rigorously refusing to speak of divine agency, the critical philosophy of history becomes a final "exoneration" of the divine, as Blumenberg puts it in summarizing Marquard, a refusal of God "so as not to tarnish the image of God" (Blumenberg,

Legitimacy, 57). Unlike modern analytical philosophy, the tradition Marquard outlines, which I would expand to include a great deal of twentieth-century narrative literature, refuses to relinquish philosophy's hold on the question of theodicy, that is, its attempt to explain what the novel has also so often tried to explain: how bad things happen to good people, or rather, a vindication of justice in the face of evil, which would take on renewed importance after 1945. (Indeed, it would not be a mistake, in my view, to read all of Heidegger's postwar lectures and essays, in all their tortured, *verwindend* attempts to explain the Nazi debacle without reference to Jews or the Holocaust, as primarily his secular, phenomenological attempt at theodicy, or at least a way of expiating shame.) It is no accident, in this regard, that Gottfried Leibniz's invention of philosophical theodicy (in his *Essai de Théodicée sur la bonté de Dieu, la liberté de l'homme et l'origine du mal* [1710]) belongs to the same age as Samuel Richardson's *Clarissa, or, the History of a Young Lady* (1747–48) and Pierre Choderlos de Laclos's *Les Liaisons dangereuses* (beginning in 1782), both novels situating the new genre as an inquiry into the issue Leibniz raises, both demanding that the reader decode the *origine du mal* embedded in human duplicity from fragmentary epistolary evidence. In thus refusing to relinquish the question of theodicy, writes Marquard, the "idealistic autonomy-position is nothing less than what is perhaps the only promising form of theodicy. Into this thesis, atheism should then perhaps be inserted as a 'methodical atheism *ad maiorem gloriam Dei*'" (Marquard, *Schwierigkeiten*, 65).[13] Marquard's invocation of Pierre-Joseph Proudhon's "methodical atheism" is not accidental, I think, and I will have reason to cite Proudhon's "anti-theism" a bit later. Here I simply want to indicate that Marquard's account of methodical atheism as a species of theodicy will have a direct bearing on my discussion of Samuel Beckett (and in later chapters Thomas Mann and J. M. Coetzee).

Marquard's observations point, for me, to a better way of thinking about Heidegger's *Verwindung* than is usually derived from Heidegger himself, that is, not as the crossing of some epochal threshold from the fallen age of the world-picture into a new age where man and Being appropriate one another in newly authentic terms, but rather as the inevitable peripeteia, if I can call it that, within the secularization narrative, a complicating swerve that distorts the grand narrative of secularization and allows, at times, for a certain recuperation of the religious, or Being, or what Charles Taylor (following Peter Berger) rather infelicitously likes to call "fullness," often complete with doctrinal and ritual accompaniments and a historical eschatology that we generally imagine have been safely put aside.[14] It seems to me that it is only on such grounds that we really begin to think productively, and not condescendingly or naively or tragically, about the great religious reawakenings that have occurred since the 1960s in a wide variety of social and cultural settings. Thinking along such lines may also be a way to begin dismantling our inherited academic and critical presumption that the only nonideological, or authentic, location for redemptive thought in a fully secularized modernity would be the neatly circumscribed and hence safely neutered space of aesthetic appearance.

In what follows, I want to approach Beckett's writing as a distorting transformation of a Calvinist, puritan religious tradition. The issue raised in Beckett's work, I argue, is not necessarily a pious return to religious belief or faith—I have no illusions on that score—but rather a far more challenging and hard-to-assimilate process by which Beckett's resolutely secular poetics appropriates and distorts a set of religious motifs in order to realize his aims most fully. One could call it a Godless Calvinism, were it not for the fact that what may have attracted Beckett to puritan thought was in fact its godforsakenness. As Deirdre Bair writes of the tendency toward "baroque solipsism" in Beckett during the two-year period (1934–36) in which he was reading Arnold Geulincx, working on *Murphy* (1938), and undergoing psychoanalysis with Wilfred Ruprecht Bion, a follower of Melanie Klein, at the Tavistock Clinic in London, "He also called himself a Puritan and, in the most important part of his self-analysis, said Puritanism comprised the simple, straightforward and dominant part of his personality, but that he had agreed to allow this part to be necessarily disrupted by analysis because he could no longer function."[15] In Beckett's remarkably religious exegesis of Proust—in which Proust emerges as someone "detached from all moral considerations," so that "there is no right and wrong in Proust nor in his world"—Beckett observes, in good puritan or Calvinist fashion, "Tragedy is not concerned with human justice. Tragedy is the statement of an expiation, but not the miserable expiation of a codified breach of a local arrangement, organised by the knaves for the fools. The tragic figure represents the expiation of original sin, of the original and eternal sin of him and all his 'socii malorum,' the sin of having been born."[16] It is this "sin of having been born" in Beckett that I want to juxtapose to Habermas's more optimistic translation of religious truths into a fully secularized modernity.

▪   ▪   ▪

Actually, I should make a small confession at this point: I do not know what the phrase "fully secularized modernity" actually means. For example, if it means leading one's life rigorously according to scientific principles—at least the ones we have produced so far—then I would say that the fully secular life is quite difficult to imagine. Perhaps one would be in the predicament of Beckett's Molloy (which is certainly not to say that such predicaments never occur in real life), who is the embodiment of that good seventeenth-century convert to Calvinism, Arnold Geulincx, and his neo-Cartesian (and proto-Leibnizian) theory that mind and matter are not finally connected at the pineal gland, but instead run independently beside one another, like clocks synchronized in preestablished harmony by the will of God.[17] Beckett borrows from Geulincx numerous times in his writing and refers to Geulincx by name on several occasions, most notably in *Murphy* and *Molloy* (French, 1951; English, 1955). In the latter we read, "I who had loved the image of old Geulincx, dead young, who left me free, on the black boat of Ulysses, to crawl towards the East, along the deck. That is a great measure of freedom, for him who has not the pioneering spirit. And from the poop, poring upon the wave, a sadly rejoicing slave, I follow with my eyes the proud and futile wake" (Beckett, *Selected Works*, 2:46). The image is from Geulincx, who had argued that the minimal freedom of the human will—Beckett calls it an "innate velleity" (Beckett, *Selected Works*, 2:81)—can be exemplified by a man walking from the bow of a ship to its stern, even as the God-powered ship moved relentlessly forward. It is hard to ignore the implication here that Geulincx helped liberate (though this is a tendentious term to use) Beckett from James Joyce's powerful, even godlike, influence, for Beckett served as Joyce's re-Joycing slave—his secretary and amanuensis—as Joyce composed his proud, futile *Finnegans Wake* (1939). It is also hard not to connect the buzzing murmur that Beckett's characters constantly hear and must learn to decipher to Joyce's voice itself. Based on what Beckett told him, James Knowlson has argued that Beckett "rejected the Joycean principle that knowing was a way of creatively understanding the world and controlling it," and that Beckett determined instead to focus on "poverty, failure, exile, and loss" (Knowlson, *Damned*, 352–53). These more ascetic virtues perfectly complement the "*humilitas*" that underlay Geulincx's theology. Called "occasionalism," Geulincx's main idea had its most famous proponent in Nicolas Malebranche, though its origins seem to lie in tenth-century Islamic theology.[18] One striking metaphor Geulincx suggests for this condition (a metaphor Beckett himself adapts at several points) is a comparison of mind and body to an infant and its rocking cradle. The infant may want the cradle to rock at the same time that its mother wants to rock the cradle, though only the mother (the stand-in for God in Geulincx's trope) could be said to cause the action, no matter what the infant may imagine, and even if the infant could imagine that its crying is what caused the cradle to rock.[19]

This also means, as Geulincx writes in his *Ethics* and Beckett translates in his notes, "I am therefore a mere spectator of this machine [that is, the world] whose workings I can neither adjust nor readjust. I can neither construct nor demolish anything here: the whole thing is someone else's affair" (Geulincx, *Ethics*, 34). Someone else is moving this mechanistic world, a machine that includes our own bodies precisely because we cannot really claim to be the efficient mover of a device the operations of which we cannot understand. The fact that this "someone" is the Christian God, as Geulincx makes perfectly clear throughout his work (though, oddly, not here) was at times ignored by eighteenth-century critics who accused Geulincx of atheism, with complaints not unlike those brought against Geulincx's immediate contemporary Baruch Spinoza—though there is no evidence the two philosophers knew each other's work or even met, despite being at times in the same city.[20] Geulincx's resolutely skeptical emendation of Descartes's mind-body argument, that is, of the occasionalism to which Descartes imagined a solution through the eventual achievement (with God's grace) of certainty via rigorous introspection, culminates in what has come to be called Geulincx's axiom of metaphysics: "Quod nescis quomodo fiat, non facis."[21] I would translate the phrase most literally as, "What you do not know how to do, you do not do."

In his notes, Beckett reproduces a related passage from the *Ethics*: "Do not say that you do what you do not know how to do" (Geulincx, *Ethics*, 331). In *Murphy*, Beckett provides an extended, three-page elaboration of Geulincx's metaphysics, at the center of which we find the following passage.

> Thus Murphy felt himself split in two, a body and a mind. They had intercourse apparently, otherwise he could not have known that they had anything in common. But he felt his mind to be bodytight and did not understand through what channel the intercourse was effected nor how the two experiences came to overlap. He was satisfied that neither followed from the other. He neither thought a kick because he felt one nor felt a kick because he thought one. . . . However that might be, Murphy was content to accept this partial congruence of the world of his mind with the world of his body as due to some such process of supernatural determination. The problem was of little interest. Any solution would do that did not clash with the feeling, growing stronger as Murphy grew older, that his mind was a closed system, subject to no principle of change but its own. (Beckett, *Selected Works*, 1:68)

In *The Unnamable* (French, 1953; English, 1958), Geulincx's axiom emerges this way: "For example, in case you don't believe me, I don't yet know how to move, either locally, in relation to myself, or bodily, in relation to the rest of the shit. I don't know how to want to, I want to in vain" (Beckett, *Selected Works*, 2:343). The axiom seems to be important to Beckett (as it clearly was for Geulincx) not simply as an assertion of skepticism or impotence, but as an injunction to humility, which for Geulincx entails both the Cartesian epistemological demand for rigorous self-inspection and a neo-Stoic moral imperative enjoining self-disregard.

In his emphasis on humility and his rejection of self-interest, Geulincx follows Calvin, as one might expect, but is also strikingly akin to his contemporary Blaise Pascal, who, after a youthful career in mathematics and physics, had a visionary experience and aligned himself with the Jansenist-leaning members of the convent of Port-Royal. Pascal was certainly devoted to the late, predestination-embracing texts of Augustine that had so inspired Saint-Cyran, Cornelius Jansen, and Calvin alike. But whether due to the papacy's declaration that Jansenism was heresy or to his own wavering belief, Pascal's commitment to Jansenism was probably in the end fairly lukewarm. As Pascal writes in *Pensées* 230, "For in the end, what is humanity in nature? A nothingness compared to the infinite, everything compared to a nothingness, a mid-point between nothing and everything, infinitely far from understanding the extremes; the end of things and their beginning are insuperably hidden for him in an impenetrable secret. . . . He is equally incapable of seeing the nothingness from where he came, and the infinite in which he is covered."[22] In this same entry displaying his skepticism toward human understanding, Pascal comes close to Geulincx's position on mind and body: "To human beings, a human being is nature's most stupendous work. They cannot understand what the body is, far less the spirit, and least of all how the body can be combined with the spirit. That is the worst of their difficulties, and yet it is their own existence. *Modus quo corporibus adhaerent spiritus comprehendi ab homine non potest, et hoc tamen homo est* [The way in which minds are attached to bodies is beyond man's understanding, and yet this is what man is (St. Augustine, *City of God*, 21:10)]" (Pascal, *Pensées*, 72).[23]

Geulincx himself was steeped in the Latin Stoics, especially Seneca, but like Pascal he diverged sharply from them on several key points, especially concerning the ancient Stoics' belief in freedom of action, which also meant the freedom to commit suicide. By contrast, for Geulincx, strictly speaking we cannot commit suicide: whether we succeed or fail at the attempt is not really up to us, but to God. It is "someone else's affair" (Geulincx, *Ethics*, 34). The moral obligation to avoid the attempt remains, however, since we have no more right to wish to control our departure from this world than we have an ability to control our coming into it—an obligation that reveals just how much moral emphasis Geulincx places on intentions rather than deeds, for it is clear to him that we control only the intentions and never the deeds, and even our control of the intentions is dependent on "someone else," as Beckett will also indicate. Not unlike Beckett, and quite opposed to many existentialist writers of Beckett's era, the physically frail and constantly suffering Geulincx was in the position of appearing to say, as Beckett so often does, most famously in the last line of *The Unnamable*, "I can't go on, I'll go on" (Beckett, *Selected Works*, 2:407).[24]

Geulincx's insistence on humility is further encapsulated in what has been called his axiom of morals: "Ubi nihil vales, ibi nihil velis," which I would translate as "Where one has no influence or power, there one should not choose, or desire, or will anything" (Geulincx, *Ethics*, 178). Geulincx paraphrased his axiom "in other words, *do nothing in vain*" (Geulincx, *Ethics*, 178; emphasis Geulincx's). It is an axiom that thus directs us only to intentions that God would approve and perhaps provide the grace to accomplish, though as the second part of *Ethics* makes clear, virtuous actions are, in some sense, also rewards in themselves. Beckett supplies two possible interpretations. In his notes, he renders Geulincx's Latin as "Wherein you have no power, therein neither should you will" (Geulincx, *Ethics*, 337). This is more or less what we find in *The Unnamable*: "I can't speak of anything, and yet I speak, perhaps it's of him, I'll never know, how could I know, who could know, who knowing could tell me, I don't know who it's all about, that's all I know, no, I must know something else, they must have taught me something, it's about him who knows nothing, wants nothing, can do nothing, if it's possible you can do nothing when you want nothing" (Beckett, *Selected Works*, 2:397).

There is some ambiguity in the phrase, however, because the Latin verb *valeo* can also mean "to be worth something," or "to be valued at a certain price," or even simply "to signify" in some way. (The two meanings are not hard to connect: in Roman society, as now, to have power is to be worthy, to signify). In *Murphy*, Beckett cites the Latin and then provides his own gloss. "In the beautiful Belgo-Latin of Arnold Geulincx: *Ubi nihil vales, ibi nihil velis.* But it was not enough to want nothing where he was worth nothing" (Beckett, *Selected Works*, 1:107–8). It is an interpretation that clearly emphasizes the quality of *humilitas*—which for the ancient Romans, as Nietzsche had pointed out, and as is exemplified by so many of Beckett's characters, would have meant not only the Christian virtue of self-abnegation but also the abasement (and perhaps ressentiment) that comes with social insignificance and low birth. One is tempted here, in stark opposition to those who see in Beckett a literary or aesthetic equivalent of a revolutionary politics, to say that the root motivation behind Beckett's sensibility (something also legible in Mann's relationship to Germany and Coetzee's to South Africa) is *shame*—that is, for Beckett, not so much the shame of being born into a long-oppressed and impotent Ireland or the shame of the violence unleashed by World War II, but, as Beckett told Bair, the "shame of having been born" at all.

In either the Christian or Roman interpretation of Geulincx's *humilitas*, what is thus at stake in Beckett is on the one hand a meditation on the seemingly inextinguishable *vanitas* of human desire. In *The Unnamable*, the narrator refers repeatedly to Mahood, or to himself, or to himself as Mahood, simply as "Worm," so that "the essential is to go on squirming for ever at the end of the line, as long as there are waters and banks and ravening in heaven a sporting God to plague his creature, per pro his chosen shits" (Beckett, *Selected Works*, 2:332). On the other hand, however, Beckett's work is a meditation on the fact that, precisely as Geulincx had claimed, a narrative voice is no more than the voice of a "mere spectator of a machine whose workings I can neither adjust nor readjust" (Geulincx, *Ethics*, 34). Or, as Beckett puts it, in somewhat pithier terms, in *Molloy*:

And in winter, under my greatcoat, I wrapped myself in swathes of newspaper, and did not shed them until the earth awoke, for good, in April. The Times Literary Supplement was admirably adapted to this purpose, of a neverfailing toughness and impermeability. Even farts made no impression on it. I can't help it, gas escapes from my fundament on the least pretext, it's hard not to mention it now and then, however great my distaste. One day I counted them. Three hundred and fifteen farts in nineteen hours, or an average of over sixteen farts an hour. After all it's not excessive. Four farts every fifteen minutes. It's nothing. Not even one fart every four minutes. It's unbelievable. Damn it, I hardly fart at all. I should never have mentioned it. Extraordinary how mathematics help you to know yourself. (Beckett, *Selected Works*, 2:25–26)

The fact that the one subject at Trinity College with which Beckett had difficulty was mathematics is surely part of the passage's larger resonance. Molloy constantly monitors the way his deteriorating body behaves, sometimes in great astonishment, but he is bereft of any ability to control that behavior, or to motivate his body, beyond an endless series of comically painful vaudevillian routines he invents to occupy his time (such as the famous, excruciatingly detailed, six-page account of the sucking-stones) and, finally, to have something to monitor and write about in the first place (Beckett, *Selected Works*, 2:63–69). A few pages on, Molloy observes, "For in me there have always been two fools, among others, one asking nothing better than to stay where he is and the other imagining that life might be slightly less horrible a little further on" (Beckett, *Selected Works*, 2:43–44). That dualism recurs throughout Beckett's work, and it is all that finally remains of anything approaching a religious faith in his writing. One could even say that, in the end, eliminating the minor distinction between the two fools is the true aim of all of Beckett's characters, for it is only then, in the words that Molloy, contemplating self-castration, borrows from Leopardi, "that non che la speme il desiderio"—that not just hope, but even the desire for it, is extinguished (Beckett, *Selected Works*, 2:31).

But the tension between the two fools is embedded in a struggle with language that turns out to be theological enough after all. When, in the wake of Beckett and then Alain Robbe-Grillet, Roland Barthes begins to formulate the idea of a "writing degree zero," he writes:

> It is not granted to the writer to choose his mode of writing from a kind of non-temporal store of literary forms. It is under the pressure of History and Tradition that the possible modes of writing for a given writer are established; there is a History of Writing. But this History is dual: at the very moment when general History proposes—or imposes—new problematics of the literary language, writing still remains full of the recollection of previous usage, for language is never innocent: words have a second-order memory which mysteriously persists in the midst of new meanings. . . . A stubborn after-image, which comes from all the previous modes of writing and even from the past of my own, drowns the sound of my present words.[25]

As Beckett told Knowlson, he decided after *Murphy* to write in French because it was thus easier to write "without style," that is, in Barthes's terms, in the mode of a zero degree of writing that was rigorously cleansed of all that might color it with the unstated connotations of a particular, historically situated, individual sensibility.[26] And in a letter Beckett writes (in his idiosyncratic German) in 1937 to Axel Kaun, to whom he had only been recently introduced—it is a letter focusing on problems of translation—Beckett elaborates in large degree what Barthes would later codify.

> Grammar and style! To me they seem to have become as irrelevant as a Biedermeirer bathing suit or the imperturbability of a gentleman. A mask. It has to be hoped the time will come, thank God, in some circles it already has, when language is best used where it is most efficiently abused. Since we cannot dismiss it all at once, at least we do not want to leave anything undone that may contribute to its disrepute. To drill one hole after another

into it until that which lurks behind, be it something or nothing, starts seeping through—I cannot imagine a higher goal for today's writer.[27]

A language full of holes—exactly what Coetzee invokes in *The Childhood of Jesus*, which I discuss in chapter 3—is Beckett's version of a writing that has abandoned the concept of a personal (which is always also historical) "style." For Barthes, the utopian pursuit of "freedom" for the modern writer is the production of a writing liberated from all intimations of past ideology, of the moral and theological crutches in our historical awareness, in our bourgeois sensibilities, in our national prejudices, our metaphors, our idioms, in the reifications of received wisdom lodged like ineradicable bedbugs in the fabric of our language. This zero degree of writing, he concluded, was "the anticipation of a homogeneous social state" itself freed from the ideological burdens of the past (Barthes, *Writing Degree Zero*, 87). Yet what Barthes describes is also, perhaps unwittingly, perfectly compatible with Auerbach's assertion that the history of the novel is itself a progressive mingling and undoing of stylistic conventions that is based (for Auerbach) on a profoundly Christian moral and political ideal, one prefigured, however unsuccessfully, by the Calvinist insistence on election that was also important to Geulincx. The secularization of literary form, aiming at the perfect freedom of a "writing degree zero," is also, however perversely, the enactment of the Christian teleology Auerbach celebrates.

What remained in the wake of this demand for writing detached from its "second-order memory" were utterly banal and mathematized routines, such as the minute description and counting of rows of banana trees (some cut down, some not) on Franck's plantation that we find in Robbe-Grillet's *La Jalousie* (1957). "For the following rows, one has: twenty-three, twenty-one, twenty-one, twenty-one. Twenty-two, twenty-one, twenty, twenty. Twenty-three, twenty-one, twenty, nineteen, etc."[28] It is a counting routine repeated several times in the novel. If Barthes is correct about such writing—and I think he is, to a large extent—then it is also the case that the difference between the secular and the religious in our literature is in fact far more difficult to pin down than we casually imagine, since as even Barthes implied, no one can write for any duration without once again becoming a prisoner of the "after-images" of his or her language (Barthes, *Writing Degree Zero*, 17). Like the inescapable and ubiquitous vestiges of the *idées reçues* that preoccupied Gustave Flaubert and then Stephane Mallarmé, the religious is so deeply a part of the language we use, as both Mann's and Coetzee's works also reveal, that one must resort to counting farts and banana trees, or perhaps watching *Keeping Up with the Kardashians*, to be confidently rid of it, though I can easily imagine repeated iterations of this last routine eventually driving one back into the arms of an established church full-time. For me, however, there is one further conclusion to be drawn from the predicament Barthes outlines, a conclusion Barthes himself would not have considered, though it is implied by Heidegger's *Verwindung* and Marquard's "methodical atheism": that the attempt to liberate our language of any and all vestiges of the theological has an uncanny way of reinscribing itself in the history of theology, perhaps unintentionally and perhaps not, in order to accomplish its end. Beckett's embrace of Geulincx's metaphysics is not so neatly detached from Geulincx's theological and moral positions, which were all of a piece for the Flemish thinker. That is, I want to suggest that even the successful achievement of a zero degree of writing would itself be a theological event of sorts, since it would reproduce in an uncanny way via its formal demands precisely the puritan severity and moral hygiene that Calvin, perhaps more than any other Protestant theologian, aimed to achieve.

I mentioned earlier that Geulincx was not merely a Cartesian philosopher—he was also, as were so many advanced thinkers of the Baroque Age, a devout (if somewhat unorthodox) Calvinist, converting to the sect after losing his first academic position, perhaps because of his too-vocal Jansenism. It is not surprising that Calvin is almost completely ignored in studies of Beckett, who seems never to have mentioned the Reform theologian in his writings.[29] It is far more surprising, I think, that neither Hans van Ruler's introduction to Geulincx's *Ethics* nor Anthony Uhlmann's introduction to Beckett's notes on Geulincx mentions Calvin even once. In this respect, van Ruler and Uhlmann follow the pattern set by the earliest—and perhaps still most astute—interpreter of the presence of Descartes and Geulincx in Beckett's work, Hugh Kenner. Kenner's *Samuel Beckett* first appeared in 1961, and in it he provides a brilliant formal analysis of the way Geulincx's Cartesian-based occasionalism not only runs throughout Beckett's writing, but also provides a comic, vaudevillian mirror of sorts for what has become of the human body in a realm of scientific abstraction and technological ubiquity. Even the humble bicycle emerges in Beckett as evidence of Geulincx's demand to *despectio sui*, to despise oneself because of the weakness of one's understanding. Mathematized experience, for Kenner, is what allows for the increasing detachment of consciousness from the way the world really works, as if the best model of how bodily motion occurs had been provided by the animators of Walt Disney's Mickey Mouse cartoons, who assembled thousands of disconnected drawings to give the appearance of continuous and intended motion.

But nowhere in his account of Geulincx does Kenner mention Calvin or anything remotely connected to Geulincx's religious claims.[30] John Fletcher expands on Kenner's insights, though again with no mention of Geulincx's Calvinism.[31] This pattern continues unbroken into more recent criticism. In a book on the "revolutionary" (both literary and political) tendencies in Beckett, Pascale Casanova offers a putatively new interpretation of Geulincx in Beckett, though she finally provides a less informed reading than does either Kenner or Fletcher, without mentioning the earlier work of either of them and, once again, without any mention of Calvin within Geulincx.[32] David Tucker's recent book is perhaps the most complete textual accounting we have so far of Beckett's references to Geulincx. And though Tucker spends far too much time hunting down Geulincxian imagery that earlier commentators, such as Uhlmann, have apparently missed, Tucker nevertheless comes closer than anyone before him to recognizing the issue of religious predestination in Geulincx (and, vaguely, in Beckett).[33] "Fundamental to Geulincx's conception of the authority of God is that it is metaphysically impossible to resist" (Tucker, *Samuel Beckett*, 121). Yet even Tucker never addresses the obvious connections linking the problem of a seemingly "tyrannical" God, the "ethical fatalism" of Geulincx's *Ethics*, and the inescapable theological source of these matters in Geulincx—John Calvin (Tucker, *Samuel Beckett*, 121).

Like all his predecessors, Tucker makes no mention whatsoever of Geulincx's Calvinism and hence (like those before him) is unable to put issues such as a "tyrannical" God or "ethical fatalism" in the proper perspective of a Calvinist Puritanism that has had (even if we accept only half of what Max Weber teaches us) an immense role in the development of Western European and American culture—indeed, in the development of something we call "modernity" itself. In this sense, it is wrongheaded from the start to imagine that what Beckett found in Geulincx's occasionalism is nothing more than an intellectual curiosity that could be put to clever uses in his fiction, since once we acknowledge the radical Calvinism at the basis of Geulincx's work, we are no longer dealing merely with a tyrannical divinity and ethical abdication, but rather with a crucial shift in the nature of belief and the meaning of redemption. The only contemporary criticism I have found that even acknowledges Beckett and Calvin in the same context does so through an odd sort of postmodern formalism in which it is argued that Beckett's style may help us to understand Calvin's rhetorical choices in the *Institutes of the Christian Religion* (1559).[34] Yet Geulincx's separation of mind and body is, in profound ways, the most rigorous form of Calvin's doctrine of human helplessness without God's grace. That is, the belief that our minds and bodies are related to one another only by the grace of God and the belief that we are in fact quite impotent to do anything without divine aid are intimately tied to one another, and it is not at all surprising to find them linked in Geulincx. Not only is the doctrine of human impotence without God's assistance part and parcel of the larger idea of election, as these joined ideas emerge in the work of Augustine and then in Calvin, but the conjunction also implies both our powerlessness to effect our own salvation and, pushed to its logical conclusion, our powerlessness to join intentions to deeds at all on earth without divine intervention.

It is only on such grounds that Max Weber could derive his sense of Calvinism's unintended consequences: that is, the psychological reaction to Calvinism's doctrinal isolation and hopelessness that prompted a compensating overconfidence in *fides efficax*, faith manifested in its effects, such that these effects were to be read as the legible signs that one had been blessed by God. Since the effects of faith were in fact produced by God and not by us, and were the necessary consequence of God's grace and mercy in our otherwise corrupt worldly existence, those effects might also eventually be taken as signs of our own final salvation—a conclusion Calvin's work itself does not support, even if Calvin held that our worldly successes and failures were themselves manifestations of God's power.[35] Calvin's notion of prayer is instructive here. We are enjoined to pray, and to pray fervently, because it is good for us: "hence comes an extraordinary peace and repose to our consciences," an inner peace that, in effect, prevents us from too curiously and presumptuously looking into the ways of God and his plan for us (Calvin, *Institutes*, 851; 3.20.2). We pray, that is, for a strengthened but blind faith, that we may better serve God without doubt. And yet, Calvin never wavers from the true source of that faith: "Faith is the work of election, but election does not depend upon faith" (Calvin, *Institutes*, 967; 3.24.3). The difficult predicament in which this leaves the helpless yet hopeful sinner, trying to strengthen a faith that may be a consequence but never a cause of salvation, is not as far from the predicament of Beckett's characters as it may at first appear.

In many usually unacknowledged ways, these same doctrinal issues haunt the entirety of Beckett's work—not only the aporia separating mind and body, but also the impotence of human will *sine gratia* (and I am tempted to imagine that over the door of Beckett's good Protestant childhood home he may have perversely envisioned the phrases *sine gratia*, *sine fide*, and *sine scriptura*). As Molloy observes during the burial of Lousse's dog, "All the things you would do gladly, oh without enthusiasm, but gladly, all the things there seems no reason for your not doing, and that you do not do! Can it be we are not free? It might be worth looking into" (Beckett, *Selected*

Works, 2:32). Yet even the numerous religiously inflected interpretations of *En attendant Godot* (French, 1952; English, 1954)—which could be translated with a more tendentiously eschatological resonance as *In the Meantime, Godot*—rarely, if ever, include Calvin in the discussion. Nevertheless, Geulincx's perfectly Calvinist account of happiness is ideally suited to *Waiting for Godot*. In Geulincx's formula, "Happiness should not be summoned, but neither should it be kept away: one must await it, not strive for it. When it thrusts itself upon you, you may embrace it; when God brings it to us, it is right to make use of it; it is fitting to accept what He sends us" (Geulincx, *Ethics*, 61). And again: "We must conduct ourselves in a merely negative way towards our own Blessedness" (Geulincx, *Ethics*, 58). As Estragon observes in the first, perfectly Geulincxian line of *Waiting for Godot*, "Nothing to be done" (Beckett, *Selected Works*, 3:3). It is a line that first appears in *Molloy* as "Nothing or little to be done" (Beckett, *Selected Works*, 2:49). *In the meantime*, that is, during what the early Church Fathers would have called the *saeculum* of a fallen existence suspended between Adam's original sin and Christ's second coming, Beckett's characters occupy themselves with the vaudeville routine we call life, as if each was no more than a "puppet" manipulated from above (Beckett, *Selected Works*, 2:49). It is the stoically humble—or comically humiliating—sort of life that is available when "the whole thing is someone else's affair," however one chooses to imagine what or who that someone might be (Geulincx, *Ethics*, 34).

In Beckett's *The Unnamable*, the "someone" goes by a large number of names. The novel, like *Molloy* and *Malone Dies* (French, 1951; English, 1956), is in many ways a catalogue of the various avatars of Beckett's narrative voice, and its narrator is perhaps indeed *unnamable* just for that reason, but such avatars wind up at the end of the novel simply identified as "they" and "them": "I didn't understand what they were trying to do to me, I say what I'm told to say, that's all there is to it, and yet I wonder, I don't know, I don't feel a mouth on me, I don't feel the jostle of words in my mouth . . . " (Beckett, *Selected Works*, 2:375–76). These voices are "someone else's affair," I believe, in exactly the same way that the intersection of mind and body, intention and deed, voice and phenomena, speech and mouth, are also "someone else's affair" in Geulincx's *Ethics*: "But his voice continued to testify for me, as though woven into mine . . . " (Beckett, *Selected Works*, 2:303). And if that is the case, then Beckett's strenuous efforts to rid his work not only of "style," but even more radically of the presumption that the narrative voices he produces are his own, cannot avoid what Barthes calls the "second-order memory," the "stubborn after-image," of Geulincx's Calvinism, by which his own voice instead emerges precisely as the effect of those that speak to him. They are voices that come, if no longer as the consequence of some identified divine grace, then by a process that is a perfect mnemonic residue, a literary photogene, of Calvinist humility in the presence of the word of God.

Rather than invoke some ill-fitting and vague negative theology that at times hovered around French existentialism, or an all-too-human cry of agnostic cosmic despair in post-Holocaust Europe, I want to insist on the importance of Beckett's formal search for an appropriate style—for a writing degree zero, which is to say for a more thoroughly secular writing than had ever before been achieved. Such a methodical secularism, if I can inflect Marquard's phrase, is what Barthes elsewhere describes as the "intransitive" writing of an écrivain rather than that of an écrivant who addresses real people, objects, and history, as if those real people, objects, and history could be affected in some way by the writer's intentions, as if they were *not* (as they are for the écrivain) "someone else's affair" (Geulincx, *Ethics*, 34).[36] But I want to emphasize at the same time that Beckett's literary answer to this search, which is one of the finest verbal manifestations of a thoroughly secularized universe we are likely to see, itself swerves back to recuperate the most rigorous and demanding theology within all of Christendom, that is, Calvin's doctrine of election as it is embodied in Geulincx's metaphysics. For me, this is *Verwindung* with a vengeance.

▪   ▪   ▪

It is somewhat routine in the study of Beckett's works to mark a break between a novel such as *Murphy*, written and published in English before the war, and the trilogy of *Molloy, Malone Dies,* and

The Unnamable, all written originally in French and published after 1945. There is much to be said for this division. *Murphy* is stylistically very different from the trilogy: it makes little attempt to achieve the "writing degree zero" anonymity and the semantically sterilized prose of the later novels, and it is filled with characters who have a fair amount of the stage Irishman about them—Neary, Celia, Wylie, Miss Counihan, Austin Ticklepenny, Mr. Willoughby Kelly, and most of all Murphy himself—caricatures that seem natural extensions of Joyce's figures. The novel is also more obviously cartoonish in its comedy, not unlike the early Thomas Pynchon in that respect. And it has a "realistic" specificity of setting utterly lacking in the trilogy. Particular sites in Dublin and London are invoked, and the novel ends in a London psychiatric hospital, the Magdalen Mental Mercyseat, where Murphy is briefly employed as an attendant before his suicide. The MMM is itself based on Bethlem Royal Hospital, dating from 1257 and long an asylum for the insane, where Beckett visited and took notes.[37] (BRH is the original "bedlam" of the English language.) Indeed, *Murphy* is the only novel where the protagonist (such as he is) commits suicide, a step longed for yet never attempted by those in the trilogy, as if even that act had proven to be beyond the diminished will—the velleity—of the later characters. "But the thought of suicide had little hold on me" Molloy tells us, even as he compares his life "to a veritable calvary, with no limit to its stations and no hope of crucifixion" (Beckett, *Selected Works*, 2:73). It is an image of penance that could have been taken from Dante's *Inferno*. Geulincx first appears in *Murphy*, however, and the MMM asylum is a perfectly Geulincxian world, in which "patients were described as 'cut off' from reality" and where "the function of treatment was to bridge the gulf, translate the sufferer from his own pernicious little private dungheap to the glorious world of discrete particulars" (Beckett, *Selected Works*, 1:107). Yet this idea of treatment was "duly revolting" to Murphy, "whose experience as a physical and rational being obliged him to call sanctuary what the psychiatrists called exile," a sentiment leading directly to the "beautiful Belgo-Latin of Arnold Geulincx: *Ubi nihil vales, ibi nihil velis*" (Beckett, *Selected Works*, 1:107)—why desire if one can do nothing about it?

Along with Geulincx comes some of Calvin's thinking on predestination. Murphy himself is "one of the elect, who require everything to remind them of something else" (Beckett, *Selected Works*, 1:41). But what Celia here sees as Murphy's idiosyncratic election becomes a sort of faith that Molloy half-seriously, half-sarcastically invokes in the trilogy's first novel: "For all things hang together, by the operation of the Holy Ghost, as the saying is" (Beckett, *Selected Works*, 2:36). When seeking a job, if only on Celia's insistence, Murphy is explicitly likened to Job. We are told that he needs no one but himself as an object of pity: those who suppose him "on the *qui vive* for someone wretched enough to be consoled by such maieutic saws as 'How can he be clean that is born'" were "utterly mistaken" (Beckett, *Selected Works*, 1:45), as if there were indeed no consolation to be found in the humanly shared inheritance of Adam's sin (as there is in, say, Nathaniel Hawthorne), and as if no one were more wretched than Murphy in any case. When Murphy proves to have great rapport and success with the asylum's patients, he takes this to mean that "nothing less than a slap-up psychosis could consummate his life's strike. *Quod erat extorquendum*" (that is, "that which was to be extracted by torture") (Beckett, *Selected Works*, 1:110). But to Murphy this also implies that the fortune told earlier by the astrologist Ramaswami Krishnaswami Narayanaswami Suk is the effect of his own personal fate, not the cause. In a remarkable sentence that both prefigures the play with verb tenses in the French text of the trilogy and simultaneously invokes and teases Calvin's notion of election, Beckett writes, "So far as the prophetic status of the celestial bodies was concerned Murphy has become an out-and-out preterist" (Beckett, *Selected Works*, 1:110). Everything depends here on the punning use of "preterist," for a preterist is both someone who lives only in the past tense (not unlike a character in a novel, one that in a traditional French novel lives in the literary past, the *passé simple*) but also someone who believes that all biblical prophecies (including those of Revelation) have already been fulfilled, a doctrine that in the form of "full" preterism also means that the *parousia* of Christ's second coming and the resurrection of the dead have already occurred as well (generally the date given for these events is prior to the sack of Jerusalem in

70 CE). It is a doctrine that surreally advances a predestined universe, for it suggests not only that events have been divinely foretold, but also that the significant prophecies *have already come to pass.* The only thing that seems to be left, as Murphy soon realizes, is to leave this world entirely via suicide.

The asylum is also a place where the dissociation of narrative voices that will be so important to the trilogy is first addressed as the "schizoid voice" of the appropriately named Mr. Endon, who insists that the single method of suicide he will pursue is the unlikely one of "apnoea" (holding one's breath). Mr. Endon's voice will become, however, over the course of the trilogy, very much the voice of *The Unnameable.* "His inner voice did not harangue him, it was unobtrusive and melodious, a gentle continuo in the whole consort of his hallucinations. The bizarrerie of his attitudes never exceeded a stress laid on their grace. In short, a psychosis so limpid and imperturbable that Murphy felt drawn to it as Narcissus to his fountain" (Beckett, *Selected Works,* 1:111–12). Murphy's kinship with Mr. Endon is then also the kinship of the voices of psychosis with the voices of grace, and the superimposition of the two is mythological as well, for it is Narcissus's excessive attraction to his reflection in the fountain that leads to his transformation (his *Verwindung*), while the formerly voiceless Echo is transformed into a stone that suddenly has the power of speech. If what Murphy enjoys in the MMM is a "vicarious autology"—a most curious phenomenon in that what he enjoys sharing with the inmates is precisely their isolation, their speaking to themselves, which is in the end precisely what a community of Geulincxian Calvinists would share—then what happens to Beckett's narrative voice, to all the interior yet simultaneously external voices that eventually overtake the trilogy, is something strangely akin to the coming of an amazing yet perverse sort of grace, one that may in fact function as a prophylactic against suicide. After a final game of chess played with and lost to Mr. Endon, Murphy does manage to blow himself up in an explosion of gas piped into his room, his cremated remains to be strewn over the filth and bodily fluids of a barroom floor. But the novels of the trilogy all end rather differently, and the oddly sustaining murmur of a schizoid voice has a crucial role to play in that change of fate.

Perhaps the most important key to the narrative voices that fill the trilogy is provided in the early pages of *Molloy*: "What I need now is stories, it took me a long time to know that, and I'm not sure of it" (Beckett, *Selected Works*, 2:9). These "stories" move from the reports provided by Molloy before he leaves to find his mother to the report provided by Moran in part 2 of *Molloy* as he is sent (accompanied by his son) to find Molloy. The plot of *Molloy* consists of two agents (and a messenger or two), charged with certain missions, both of whom seem unclear as to the whys and wherefores of their tasks. It is not unlike, from what we can deduce, Beckett's own experience of the underground in France during World War II, where (he tells us) he spent much of his time occupying without any heroism a farmhouse in which munitions had been stashed, waiting for other agents to appear and claim them. "Are you on night patrol?" Moran asks the small, thickset man who invades his campsite, just before bludgeoning the stranger to death (Beckett, *Selected Works*, 2:145). And earlier, when Moran in exasperation dispatches his uncomprehending son to Hole to buy a bicycle, we read, "Who is this bicycle for, I said, Goering?" (Beckett, *Selected Works*, 2:137). What is important here is that, in the course of the trilogy, Beckett's own status as "secret agent" in the underground becomes that of a narrative agent, an agent who is no more than the mouthpiece of others, perhaps military commanders at first and "authors" later, behind him. "Saying is inventing. Wrong, very rightly wrong. You invent nothing, you think you are inventing, you think you are escaping, and all you can do is stammer out your lesson, the remnants of a pensum one day got by heart and long forgotten, life without tears, as it is wept" (Beckett, *Selected Works*, 2:27). The word *pensum* here has a specific, though generally unnoted, resonance with Calvin. The nominative *pensus*—derived from the verb *pendo*, meaning "to weigh" (via suspension); "to dole out," as an amount of wool to be spun; "to ponder"; "to value"; or "to have value or weight"—comes to mean the equivalent of a day's labor, or any task in general, though it later also came to refer to a punishment meted out in schools. In Beckett it seems to be borrowed most directly from Arthur Schopenhauer's Doctrine of Suffering in his *Parerga and Paralipomena*: "Life is a task of working at something (or a debt to be worked off): in this sense having discharged one's duty is a more beautiful expression."[38] But the idea of life as a duty or task to be discharged is also deeply Calvinist, and in a way that resonates tellingly with Murphy's search for a paying job, which finally leads him to the sanctuary of an asylum, and with the obscure assignments, fruitless efforts, and terminally weak wills of Molloy and even the seemingly Catholic or Church of Ireland Moran, who craves private communion after missing Mass at the start of his tale and wonders at the end how long he had gone "without either confession or communion" (Beckett, *Selected Works*, 2:162). "Again, it will be no slight relief from cares, labors, troubles, and other burdens for a man to know that God is his guide in all things. . . . From this will arise a singular consolation: that no task [opus] will be so sordid and base, provided you obey your calling in it, that it will not shine and be reckoned very precious in God's sight" (Calvin, *Institutes*, 725; 3.10.6). In Beckett, this "sordid and base" task, or duty, or penance, ultimately becomes writing itself, that is, the finding of "stories."

In the course of *Malone Dies*, these stories, once started, quickly become almost too ridiculous in their inevitable recourse to recycling and cliché to pursue—though, as Malone eventually demonstrates, they also manage to lead up to, and end with, the narrator's murder (a self-consuming strategy that Coetzee will repeat in *Age of Iron*). Malone's narrative, which begins with his certainty that he will soon be dead and is composed from a sort of hospital or asylum bed in which he inexplicably finds himself, is made up of stories that, paradoxically, are not so much designed (as in narrative strategies from *The Thousand and One Nights* to those outlined by the psychoanalytic narrative theory of Peter Brooks) to defer the narrator's or the protagonist's inevitable death via digressions and interpolated subplots.[39] Rather, they are designed as if *en attendant*—that is, something to fill the meantime, the *saeculum* before death comes—and eventually, perhaps, to hasten the arrival of a narrated death, as the story Malone tells finally does. The stories, however, repeatedly turn out to be almost as unendurable as the waiting itself. Malone interrupts his story of Saposcat (one who knows scat, or shit) and the Lamberts with authorial asides: "What tedium" or "no, that won't do" or "This is awful" or "no, I can't do it" or "Mortal tedium" (Beckett, *Selected Works*, 2:181, 183, 185, 190, 211). Sapo is renamed Macmann (son of man), who is reduced to crawling and then to rolling for his locomotion, "coming to," finally, in a bed "in a kind of asylum"—not unlike Malone himself (Beckett, *Selected Works*, 2:248). At which point Lemuel (shade of Jonathan Swift's Gulliver) enters the story, leading Malone eventually to an island excursion with the philanthropist Lady Pedal and some attendants, where Lemuel murders the entire party with a hatchet.

But before all this occurs, Macmann has time for some theodicy of a sort. Lying on his back, pelted by the rain, Macmann reflects on the cause of his inexorable decline.

> The idea of punishment came to his mind, addicted it is true to that chimera and probably impressed by the posture of the body and the fingers clenched as though in torment. And without knowing exactly what his sin was he felt full well that living was not a sufficient atonement for it or that this atonement was in itself a sin, calling for more atonement, and so on, as if there could be anything but life, for the living. And no doubt he would have wondered if it was really necessary to be guilty in order to be punished but for the memory, more and more galling, of his having consented to live in his mother, then to leave her. And this again he could not see as his true sin, but as yet another atonement which had miscarried and, far from cleansing him of his sin, plunged him in it deeper than before. And truth to tell the ideas of guilt and punishment were confused together in his mind, as those of cause and effect so often are in the minds of those who continue to think. And it was often in fear and trembling that he suffered, saying, This will cost me dear. (Beckett, *Selected Works*, 2:233)[40]

It is a richly Calvinist speech: the constant trial of postlapsarian life; the impossibility of real atonement, in that, as Calvin pointed out, and as Coetzee will too, confession and penance are in their own ways just more occasion for sin, hence requiring more atonement, endlessly; the unmerited nature of punishment and grace; the causal confusion of guilt and punishment (like the causal confusion of faith and grace); and—though only in Beckett's English—the Kierkegaardian "fear and trembling" that suggest that suffering itself will be punished.

At this point, the task, the *pensum*, of writing in *The Unnamable* turns into an endless, if bewildered, listening to the multiple schizoid voices that speak to the narrator, though his autology, his "psychosis," also turns out, as in *Murphy*, to be quite indistinguishable from a twisted, contorted sense of grace. It is what allows the narrative, if that is what it can be called—and perhaps allows Beckett as writer— to "go on" when there is no longer reason to do so. It is the silence that must be filled with words, but also the silence that allows (or invites) words to fill it. In the final, often-cited lines of *The Unnamable*, as the narrator worries that the voices speaking to him will abandon him, will stop coming altogether, we read:

> You must say words, as long as there are any, until they find me, until they say me, strange pain, strange sin, you must go on, perhaps it's done already, perhaps they have said me already, perhaps they have carried me to the threshold of my story, before the door that opens on my story, that would surprise me, if it opens, it will be I, it will be the silence, where I am, I don't know, I'll never know, in the silence you don't know, you must go on, I can't go on, I'll go on. (Beckett, *Selected Works*, 2:407)

In *Murphy*, Mr. Endon proved to be unable to distinguish between the "limpid and imperturbable" psychosis of his hallucinations and his sense that this affliction was itself a product of grace. This is not exactly where the narrative voice of the trilogy ends up. But it seems impossible to avoid the conclusion that what had been the enclosed sanctuary of the MMM in *Murphy* becomes in the trilogy—for a variety of reasons, of which perhaps the senseless suffering of the war years is one, though hardly the only one—the condition of what Giorgio Agamben has called in a rather different context "bare life" in general.[41] Long before Agamben, and more in keeping, I think, with Beckett's point of view, Charles Baudelaire referred in 1859 to the "hospital" of everyday life, and Beckett's trilogy would seem rather directly to put that observation to the test.[42] Mr. Endon's voice in the asylum, in that sense, becomes narrative voice per se for Beckett, which means that we are left to wonder whether Mr. Endon's belief that his hallucinatory condition is also a form of sanctuary, of fugitive grace, is an insight to be applied to *The Unnamable* as well.

Beckett's decision to write in French after *Watt* (1953) and beginning with *Mercier et Camier*, which was written in 1946 but not published until 1970, brings with it certain complications, none more significant than verb tense. After *Molloy*, translated with Paul Bowles, Beckett alone translated all of his subsequent works. But Beckett turned to French at a significant moment in the literary appearance of that language, the moment at which the defining marker of French fictional (and traditional historical) narrative—the *passé simple*, which indicates the occurrence of an event at a definite time in the past—was falling out of use in favor of the more informal and conversational *passé composé*, which indicates that an event occurred at some indefinite time in the past, and the *imparfait*, which may indicate habitual or lasting action, an event simultaneous with another, or a persistent condition. Both are dependent on context for precise meaning. Since there is no equivalent of the *passé simple*, or literary past, in the English novel, there was no way for Beckett to translate his play with French verb tenses—some "literary" and some not—into English. On the whole, like other French writers of the era, Beckett eschews the *passé simple*, but not always. *Molloy* begins in the present tense, but when the narrator initiates his tale of A and C (A and B in the French text), Beckett uses the literary past, the *passé simple*. But this pretense to literary narrative is soon abandoned for the more informal *passé composé* and *imparfait*. Again, when Molloy tells us the tale of how he helped Lousse bury her dog (which he had run over with his bicycle), the *passé simple* briefly reappears. The result is that, in French, Beckett can make his various narrative voices signify overtly both that they are not composing something called "literature" and also that they periodically feel the demand (or need) to appear as if they are. In part 2 of *Molloy*, after Moran has awakened to the fact that he has apparently smashed to a pulp the head of a man (in a double-breasted suit, long dark muffler, and hat with a fishhook and artificial fly in the band) who earlier intruded upon his campfire, we read, "I do not know what happened then. But a little later, perhaps a long time later, I found him stretched on the ground, his head in a pulp. I am sorry I cannot indicate more clearly how this result was obtained, it would have been something worth reading. But it is not at this late stage of my relation that I intend to give way to literature" (Beckett, *Selected Works*, 2:145–46). The implication is that the literary past tense might have allowed a more detailed representation of the man's beating at the hands of Moran—though Beckett has doubled the irony here, for in the French, the text slips momentarily into the *passé simple* when the discovery of the body occurs, even as the temporal clarity of the discovery is all the same called into question—as if to indicate that such a melodramatic event is inherently a "literary" device. "Mais un peu plus tard, peut-être beaucoup plus tard, je le trouvai étendu par terre, la tête en bouillie" (Beckett, *Molloy*, 201). What is clear, however, is that the demand or need to write—to write "reports" in *Molloy*, "stories" in *Malone Dies*, and an increasingly disembodied spiritual autobiography in *The Unnamable*—is in constant tension with the idea of having to write "literature," and the periodic recourse to the *passé simple* makes this tension all the more resonant in French.

And yet the primary issue for Beckett, I think, is that of past-ness itself, or rather, the idea that a narrative has been allowed to go on (as in a novel) long after the events being recounted have supposedly ended—indeed, such events can be repeated endlessly, exactly as before, even after they have stopped, even if they or anything like them had never occurred. Beckett's concern with the puzzling dimensions of a literary past sometimes appears openly as worry over the precise *sort* of past-ness his narrative requires: "This should all be re-written in the pluperfect" (Beckett, *Selected Works*, 2:12), Molloy observes at one point. After all, it is precisely the past as something narratively or historically available to us through our verb tenses that is constantly undermined by Beckett's periodic recourse to the present tense (and often the future) in order to speak of the past, rather than to the past tense itself. At one point, Molloy calls this "the mythological present, don't mind it" (Beckett, *Selected Works*, 2:22). But this odd temporal condition is neither more nor less than the temporal condition of all narrative "literature"—a kind of past that is always present, that we speak of as if it were present, and that is marked by a unique tense in French.

When we are told that Murphy has become a "preterist," his "pastness" is at the same time the grammatical condition of the novel in general and the theological condition that arises *once all prophecies and apocalypses have been fulfilled*—that is, the condition of actually living on in a kind of afterlife, one in which there is nothing left to be achieved, or at least one in which the end of narratable time has already occurred. Early in *Molloy*, Molloy suddenly yokes the technical problem of narrative verb tense to the theological problems of "preterism" and Calvinist election in a way that neatly sums up the entire problem of narrating in a divinely abandoned *saeculum*, for which the only "event" to be awaited is death and the only means of occupying the "meantime" is the story: "My life, my life, now I speak of it as of something over, now as a joke which still goes on, and it is neither, for at the same time it is over and it goes on, and is there any tense for that?" (Beckett, *Selected Works*, 2:31). Such a time might be superficially described as the time of a death-in-life (as in Jean Rhys's late novel *Wide Sargasso Sea*, from 1966), or a ghostly time before which the apocalypse has already arrived. It might also be the time between death and the onset of rigor mortis, since from Molloy on each of Beckett's characters in the trilogy begins to stiffen, one leg at a time, until we are left only with a limbless torso and head. But for me this understanding of temporality bears a more striking resemblance to what must have been the isolating and psychologically debilitating significance of Calvin's doctrine of election in its original and unameliorated form. Taken in its most radical expression, rather than in the diverse and more human-centered interpretations developed by Nicolaus Zinzendorf and August Hermann Francke, by John Wesley and George Whitefield, and by the Presbyterians, Congregationalists,

Pietists, Methodists, Baptists, Moravians, Mennonites, and Quakers, for whom over time some *certitudo salutis* (assurance of salvation) became a guarantee for the faithful, Calvin's doctrine of predestination is perfectly captured by the impossible verb tense Molloy and Beckett seem to require.[43]

In *The Unnamable*, the narrator is by the end quite literally reduced to a talking head, or rather a talking ear. He has come to be stuffed up to his mouth into a big jar, like flowers in a vase, his slowly withering body limbless except for his now useless manhood, a body supported inside the jar by sawdust, which is periodically changed to clean the filth by the proprietress of a restaurant across the street. The jar itself serves as a kind of sidewalk spectacle; the chophouse owner, who has attached a menu to it and lit it with Chinese lanterns, occasionally puts bones into the narrator's mouth and is kind enough to cover the jar with a tarp in winter. Eventually, what is left of this narrator is no more than an ear, but (as one might expect, given the interminability of Beckett's narrative dilemma) this ear soon regrows a head of its own.

> No, in the place where he is he cannot learn, the head cannot work, he knows no more than on the first day, he merely hears, and suffers, uncomprehending, that must be possible. A head has grown out of his ear, the better to enrage him, that must be it. The head is there, glued to the ear, and in it nothing but rage, that's all that matters, for the time being. It's a transformer in which sound is turned, without help of reason, to rage and terror, that's all that is required, for the moment. (Beckett, *Selected Works*, 2:349)

The phrases "for the time being" and "for the moment" look forward to the *en attendant*, the "in the meantime," of *Waiting for Godot*, and what fills this secular time are the stories the narrative voice both longs to finish and cannot stop telling. "No point either, in your thirst, your hunger, no, no need of hunger, thirst is enough, no point in telling yourself stories, to pass the time, stories don't pass the time, nothing passes the time, time doesn't matter, that's how it is, you tell yourself stories, then any old thing, saying, No more stories from this day forth, and the stories go on . . ." (Beckett, *Selected Works*, 2:378). If a reader is in a certain mood, the comedy here is quite marvelous: the writer, stinking, immobile, and impotent, his head covered in pustules and flies, having become no more than an unstoppable ear and an unstoppable inner voice, serves as a decorative curiosity no different from a rotting floral arrangement for the denizens of a quiet street "near the shambles" (Beckett, *Selected Works*, 2:321)—which is to say, near the slaughterhouse, perhaps of horse meat, not exactly where the bourgeoisie would choose to dine.

Yet even at this point, the voices that fill our narrator's head are overwhelming in their plenitude: they represent "consciousness" as a kind of terminal disease, as though those plagued by it (even in the dreams of sleep) long only for an unattainable respite from it. This vocal plenitude raises a rather uncomfortable (and unanswered) question that appears early on in *The Unnamable.* Near the novel's start, the narrator has decided that, unlike the named voices of previous novels, "perhaps it is time I paid a little attention to myself, for a change" (Beckett, *Selected Works*, 2:294), and he tells us, "I am Matthew [another M-name to join Murphy, Mercier, Molloy, Moran, and Malone] and I am the angel, I who came before the cross, before the sinning, came into the world, came here" (Beckett, *Selected Works*, 2:295). Like Flannery O'Connor's Hazel Motes in *Wise Blood* (1952), this angel sees the redemptive crucifixion as the *cause* of our sense of sinfulness, of sin itself, rather than sin's *effect* and erasure. But the possibility of the narrator's self-identification—he is he, before all the others, like God's angel—is soon undone, so that this narrator once again becomes the invention of another. Even he, the unnamed one, is in the end "someone else's affair," not unlike Murphy and Molloy and all the rest, and perhaps not unlike even the apostle and gospel writer Matthew, who is after all not supposedly *inventing* stories but actually *listening* to the word of God being channeled through him.

> But let us first suppose, in order to get on a little, then we'll suppose something else, in order to get on a little further, that it is in fact required of me that I say something, something that is not to

be found in all I have said up to now. That seems a reasonable assumption. But thence to infer that the something required is something about me suddenly strikes me as unwarranted. Might it not rather be the praise of my master, intoned, in order to obtain his forgiveness? Or the admission that I am Mahood after all and these stories of a being whose identity he usurps, and whose voice he prevents from being heard, all lies from beginning to end? And what if Mahood were my master? I'll leave it at that, for the time being. (Beckett, *Selected Works*, 2:305)

Or, to paraphrase: in writing of myself, I may actually be writing in the hope of divine forgiveness of my guilt; or, I may be writing as a kind of authorial divinity, so that the entire conceit (running throughout *The Unnamable*) that the narrator's voice is one that is constantly usurped by another's speaking through him (Mahood in this case) is a fiction, since I am Mahood; or, I may be writing in such a way that this character I have supposedly invented, Mahood, is in fact my master, and I am merely his agent, or messenger, or channel, not unlike Matthew the Evangelist, and "I" am that which is always "someone else's affair."

These are, one could say, recognizable theological positions, from prayerful petitioning for grace, to the anthropological recognition that one is always already one's divinity, to the possibility that everything one takes as cause and effect might need to be reversed, since in a Geulincxian narratology, we are the effects of external causes. If we take all of this seriously—always a leap of faith in Beckett—it means that every story is in fact an atonement, a *pensum* to be endured, a penance to be worked out, not unlike life; that all fictional personae are puppets, manipulated like so many predetermined destinies in a Calvinist universe; and that the authorial "I" is the most salient puppet or actor of all, since he is never anything other than the personae that come to life through him, unbidden, perhaps unendurable, and yet inescapable, as if guided always by the "prompters" of a theatrical performance from which he is helpless to escape. And as in Calvin's theology, the will's velleity is entwined with its innate sinfulness. Beginning with Molloy, the narrator's sense that he is no more than the mouthpiece of another is accompanied by an inexplicable feeling of guilt. As he grinds to a halt in the forest, Molloy wonders whether he could simply remain there "without the painful impression of committing a fault, almost a sin. For I have greatly sinned, at all times, greatly sinned against my prompters" (Beckett, *Selected Works*, 2:80). When *The Unnamable* ends, it ends with a whisper, not a bang, in a space dominated by nothing more than a weak murmur, by the velleity that precedes language, and by "the words that remain": "all this time I've journeyed without knowing it, it's I now at the door, what door, what's a door doing here, it's the last words, the true last, or it's the murmurs, the murmurs are coming, I know that well, no not even that, you talk of murmurs, distant cries, as long as you can talk . . ." (Beckett, *Selected Works*, 2:406–7). Leaving the stage, as it were, Beckett's narrator still hears and performs the words of a play that was being produced before he arrived, and that will continue to go on, as will he, afterwards.

■　　　■　　　■

As my subsequent chapters demonstrate, both Thomas Mann and J. M. Coetzee elaborate, in different ways, on these themes, Mann in the terms of a somewhat more conventional narrative loop, where the narrator's all-too-human voice turns out to be both the cause and the effect of a demonic narrative's plot and protagonist; and Coetzee in his self-conscious invocation of Beckett's work, as authorial voices become narrative voices become characters, and as the novel wrestles with the Calvinist problem of what Coetzee calls "secular confession." But in all three cases, I believe, the question of narrative form becomes once again inseparable from deeper questions posed by theology and theodicy, so that this particular tradition of novels after 1945 oddly reproduces the photogram of a religious history one expects would have been left behind long ago.

Pierre-Joseph Proudhon, who refused the label of vulgar atheist as well as materialist humanist, and who insisted instead on being known as an anti-theist or a "methodical atheist," maintained a sense of dialectical opposition between God (as a heuristic principle necessary to human reason, and not as a dogmatic idea provided by revelation or an empty consequence of Deistic abstraction) and man, though it is an opposition that would never enjoy a Hegelian resolution.

> Man, as man, is never able to find himself in contradiction with himself; he only feels confusion and anguish through the resistance of the God who is within him. In man is reassembled all the spontaneity of nature, all the instigations of mortal Being, all the gods and demons of the universe. In order to subdue these powers, to discipline this anarchy, man has only reason, his progressive thought: and here is what constitutes the sublime drama the vicissitudes of which form, through their admixture, the ultimate justification for all existence. The destiny of nature and of man is the transformation of God: but God is inexhaustible, and our struggle eternal.[44]

Proudhon's language powerfully describes an intractable relation between the progressive human "transformation" (*metamorphose* for Proudhon, *Verwindung* in German) of theology—what Habermas called the translation of theology's enduring semantic energies—and the "inexhaustible" nature of the thinking of God that produces for Proudhon a necessary "struggle" that he refuses to abandon in favor of reductive materialism. Although perhaps not in exactly the way the French utopian imagined, much of Beckett's work and, as I outline in later chapters, of the work of Thomas Mann and J. M. Coetzee as well, would seem to prove Proudhon's point.

Thomas Mann, Augustine, and the "Death of God"

I ended the previous chapter with the suggestion that Samuel Beckett's numerous borrowings from Arnold Geulincx were also intimately wrapped up in Calvin's doctrine of election and the moral severity and radical humility that doctrine entailed. Beckett's borrowings include, most notably, Geulincx's neo-Cartesian insistence on the aporia between mind and body (or mind and world), by which mind only appears to us to cause changes in the body and the world that are due instead to God's preordained synchronization of spirit and matter. Beckett's incorporation of Geulincx's inhuman and serendipitous metaphysics in his version of what Barthes calls a "writing degree zero" is then, paradoxically, also embedded in a meditation on the inhuman and serendipitous dispensation of divine grace among corrupt humanity, and hence an example of what I mean by a Heideggerian *Verwindung* in which the attempt to "step back" away from the Christian tradition also involves the distorted recuperation of the most radical and rational (or rationalized) forms of that tradition.[1]

But Beckett's minimalist reduction of the novel's voice to a mere murmur intruding on the narrative from somewhere offstage, as if it were someone's else's affair altogether, was only one way in which the *Verwindung* that concerns me here—that is, the overriding sense of arbitrary election, the shame of having been born, radical humility and humiliation, in short, an oddly religious world without grace—was figured in the postwar novel. Thomas Mann's *Doktor Faustus*

(1947), a novel that retains most of the earlier realist trappings discarded by Beckett, is nevertheless a crucial example of the endless secularization I want to emphasize. For Mann's achievement in his late novel is, in effect, wrapping the story of one trajectory of aesthetic development—the formal evolution that for Mann ends in Adrian Leverkühn's tragic betrayal of his own soul to atonal demonic powers, which is the same strain that for Beckett ends in the darkly comedic, atonal routines of a zero degree of narrative voice—within another story: that of Serenus Zeitblom, the good bourgeois historian who, a bit like Mann, is simultaneously enraptured by Leverkühn's art and horrified by what that art seems to signify. In *Doktor Faustus*, in other words, Zeitblom, our conventionally humane narrator, registers for us everything that might be suggested by the vaguely allegorical and apocalyptic landscapes (both moral and material) of Beckett's fiction, but never in fact are. At the same time, Mann's last novel, *Der Erwählte* (*The Elect*), which is itself an otherworldly parody of medieval allegory, takes on more directly the dark humor of Beckett's perspective and makes clearer, as its title suggests, many of the distorted echoes of theology that are easily missed in *Doktor Faustus*. In the final section of this chapter, I turn briefly to a this-worldly example of what "election" came to mean in the postwar era by examining what was popularly called the "Death of God" movement of the 1960s.

■   ■   ■

In *Doktor Faustus*, I am not particularly interested in parsing the much-discussed political allegory of this novel, nor even in those elements that overtly derive from Scripture, such as the penultimate chapter's reproduction of the Garden of Gethsemane.[2] The latter episode comes complete with Leverkühn's version of "Watch with me!" as he descends into the final phases of syphilis, surrounded by thirty or so of his friends, and collapses (after a brief "sermon") while playing a "strong dissonant chord" from his *Lamentation of Dr. Faustus*.[3] This climactic scene, which, like so much in the novel, is half parody and half in earnest as Leverkühn reveals to disbelieving ears his twenty-four-year pact with the Devil while becoming increasingly Christlike in appearance, is certainly fascinating, but it does not get at the heart of my concerns. Something observed in the final lines of the book by our all-too-*gemütlich* narrator, Zeitblom, that earnest high school instructor of Latin and Greek, does provide a starting point of sorts, however. While gazing on the dying face of his friend Leverkühn, our narrator remarks, "What a sardonic trick of nature, one might well say, that she is able to create the image of highest spirituality where the spirit has departed" (Mann, *Doctor Faustus*, 533).[4] On the surface, it is just what one would expect from Zeitblom: a pale, insipid, humanistic attempt at finding a redeeming virtue in an otherwise horrifying tale. But in it one also finds a version of *Verwindung*, of transformation or recuperation that is at heart also a distortion, and it is something that runs throughout the secularizing impulses of Leverkühn's life as a composer, or more accurately a *Tonsetzer*. This latter is an obsolete term for "composer" (*Komponist* would be the usual modern German), a deliberate archaism like much of the "medieval" prose in Mann's novel. It literally means "tone-setter," not unlike a typesetter (or *Schriftsetzer*), which is to say someone who sets down in ink what has already been written or composed by—or as if by—someone else, as if the music itself were "someone else's affair" before it was that of the *Tonsetzer*. As Leverkühn observes in the earlier days of his theological studies, "Apostasy is an act of faith, and everything is and happens in God—falling away from Him most especially" (Mann, *Doctor Faustus*, 140).[5] It is a sentiment that echoes both Geulincx's occasionalist Calvinism and the distorting swerve of Beckett's prose as Beckett recovers Geulincx and Calvin in the process of his own "falling away." In the case of Mann, however, the true source of Leverkühn's sentiment is much more the writings of Augustine, a distant if important precursor to both Luther and Calvin.

Mann was born to a Lutheran father and a Catholic mother, and was baptized into the Lutheran church. But the confessional distinction between his parents was preserved in the relation of Zeitblom, a Catholic, and Leverkühn, a Lutheran. (To Leverkühn's father Mann attributes not only a devout dedication to Luther and Luther's mysticism, but also a deep fascination with quasi-magical speculation in natural philosophy—a background that provides the first hint of Leverkühn's later demonic fate.) Zeitblom may be far more the good bourgeois humanist than his friend, and fairly unwilling to engage in theological speculation, but he is also much more optimistic. He tries desperately to hold on to hope not only about the disposition of Leverkühn's soul but even about the German war effort, which he rather naively imagines might be brought to a halt before Germany's complete destruction; he must also deal, finally, with his terrible shame about the war itself. In many ways, Augustine provides a suitably ambiguous theological foundation for the novel, in that his writings are so famously suspended over the question of free will (which he embraced in his early arguments against the theological and moral dualism of the Manichees and which he continued to support in defense of nascent Church doctrine as Archbishop of Hippo) and predestination (which he later turned to in refuting Pelagius's denial of original sin and consequent emphasis on human self-sufficiency).

Augustine had appeared earlier in Mann's *Der Zauberberg* (1924), in the arguments of the Jewish-Jesuit Naphta (based on Georg Lukács), whose dogmatic rationalism depends on both Augustine's insistence on the impotence of man without God's grace and the desire for a "city of God" that could be reproduced by an authoritarian communalism here on earth. (Naphta is opposed by a far less interesting, Zeitblom-like humanist named Settembrini.) In *Doktor Faustus*, Augustine plays a perhaps more complicated role. On the one hand, he is the source of Zeitblom's faith, gained in his childhood from his Lutheran teacher Schleppfuss, in the possibility that good might come out of evil, since "Augustine at least had gone so far as to say that the function of the bad was to let the good emerge more clearly, making it all the more pleasing and thus praiseworthy when compared to the bad"—a good Lutheran sentiment that Zeitblom will maintain, despite his friend's bargain with evil, as he continues until the end to imagine something positive emerging from Leverkühn's moral corruption and inhuman (or post-humanist) aesthetics (Mann, *Doctor Faustus*, 112).[6] On the other hand, even here, early in his tale,

Zeitblom notes that Aquinas had warned of the moral hazard of Augustine's idea, since it implied that God thus wanted evil to occur. In this Zeitblom points to the other side of Augustine, the side that seems to embrace the idea of the *massa damnationis* (the condemned masses; see Augustine, *City of God*, 21:12), the complete corruption of humanity because of original sin, the (eventually Calvinist) notion of the impotence of the human will to effect salvation, and finally God's seemingly arbitrary, or at least humanly unfathomable, predestination of human beings into opposed camps of the saved and the damned.

Calvin insists on a double election, by which the fates of both the chosen and the abandoned are predetermined by God. By contrast— and for Mann, I think, it is an important difference—Augustine emphasizes a single election of those chosen to receive God's grace, while the damned are damned, as it were, by nothing more than the default of original sin. That is to say, in Augustine's notion of election, God does not choose to damn anyone: if someone falls, it is simply because of the weakness of will (not unlike Beckett's "velleity") caused by Adam's sin. Adam, who had been given the gift of free will in Augustine's account, actively chooses sin and thereby condemns his progeny. Calvin's discussion of free will in Adam is much more ambiguous: he tends to speak of righteousness rather than free will, originally bestowed upon Adam, which was then corrupted "through natural vitiation, but a vitiation that did not flow from nature," that is, from God. That original corruption is what we inherit, so that with Adam's sin, Calvin writes, "the will, because it is inseparable from man's nature, did not perish, but was so bound to wicked desires that it cannot strive after the right"—that is, unless blessed by God's grace and assistance.[7] In this sense, Zeitblom is morally suspended, very much as I think Mann intends, between two sides of an Augustinian–Catholic–Lutheran dilemma. On the one hand, there is Zeitblom's near-desperate desire to overcome the profound disgrace he feels because of the German war effort—a disgrace that grows and festers as his narrative proceeds—by means of Leverkühn's putative, Christlike sacrifice and final redemption (one in which the earnest and unassuming sisters Else and Clementina Schweigestill, who care for Leverkühn to the end in their rural home, assume a sort of *mater dei* presence). On the other hand, there is the specter of complete moral impotence, the possibility that the guilt and shame he feels, because of the war and his friend's bargain with evil, may be beyond any form of redemption that either he or the suffering Leverkühn can effect. In the apparent severity with which the late Augustine insisted that neither human will nor merit was of consequence in the matter of God's dispensation of grace to the elect and his refusal of aid to the damned, we come close, as Calvin himself pointed out endlessly in *Institutes of the Christian Religion*, to later Puritan notions of election.[8] But all of this is worked out in terms of the career of the skeptical, secular Leverkühn, who gives up his theological studies in order to pursue a career in music—though he never relinquishes his belief in the deeper relation between the two vocations.

Leverkühn the secularizing *Tonsetzer* is in fact a version of Samuel Beckett the writer. After all, it is Beckett himself who points out that literature in his time has long been surpassed by musical composition and painting in formal terms, and in their realms both arts necessarily supersede Joyce's "apotheosis of the word." In the letter Beckett writes in 1937 to Axel Kaun (cited in chapter 1), Beckett makes explicit his sense that modern music has long relinquished the sacred regard for its elegant, continuous, and organically nonporous surface that literature still earnestly attempts to maintain, that is, a desire for a narrative surface in which there are no holes.

> Or is literature alone to be left behind on that old, foul road long ago abandoned by music and painting? Is there something paralysingly sacred contained within the unnature of the word that does not belong to the elements of the other arts? Is there any reason why that terrifyingly arbitrary materiality of the word surface should not be dissolved, as for example the sound surface of Beethoven's Seventh Symphony is devoured by huge black pauses, so that for pages on end we cannot perceive it as other than a dizzying path of sounds connecting unfathomable chasms of silence? An answer is requested. (Beckett, *Letters*, 1:518)

Leverkühn wants to eliminate from sequences of musical tones every humanist—and ultimately religious—echo or connotation that Beckett the secularizing writer wants to eliminate from sequences of words. That Leverkühn himself takes his final cue from Beethoven—his crowning achievement is a hellish twelve-tone reconstruction of Beethoven's Ninth Symphony, and the "Ode to Joy" is what is implied—rather underlines the link to Beckett's perspective. These are remarkably commensurable endeavors. The twelve-tone row of Arnold Schoenberg, who later admitted that he was the model for Leverkühn, becomes the subject of Mann's chapter 22, a chapter closely informed by Theodor Adorno's music criticism and by Adorno's personal conversations with Mann in Los Angeles. "The polyphonic value of each tone building a chord," Leverkühn tells his friend, "would be assured by the larger constellation. The historical results—the emancipation of dissonance from resolution, so that dissonance achieves absolute value, as can already be found in some passages in late Wagner—would justify every cluster of sound that can prove its legitimacy to the system" (Mann, *Doctor Faustus*, 207).[9] In short, musical sound would be renewed precisely to the extent that it had been cleansed, except in those rare instances where the "constellation" of the "system" demanded them, of all banal events, of "consonance, the harmony of the triad, the cliché, the diminished seventh," just as Beckett's prose had been reduced to Barthes's "writing degree zero" (Mann, *Doctor Faustus*, 207).[10] (For Mann, perhaps only partly understanding Adorno, it is J. S. Bach who emerges in the novel as the switch point in musical history, because it is Bach who takes the truly independent, contrapuntal, but rigorously rule-governed voices of sixteenth-century polyphony, as in the four-part motets of various Kyries, and transforms them in clever ways to produce harmonic variation, with dominant and subordinate voices, for a new, bourgeois audience.)

But why should we trust Zeitblom's memory for such details? After all, there is the autobiographical "document" describing Leverkühn's interview with the Devil, which Leverkühn left behind for Zeitblom. In it, the Devil summarizes an aesthetic—not yet fully realized by Leverkühn—that would become the basis of Leverkühn's art.

"Certain things are no longer possible. The illusion of emotions as a compositorial work of art, music's self-indulgent illusion, has itself become impossible and cannot be maintained—the which has long since consisted of inserting preexisting, formulaic, and dispirited elements as if they were the inviolable necessity of this single occurrence" (Mann, *Doctor Faustus*, 256–57).[11] The Devil continues, "The subordination of expression to all-reconciling generality is the innermost principle of musical illusion. And that is over" (Mann, *Doctor Faustus*, 257).[12] But with the end of this bourgeois musical illusion comes the end of the bourgeois composer's freedom, which, after all, was only ever guaranteed by the conventions of (post-Bach) harmonic resolution. And what Leverkühn argues can be closely linked to Geulincx's occasionalism: the freedom of the composer is in fact an illusion, for the actual organization of the form depends only on each element's "legitimacy to the system," which is finally like saying that it is "someone else's affair." As Zeitblom remarks to his friend, "it ends up being like a kind of composing prior to composing"—which rather neatly implies that the second act of composing is akin to that of a *Tonsetzer* (Mann, *Doctor Faustus*, 207).[13] The only rub, it seems, is that whereas for the medieval and early modern (pre-Bach) *Tonsetzer* the "someone else" was God, for the modern, post-bourgeois Leverkühn it is only the Devil who can fill that role—and that displacement becomes the unstated basis of Leverkühn's Faustian pact. What remains is the fixed mathematics of the tone row and its seemingly endless series of—what shall we call them?—*routines*, or tonal games, including four kinds of inversion, each with its own multiple variations, played on precisely the same level that Molloy plays the game of the sucking-stones. But this too turns out to be a highly religious issue. As the Devil tells Leverkühn, "A highly theological matter, music—just as is sin, just as am I" (Mann, *Doctor Faustus*, 257).[14] And a significant part of this "matter" for Leverkühn is not unlike what one finds lurking behind Beckett's Geulincx, that is, a particular and rigorous form of Augustine's (and later Calvin's) doctrine of election.

Leverkühn's origins as a *Tonsetzer*, we are told, lie in the deeper recesses of Anabaptism—that movement with murky origins in Switzerland and the Tyrol, yielding Pietists, Mennonites, Hussites, Moravians, Quakers, and Amish, whose radically egalitarian tenets coincided with a fierce resistance to change and modernity. This German Pietist tradition owes much to Calvin; as Weber noted, "historically the doctrine of predestination is also the starting point of the ascetic movement known as Pietism. In so far as the doctrine remained within the Reformed Church, it is almost impossible to draw the line between Pietistic and non-Pietistic Calvinists."[15] Leverkühn is infused with their spirit via his mentor Kretzschmar, who at one point relates the story of one Johann Conrad Beissel, an orphan who emigrates from Germany to Pennsylvania and then winds up as head of a new sect, the Seventh Day Baptists. In Pennsylvania, Beissel realizes that theology is not enough—he must also become a composer, or rather a *Tonsetzer*. Beissel's music eliminates the "all too complicated and artificial" melodies of music imported from Europe: "he wanted to begin anew, to do things better, produce a kind of music more suited to the simplicity of their souls," a music with certain "'masters' and 'servants'" ("Herren" und "Diener") in every scale, and a method that could be easily mastered by anyone (Mann, *Doctor Faustus*, 73).[16] But Leverkühn's compositions evolve from this into something far more rigorously akin to Augustinian notions of election—that is, they move from the populist, *völkisch* simplicity of Beissel's premodern sect or cult, in which the masters and servants are themselves no more than a pseudo-egalitarian feudal trope, to something that emphasizes both the austere rationalism and the radically predetermined nature of the musical logic Leverkühn embraces. Leverkühn builds on Beissel to create something that is beyond the received bourgeois wisdom of the Western musical tradition's emotional—and ultimately theological—sources and trajectory, just as Beissel's theories harken back to an idiom that precedes that tradition.[17]

Much of this is made explicit in Leverkühn's casuistic attempt to rebut the Devil's seductive reasoning on the efficacy of contrition in winning salvation, a contrition of which the Devil deems Leverkühn, in all his pride, incapable. "*Contritio* without hope," Leverkühn remarks, "and as utter unbelief in the possibility of grace and forgiveness, as the sinner's deep-rooted conviction that he has behaved too grossly and that even unending goodness will not suffice to forgive his sins—only that is the true remorse, and I would remember you that it is to redemption most proximate, to goodness most irresistible" (Mann, *Doctor Faustus*, 262).[18] Leverkühn concludes his argument with what must be the most theologically significant aphorism of the entire post–World War II era—though in its deeper recesses, it is no more than a certain rigorous Augustinian logic taken to an extreme (that is, to the extreme Aquinas warned against). "A sinfulness so unholy," Leverkühn says, "that it allows its man fundamentally to despair of salvation is the true theological path to salvation" (Mann, *Doctor Faustus*, 262).[19] Yet Mann, however much he might want to agree with Leverkühn here, and hence with Zeitblom's efforts to save at least the memory of his friend, is careful to allow the most important line in this debate to the Devil, who does nothing more than out-rationalize Leverkühn. "Is it not clear to you that purposed speculation on the charm that great guilt exercises upon goodness renders the very act of its grace utterly impossible?" (Mann, *Doctor Faustus*, 263).[20] The Devil's rebuttal is in fact a more precise version of Geulincx's Calvinist admonition that "we must conduct ourselves in a merely negative way towards our Blessedness"—in short, no purposed speculation on the ability of either goodness or guilt to charm God is allowed. Leverkühn tries to insist once again that the "most reprobate guilt" (verworfensten Schuld) proves to be an "irresistible provocation of infinite goodness" (unwiderstehlichsten Herausforderung an die Unendlichkeit der Güte), but the Devil wittily replies, "Not bad. Truly ingenious. And now I shall tell you that precisely minds of your sort constitute the population of hell" (Mann, *Doctor Faustus*, 263).[21] It is a line almost designed to make Jesuits shudder and Jansenists dance in the street. What Leverkühn believes he has discovered, in a sense, is what Nietzsche had somewhat sneeringly called the air of good, honest atheism that he felt the more intelligent bourgeoisie around him already inhaled. That is, Leverkühn wants to believe that his devotion to the truth, even to the truth that there can be no salvation for him, is of greater value than divine grace itself. In that sense, Nietzsche argues, the bourgeois atheist's rejection of religious salvation is ironically the most severe and pseudo-religious *ascetic ideal* in a nutshell: the unvarnished truth, the bourgeois atheist mistakenly believes, even the brutal truth about one's own disbelief, shall set you free, shall be, in effect, your redemption. And it is the Devil's pleasure, as it was Nietzsche's, to unravel the ruse involved in Leverkühn's way of thinking.

But Mann himself is not so eager to abandon his hero completely to the Devil's ridicule, despite the obvious desperation of Leverkühn's attempt to turn his rejection of salvation, his turning his back on God, into a higher sort of morality. Near the end of the novel, Leverkühn meets his young nephew, Nepomuk Schneidewein, whose unearthly innocence and saintly simplicity are impossible for him to resist. (Somehow, Leverkühn imagines that the Devil's contractual prohibition against loving anyone only applies to loving a woman, an act that has already been Leverkühn's quite intentional undoing. But sexual desire is never that simple in a Thomas Mann novel, and it is a sort of innocent, homosexual love that Leverkühn mistakenly thinks he can still allow himself.) The child is nicknamed both Nepo and Echo, and while the latter name may function in part mythically as a complement to his uncle's intractable and deadly narcissism, it is even more a sign of the child's influence as muse for his uncle's final composition. (The name of the saintly Nepo likely refers to the fourteenth-century Czech martyr and saint, John of Nepomuk, but perhaps also to his musical namesake, Johann Nepomuk Hummel, a onetime student of Mozart whose elegant works for the piano were quickly overshadowed by Beethoven and the romantic composers who followed.) As Zeitblom finally interprets it, Leverkühn's *Faustus* cantata is itself a form of primitive mimesis paradoxically embodied by the most rationalized form of musical art—a point Mann borrows quite deliberately from Adorno's interpretation of modern art as rationalized mimesis.[22] In Zeitblom's words, "The echo, the sound of the human voice returned as a sound of nature, revealed as a sound of nature, is in essence a lament, nature's melancholy 'Ah yes!' to man, her attempt to proclaim his solitude . . ." (Mann, *Doctor Faustus*, 510).[23] The child's rather saccharine prayers in the days before he dies in horrible pain from the headaches and vomiting caused by meningitis thus allow Mann to reveal, in somewhat more straightforward terms, the content of this "lament," which includes an affinity with Augustine's awkwardly twinned notions of divine mercy and irrevocable election that, though more generous and humane than the unforgiving Calvinism of Beckett's Geulincx, nevertheless raise similar issues.

One of Echo's prayers suggests precisely the sort of conundrum that lies at the heart of theology's struggle with notions of grace and election. Zeitblom refers to the prayer as being "remarkable for its unmistakable coloring of predestination":

> No man be given leave to sin
> But that there be some good therein.
> No man's good deed will be forlorn,
> Save that to hell he hath been born.
> May those I love all-ready be
> Made blissful for eternity! Amen.
> (Mann, *Doctor Faustus*, 494)[24]

The prayer is itself perfectly Augustinian in its mixed message: while the first two lines suggest the possibility that, via grace, good may always emerge out of evil, the next four lines clearly suggest the harsher doctrine of a "double election," so that those dear to Nepomuk, he hopes, will already be saved, one way or the other. The poem is thus congruent on the one hand with Zeitblom's earlier affection for Augustine's more forgiving belief in the power of human will supported by a grace available to all, and on the other with Augustine's later and sterner embrace of election. The "strict style" of what Zeitblom calls Leverkühn's final *de profundis*, that is, his atonal, a-theological inversion of Beethoven's Ninth Symphony in his *Faustus* cantata, which Zeitblom calls a "lamentation of the son of hell, the most awful lament of man and God ever intoned on this earth," is a composition Zeitblom also describes as a possible "breakthrough" (Durchbruch), and it allows Zeitblom yet one more turn of the screw in the theological debate over the charm of sin that appears in Leverkühn's interview with the Devil (Mann, *Doctor Faustus*, 509).[25]

"Does it not imply," Zeitblom observes, "the recovery, or, though I would rather not use the word, for the sake of precision I shall, the reconstruction of expression, of emotion's highest and deepest response to a level of intellectuality and formal rigor that must first be achieved in order for such an event—the reversal, that is, of calculated coldness into an expressive cry of the soul, into the heartfelt unbosoming of the creature—to occur?" (Mann, *Doctor Faustus*, 509–10).[26] The "reconstruction of expression" and "the reversal . . . of calculated coldness into an expressive cry of the soul" is a version of what I mean by the *Verwindung* of secularization in *Doctor Faustus*. (That Mann seems to be anticipating the use of "event" or *Ereignis* as also a transformative reversal in Heidegger's late essay "The Principle of Identity" is surely coincidental, though Zeitblom's hesitation over the word *Rekonstruktion*, with its obvious reference to the rebuilding of postwar Germany, is I think no accident.)[27] The Faust cantata is a site where, through the elimination of expression via the use of "pre-organized material" (a version of occasionalist thought, in the end), expressivity as lament is reborn. It is as if Mann also invites us to see all of Beckett, too, as a site where, despite the seemingly meaningless routines, a certain expressivity is reborn in the black comedy of lament.

The purer, early modern polyphony of Leverkühn's prior work is now softened somewhat by the sense that counterpoint here allows the secondary voices, though still independent, to be "more considerate of the principal voice" (Mann, *Doctor Faustus*, 513).[28] Yet the larger notion that Leverkühn's final masterwork is a negation of the divine harmonic resolutions of Beethoven's Ninth remains its most powerful religious statement in Zeitblom's account, what we might call his ultimate argument for the expiation of guilt, shame, and disgrace, for the demonic Leverkühn, for himself as a good German with good German sons in the military, and for Germany as a nation.

But it is not merely that more than once it performs a formal negation of the Ninth, takes it back into the negative, but in so doing it is also a negation of the religious—by which I cannot mean, its denial. A work dealing with the Tempter, with apostasy, with damnation—how can it be anything but a religious work! What I mean is an inversion, an austere and proud upending of meaning, such as I find, for example, in the "friendly appeal" by Dr. Faustus to the companions of his final hour that they should go to bed, sleep in peace, and be not troubled. Given the framework of the cantata, one can scarcely help viewing this as the conscious and deliberate reversal of the "Watch with me!" of Gethsemane. . . . Linked with this, however, is the reversal of the notion of temptation, in that Faust refuses the idea of salvation as itself a temptation—not only out of formal loyalty to the pact and because it is "too late," but also because with all his soul he despises the positive optimism of the world to which he is to be saved, the lie of its godliness. (Mann, *Doctor Faustus*, 514)[29]

That "lie of its godliness" is what Zeitblom calls its "false and flabby bourgeois piety" (Mann, *Doctor Faustus*, 515).[30] Oddly, what Zeitblom captures in his remarks about the modern hypocrisy of "bourgeois piety" is a sentiment very close to Geulincx's seventeenth-century perspective. Religion, Geulincx observes at one point, "is encompassed by dangers and dreadful precipices; so that it is well said that *it is preferable for men to have no Religion at all than such as most people have.*"[31]

Zeitblom's response to Leverkühn's opus emphasizes Augustine's implied rejection of a godliness based on the strategy that one might somehow *earn* one's salvation—a principle that in Calvin will reach a sort of apotheosis. Yet Zeitblom is not willing to abandon the idea—also implied by Augustine—that even in, or perhaps because of, the depravity of one's evil and the depth of one's despair, God's mercy will be shown, which is precisely the conundrum, the moral hazard of mixed motives, that the Devil smilingly unpacks for Leverkühn. The final lament of Leverkühn's "dark tone poem" (dunkle Tongedicht) is another reversal, one that in effect mirrors the odd determinism of what must be God's lament for his lost and fallen creation—that is, "I did not will this" (Ich habe es nicht gewollt), as if even God ultimately had no ability to enforce his will, as if creation itself had gone awry. But it is a divine lament that, by permitting no consolation, reconciliation, or transfiguration, forces Zeitblom to ask, "But what if the artistic paradox . . . corresponds to a religious paradox, which says that out of the profoundest irredeemable moral corruption [Heillosigkeit], if only as the softest of questions, hope may germinate? This would be hope beyond hopelessness, the transcendence of despair—not its betrayal, but the miracle that goes beyond faith" (Mann, *Doctor Faustus*, 515).[32] Mann's *Heillosigkeit*, which denotes the collapse of all moral capacity in a fit of anti-Semitism so debasing as to make genocide itself seem to the perpetrators a heroic task, also connotes etymologically a state of healthlessness—disease—and, as elsewhere in Mann's work, disease in *Doctor Faustus* becomes a multifaceted predicament that may often be oddly productive, even transformative. The running motif of the *hetaera esmeralda* in the novel, a term signifying both the prostitute from whom Leverkühn knowingly contracts his fatal syphilis and a species of butterfly, the insect known for the centrality of metamorphosis in its life cycle, is thus recalled in Zeitblom's meditation on the possible consequences of his friend's "corruption." Allegorically, Zeitblom's question is finally also about Germany itself: that is, can there be hope for a people so corrupt, so completely lacking in any moral capacity despite their obvious spiritual achievements (especially in religion and music), that their damnation seems to have been foreordained in Augustinian terms?[33] The sort of consolation Zeitblom seeks may be nothing more than his own version of flabby bourgeois piety, and I think Mann wants us to understand it that way. But it is, for better or worse, Mann's piety as well.[34] And it points, I think, to the same *Verwindung*—the same distortion of tradition (and what better way to do this than through the twelve-tone row's mournful, rationalized rewriting of the "Ode to Joy") that winds up recuperating the religious precisely through its most strenuous, neo-Augustinian rejection of routinized piety in pursuit of something like the miracle of a grace that is "beyond faith" itself.

▪   ▪   ▪

That one of Mann's last novels was simply titled *Die Erwählte*— *The Elect*, or *The Chosen One*—cannot be ignored at this point.

Moreover, the title of the only English translation, *The Holy Sinner*, obscures precisely what it should reveal. Mann takes his story from a German epic of the Middle Ages, *Gregorius vom Stein*, by Hartmann von Aue (1165–1210), though even this version is based on earlier French and Latin versions. Hartmann's tale is in its most overt form a retelling of the Oedipus tragedy in the guise of the biography of Pope Gregory I, except that in his version the crime of incest is doubled, and it is the work of the Devil. In the telling of Mann's wry narrator, Clemens the Irishman, Gregory's parents are twin siblings, Wiligis and Sibylla, and Gregory himself later produces children with his estranged mother. Mann makes the Devil less prominent than he is in Hartmann's tale—Satan is invoked only at the very end—but whether this returns us to the sense of fate accepted by Sophocles or instead to the sense of election developed by Augustine is another question. Perhaps more important, Mann turns Hartmann's saintly biography into a comedy, though it is a comedy with a fairly dry sense of humor. When Gregory and Sibylla realize that, after having been separated for almost two decades, they have become husband and wife, mother and father, they retreat to opposite sides of their room and plant their heads on the walls in a mimicry of shame—no one's eyes are destroyed. Still, Mann's ironic treatment of the Oedipus myth in relation to the origins of the man many consider to have been the first great pope after Peter is curiously significant. Russell Berman, in reading the novel as Freudian allegory, argues in his introduction to *The Holy Sinner* that Mann rejected both Greek fate and Augustinian predestination in favor of a Spinozistic or humanistic sense of natural, rather than divine, election: the twins are narcissistically attracted by their sameness, as if no one else could be worthy of them, and it is only through the gradual splitting of their self-identification—first via fraternal incest, then as Oedipal incest, and finally as the ascension of the penitent Gregory the Great into the position of an individual, the pope, who is also universal—that his mature self-consciousness is attained. But the novel, I think, implies much more than a humanist, humorous Freudianism in the guise of Christian hagiography.

The earliest reception of Mann's novel certainly assumed that his tale concerned the "good sinner Gregorious" and the necessity of a belief in Christian humanism. William McClain, for example, writes, "*Der Erwählte* exemplifies supremely the new humanistic *Weltanschauung* expressed in 'I believe,' the 'third humanism' which, while preserving the spiritual and humanitarian values of Christianity, transcends the fundamental dualism of Christian thought arising from its antithetical concepts of body and soul, flesh and spirit, and this points the way to a new and more harmonious outlook."[35] But the abiding problem with these earlier attempts to collapse Christianity and humanism into one creed after World War II is that they never seem to address *which* version of Christianity is at issue in the conflation. This is as true of McClain vis-à-vis Mann as it is of the majority of Beckett's early readers, who found an existential-religious sentiment in his work. My claim is simply that taking the attitudes toward predestination and the inexplicability of grace in Augustine and Calvin seriously—as, in my view, both Mann and Beckett did—makes the conflation of Christianity with humanism a far harder task than it might seem, for humanism is, prima facie one might say, not a natural ally of divine election.

Certainly, Mann is attracted to Gregory because of his legendary sense of clemency. "Seldom is one wholly wrong in pointing out the sinful in the good, but God graciously looks at the good deed even though its root is in fleshliness"—a theological perspective, found in Augustine and in *Doktor Faustus*, in which good may not only emerge from evil, but might even be understood to require evil in some inexplicable sense.[36] Yet Mann's tale (like Hartmann's) is hardly a model of worldly humanism. It frankly, if half ironically, depends on the miraculous, as if to say that Gregory's quite human absolution for his crimes and his subsequent election to the papacy are inseparable from another kind of election, one completely dependent on God's unwarranted grace. After separating from his mother-wife, Gregory has himself bound with a leg iron for seventeen years on a rock jutting up in a lake near the North Sea, during which time he shrinks to a creature of indeterminate species no larger than a hedgehog—"wenig

größer ein Igel" (Mann, *Der Erwählte*, 224)—surviving on nothing
more than a sort of earthy milk that he sucks from a spring on his
breast-like rock. He is quite literally preserved by an earthen mother
in the form of a *petrus*, that is, the rock of Peter on which the Church
was founded.

Back in Rome, in the middle of a somewhat slapstick papal crisis
in which the candidates of two rival factions competing for the Chair
of Saint Peter wind up dead, the pious noble Sextus Anicus Probus is
visited by a bleeding lamb, who informs him that a pope has, in fact,
already been chosen. The lamb tells Probus—in direct parody of the
traditional "habemus papam" (we have a pope) of papal election—
that he has an announcement: "Habetis papam. A pope is chosen unto
you" (Mann, *Holy Sinner*, 257).[37] When Probus asks for an explanation, the lamb replies, "Only believe! The Chosen One also must
believe, however hard he may find it. For all election is hard to understand and not accessible to reason" (Mann, *Holy Sinner*, 258).[38] Neither Augustine nor Calvin had ever described election any more
clearly. Probus and the prelate Liberius (who had experienced a similar miraculous encounter with the Lamb of God), having trekked
through a Germany ravaged (not accidentally) by five years of war,
finally locate Gregory on his mother-rock. They restore to him the
key (and hence the ability to loose and bind) that unlocks his no-
longer-fitting shackle, the key that had been thrown into the lake seventeen years earlier and is only now miraculously rescued by a large
pike caught by the fisherman who initially helped Gregory to his desired penitential exile, his Beckettian *pensum*. Gregory reassumes his
human form once given proper human nourishment and is returned
to Rome, where he assumes the papacy by popular acclaim.

But even here, after all his sins, his superhuman penance, his miraculous survival, and his final act of faith, Gregory cannot help but
emphasize that in the end his election has nothing to do with his wor-
thiness or unworthiness, and he repeats a basic Augustinian theme.
"For he said no one was worthy and he himself on account of his flesh
most unworthy of his dignity and only through an election which
bordered on the arbitrary had been elevated to it" (Mann, *Holy*

Sinner, 308).[39] That the election only "bordered" [grenze] on the arbitrary is perhaps what separates Augustine from Calvin for Mann. Just *how* unworthy Gregory really is, however, does not become clear until the end, when he grants an audience to Sibylla, who has come to confess her own sin to the new, magnanimous pope. In her audience, which is in many ways written as the most sardonic comedy of the entire book, they eventually confess to one another that they had half-known all along exactly whom they had married decades earlier. Gregory's explanation—"We thought to offer God an entertainment" (Mann, *Holy Sinner*, 332)—is an obvious tease of orthodoxy, and his subsequent comment to Sibylla when he sees their two teenage daughters is hardly more reassuring, morally speaking.[40] "So you see, revered and beloved, and God be praised for it, that Satan is not all-powerful and that he was unable to wreak his uttermost will till I had to do with these as well and even had children by them, whereby the relationship would have become a perfect sink of iniquity. Everything has its limits—the world is finite" (Mann, *Holy Sinner*, 334).[41] To say that Gregory is a tolerant man may thus be an understatement, if we are to credit his claim that (with a bit more deviltry) his potential lust for his daughters (Sibylla's half-granddaughters?) might have produced, as a literal translation would have it, "a more perfect abyss" (ein völliger Abgrund) than the one in which he had been already consumed. Mann's Clemens ends his tale with an account of all that Gregory does to bring peace and stability to Rome and the empire, largely through his ability to temper justice with mercy and tolerance: pagan temples are not to be destroyed (though the idols should be removed); and even a polygamous Turk will be allowed to convert without giving up his multiple wives. Yet by this point, as Mann surely knew, it would be hard to take very much of this with a straight face. Gregory's final account of himself relies on his gratitude that Satan did not make of him an even worse scoundrel than he was. This is, one might say, still a version of sorts of Augustine's *Confessions*, but, for the sake of comparison, it is a version where a not quite truly reformed Augustine beds his mother, Monica welcomes the attention and returns his love, and it becomes impossible to know whether we should understand the narrative as humorously recovering or simply satirizing the redemptive biography of the church father. Like the tone of Flaubert's brilliant but inscrutable religious *conte* "Un cœur simple," *The Holy Sinner*'s humanistic irony is a fuzzy and impossible creature, not unlike the monstrous *Igel* that Gregory (a postwar Gregor Samsa, in this sense) becomes in all his seemingly irreparable shame: an entertainment for God indeed.[42]

Despite (or perhaps because of) the Oedipal, and hence Freudian, underpinnings, Mann's novel is every bit as much an allegory of Hitler's Germany as was *Doktor Faustus* before it. The dominant, doubled, and proleptically *tripled* topos of incest is itself the purest version of the pursuit of racial purity—hence Clemens's commentary that the relationship of Sibylla with her son had been known, yet disavowed, even up to the moment of the transgression's revelation. This allegory of disavowal also explains the farce of heads pressed against walls rather than the tragedy of ruined eyes, for in Mann's view, it seems, Nazism's terror in no way deserved the name of tragedy, of a fall from greatness through the error of hubris. "For on top the soul pretends and makes to-do about the diabolical deception practiced on it, but underneath, where truth abides in quietness, [there had been no deception, rather] the identity had been known at the first glance, and conscious-unconscious she had taken her child for husband, because again he had been the only one equal in birth" (Mann, *Holy Sinner*, 328; I have restored a phrase dropped in the Lowe-Porter translation).[43] It is impossible, I think, not to read this as Mann's commentary on the German people's mass disavowal of knowledge of the evil committed in their name under Hitler, and the disingenuousness of so many after the war who decried the "diabolical deception" (teuflicher Täuschung) practiced on them. And it is a situation repeated rather exactly, as I note in chapter 3, in Coetzee's *Age of Iron*, where the issue is the disavowal of what has been perpetrated in the name of white South Africans. The Kafkaesque transformation of Gregory into a rodent suckled by the earth is thus no less explicit a vehicle for Mann of a political guilt and shame for which there can be no reparation than is the despair of Serenus Zeitblom at the collapse of a German war machine that has abandoned all sense of humanity. Yet in *Der Erwählte*, far more than in *Doktor Faustus*, Mann does indeed entertain the possibility of penance and the promise of redemption, if only by means of the account of Gregory provided by Clemens the Irishman, which borders on satire: Gregory is not only forgiven, but also given the power to forgive, and from a most theologically exalted position, that of pope. After equally long penance, Sibylla confesses to her son/husband (even as she reminds him that they are in fact still wedded!), whereupon Gregory, tolerant as ever, absolves her too. It is a happy, if ridiculous, ending. But its ridiculousness is not just a political satire about the disavowals and desire to forget of postwar Germany. Mann's perspective here is also of a piece with the sense of election—not of a pope now, but in the conflicted terms of Augustine—that one also finds in the Geulincxian Calvinism of Beckett's equally seriocomic prose. That is, the only authentic humility in Gregory's story derives not from his sense of guilt, nor from his extraordinary penance, both of which are in the end as absurd as his admission that, after all, it could have been worse: he might have had sexual relations with his children, too. Rather, the only humility we can credit derives from his sense that his election—in all senses of the term—is in fact the *Willkür*, the arbitrariness, of grace itself.

In this way, I think Mann is again suggesting, as he had in *Doktor Faustus*, that thinking about guilt, penance, and redemption as humanly achievable events is—at least for Germany after Auschwitz—no longer viable on either moral or theological grounds. While it is possible to see Gregory's regard for clemency (like the name of our narrator) as a plea, however attenuated, for clemency toward Germany on the part of the victorious allies and a rejection of the ill-conceived demand for reparations at Versailles after World War I, it is also clear that, in any case, such clemency can no longer be earned by penance. Despite the seemingly happy ending of *The Holy Sinner*, there is actually no real possibility of atonement—a position that Beckett and Coetzee also adopt—in this fantastic parody of medieval sin and redemption. Instead, what Mann gives us, as his title clearly states, is the principle of election, though this too leaves us with a double-edged sword. For it was precisely the sense that they, and they alone, were *of* the elect that brought Wiligis and Sibylla, and later Sibylla and Gregory, together in the first place, and this sense of election surely bears a close resemblance to that held by the racial purists of the Nazi era. But it is perhaps a mark of the perplexity of Mann's own shame that the only possibility for any redemption from such crimes is a grace that comes, if it comes at all, out of nowhere—unbidden, unearned, and finally unfathomable. As the bleeding lamb tells Probus, "all election is hard to understand and not accessible to reason," and that may be a fair way of describing what Mann means, in its deeper recesses, when Clemens says at the beginning and end of his narrative that the real cause of the events he recounts is "the spirit of story-telling" (Mann, *Holy Sinner*, 4 and 302).[44] Like the vocal murmur in Beckett that is always somehow "someone else's affair," and as we shall see in Coetzee's understanding of fiction as an event that simply descends upon both character and author, the "spirit of story-telling" in Mann is something like an act of grace, a product of election in its own right, even if it often comes, as Serenus Zeitblom understood, at an immeasurable cost.

▪   ▪   ▪

I want to conclude this chapter with a somewhat heterodox coda, one that nevertheless illustrates the importance of the moral challenge of Calvin and election after World War II, by turning briefly to the depths of the 1960s, to that moment when *Time* magazine asked in blazing red lettering on a funereal black background, "Is God Dead?" The issue appeared during Holy Week, designed to coincide with Easter. But the date of the issue, April 8, 1966, was also Good Friday (the holy day on which Beckett was born in 1906) that year, so the seemingly alarming question on the issue's cover actually had an obvious answer for believing Christians: "Yes, of course he is dead," they would say; "He dies every year at this time." The article itself, despite its attention-grabbing headline, is structured along a similar ambiguity, for in substance it is focused not so much on atheism pure and simple as on what had become the Death of God movement among certain Christian theologians of the era. The most immediate sources of the magazine's information were essays by Thomas J. J. Altizer and William Hamilton that were being collected in the book *Radical Theology and the Death of God* that same year.

While I cannot do justice here to the complexities of the entire movement, much of which derived from the humanist theology found in the prison papers of Dietrich Bonhoeffer (which appeared in English in 1962) and the postwar writings of Rudolf Bultmann, Paul Tillich, and Martin Heidegger (though Heidegger remained problematic in theological terms), I do want to single out the arguments of Hamilton, who is arguably the most important source for the magazine article.[45] What unites many of the Death of God figures, most of whom were American and German Protestant theologians, was the denial that there was any man–God relationship about which one could speak, a denial then joined with firm Christological ethical commitments, or, as *Jesus Christ Superstar*'s Mary Magdalene would soon sing about Christ as a human ethical ideal, "He's just a man."[46] In the postwar period, one could perhaps trace the literary roots of such Christological commitments in the face of theological skepticism to Nikos Kazantzakis's very popular *The Last Temptation of Christ*, published in Greek in 1951. In short, the entire episode, from Hamilton's academic theology based on irreligious secular Christianity to the *Time* magazine essay to the popular rock-opera recording and subsequent Broadway hit, produces an "event," if I can use so Heideggerian a term, that once again reveals the tendency toward *Verwindung* in the narrative of progressive secularization.

For, as Altizer and Hamilton are supremely aware, they write in the midst of the intellectual triumph of the standard "secularization thesis" in the academies. Harvey Cox's *The Secular City* and Hermann Lübbe's *Säkularisierung: Geschichte einen ideenpolitischen Begriffs* had appeared in 1965; Peter Berger's *The Sacred Canopy: Elements of a Sociological Theory of Religion* and Thomas Luckmann's *The Invisible Religion* would appear in 1967; and Robert Bellah's *Beyond Belief: Essays on Religion in a Post-Traditional World* (summarizing earlier views) would be published in 1970. These books, and many books and articles like them in both Europe and the United

States beginning in the 1950s, had by the end of the 1960s secured the sociological hegemony of the standard "secularization thesis"—that is, the fundamentally Weberian claim that modernization, which included increased social differentiation, increased dependence on societal structures of administration, and increased rationalization of religious beliefs, was inevitable and universal, and signaled the historical triumph of secularism and the death of religious thinking.[47] Altizer and Hamilton were in no sense opposed to this thesis—their work is generally seen as an important part of the consolidation of the secularization thesis in the period. But what they also reveal is the (for me) equally inevitable swerve, the peripeteia, of the secularization story, at least in the West, whenever it seems to near some sort of closure.

The swerve in the story is due to the same impulse one finds in Beckett and in Mann. That impulse is precisely the culmination of the logic built into Augustine's version of predestination and of Calvin's later rigorous and rationalizing theology, a theology specifically designed to prevent us from imagining—or even hoping—that we can, as it were, do business with God. Such logic leads inexorably to the religiously counterintuitive claim that an authentically religious posture would emerge only once one had completely *severed* humanity's personal connection with any sort of God, had negated all human ability to bargain with God for salvation, had disallowed one's ability to petition God for assistance, to please him or displease him, in short, to do *anything* whatsoever in service of the disposition of one's eternal soul or one's fate in this life. Weber correctly concluded that "quite naturally this attitude was impossible" for Calvin's followers, almost right from the start, because of the "deep spiritual isolation" it implied, which for him led to all the "unintended consequences" we call modern capitalism (Weber, *Protestant Ethic*, 66, 63). But Calvinism's seemingly impossible spiritual isolation from any God to whom one might appeal is at the same time precisely what the Death of God theologians want to insist upon. This isolation, I would claim, occupies the same space inhabited by Molloy's Geulincxian helplessness in regard to his own body and by Leverkühn's project of a musical lament that is ruthlessly purged of all human emotion and divine consolation and may thus be read, paradoxically, as the kind of redemption made available by the denial of redemption itself. In short, in all three cases, the only possibility of redemption that remains, according to a logic that actually and ironically begins with Augustine and Calvin, is the redemption in which one ceases to believe. It is, for me, the literary and social embodiment of Kafka's most famous aphorism. Remarking to Max Brod that we are merely "nihilistic thoughts that came into God's head," no more than the products of a divine "bad mood," Kafka then agrees with Brod on the likelihood of redemption in worlds other than this one: "Plenty of hope—for God—no end of hope—only not for us."[48] And indeed, in paradoxical theologies such as Hamilton's, there is hope only because—and only if—we have actually forsaken the hope of all divine salvation.

Hamilton's ethical Christology is thus interesting for me not so much in itself, but rather because of the rigor of its determination to do without the God concept altogether. Not even the remnants of mystical thinking that one still finds in Altizer, for example, are permissible for Hamilton. Hamilton is also worth our attention because of his emphasis on taking the movement from cloister to world in Luther's work to its most extreme point—for Hamilton, the worlding of the Christian tradition must be finalized, and in this sense he comes closest of all to Habermas's later argument for the translation of religious into purely secular philosophical truth. The civil rights movement of the 1960s, with its heavy dependence on the African American Protestant tradition, is for Hamilton the proof that only a form of Christianity that embraced its worldliness in the absence of God was of any value from that point forward. (Hamilton was also convinced that "post-modern" society must be both religion-less and post-Oedipal in nature—that is, that it must transcend its struggle with the father precisely by killing him off—but that is the subject for a different discussion.)[49] What I want to emphasize most here is Hamilton's rigorously Calvinist and, as he readily admits, puritan understanding of why the God concept and all God-based thought must end. "I take religion to mean not man's arrogant grasping for God (Barth) and not assorted Sabbath activities usually performed by ordained males (the moderate radicals), but any system of thought or action in which God or the gods serve as fulfiller of needs or solver of problems. Thus I assert with Bonhoeffer the breakdown of the religious *a priori* and the coming of age of man" (Altizer and Hamilton, *Radical Theology*, 40). Although many of us might reasonably ask whether, after all, the "age of man" did not begin some time ago with the humanists and materialists of the Enlightenment, Hamilton's insistence on trying to get to that point all over again, as if it had not yet truly occurred, may be the most overt embodiment I have cited so far of what I mean by Heidegger's *Verwindung*. For what Hamilton posits as the *end* of religion and the death of God is precisely what Calvin had considered the most authentically religious doctrine of all—that is, the removal, via the doctrine of election, of humanity from a God who could in any way be a "fulfiller of needs" and a "solver of problems," which is to say a God who might in any sense be in a position to serve humanity. For Calvin, it was on the contrary more than obvious that humanity was designed to serve God. In effect, what Hamilton and others had discovered was that the very best way to serve God was to do without him altogether—only then could we be absolutely certain that we would never be able (as Heidegger might have said) to put him to use, to treat the God concept instrumentally. Under Hamilton's secular regime, even the sly effort to win God's approval, and perhaps salvation, via the inherent charm of the lament of utter despair that the Devil ridicules in Adrian Leverkühn's theological reasoning is itself impossible, for Hamilton's theology demands not merely the Calvinist God who is of absolutely no avail to humanity, but the God who has died to humanity altogether. Now *that*, one can almost hear Hamilton saying to himself, will *really* guarantee that we do things only for the "right" reasons, that virtue truly will be neither more nor less than its own reward (which of course may be no discernable reward at all), and that neither faith nor works will ever be merely an opportunity for furthering our chance at salvation.

Such peripeteia are basic, I think, to the story of Western secularization: the distorting swerves and returns of the repressed that seem inevitably to bedevil it (if you can pardon the pun) and, perhaps more importantly, the way the impulse toward secularization itself tends to remotivate a logic of theological speculation that it strives to supersede. I imagine that these attempts to "get over" the religious tradition are perhaps destined to recur inevitably. Religion, in ways that are not finally inimical to either Beckett's or Mann's thinking, is a sort of incurable infection, especially if one considers how seriously Mann took the idea that disease itself can be a productive, creative force. You can contain it, you can manage the unwanted symptoms that it might cause, you can even (for a time) force it into latency, but (as in the creative and destructive life of Adrian Leverkühn) it is a virus that, once caught, may be impossible to eradicate. Even if we could somehow bring that religious tradition to an end, it seems to me that only the most desiccated minds among us would be willing to do without Beckett and Mann—or to read them with one eye closed, as it were—simply in order to complete what Habermas once called the unfinished project of modernity. Our hesitation—that is, our choice, in this most secular age, to engage with Beckett and Mann despite the theological work they demand of us when we read carefully—is ultimately the completion and larger significance of Serenus Zeitblom's argument about the diabolical yet transformative potential of Adrian Leverkühn's musical response to his irredeemable fall from grace.

The Ambivalent Puritan: J. M. Coetzee

What should we think about the now quite celebrated oeuvre of J. M. Coetzee? He is a recipient of the Nobel Prize (and the Booker [twice], CNA [three times], James Tait Black Memorial, and Jerusalem, along with numerous other prizes), feted in Stockholm for his moral and political sensitivity to the condition of the "outsider." Yet he is also a writer whose novel *Disgrace* was denounced by the African National Congress as racist and condemned by Salman Rushdie as irresponsible because it "merely becomes part of the darkness it describes."[1] He is a strikingly original, discomfiting, even brutal novelist (*In the Heart of the Country, Waiting for the Barbarians, Disgrace*) who has nevertheless made his reputation in part on that tried-and-true post-modern shtick of metafiction, of rereading and rewriting canonical writers whom he has brushed against the grain (*Foe, The Master of Petersburg, The Life and Times of Michael K*). He is a widely praised writer of fiction, though trained as a mathematician and computer programmer, who began his professional academic life as a Ph.D. in linguistics, digitally analyzing the deep structure and editorial transformations of the writing of Samuel Beckett (on whom he wrote his doctoral thesis). He is a white Afrikaner who was publicly opposed to apartheid, which in his lifetime was dismantled much less horrifically than one might have expected, given its history. But Coetzee is an Afrikaner who also left his native South Africa to pursue a politically less engaged intellectual and academic life in London, the United States, and now Australia.

Rushdie's rather dismissive review of *Disgrace* (1999), wittingly or not, perfectly reproduces the position adopted by Georg Lukács in his later years in his demand for "critical realism" (as in the work of Thomas Mann) in contrast to the modernism of figures such as Kafka and Beckett, who were being championed by Theodor Adorno. For Lukács, as for Rushdie it seems, when a novelist fails to provide a sociohistorical context that sufficiently explains the failings, crimes, or ethical shortcomings of his or her characters, and especially a protagonist, he or she thereby abdicates the responsibility to, as Rushdie puts it, "shine a light on darkness" (Rushdie, "May," 340).[2] One of my concerns in this chapter is not only to show that Rushdie is right to situate Coetzee in the company of Beckett and Kafka, but also to explain, on grounds somewhat different from those of Adorno's "immanent criticism," why Coetzee's writing is worth the reader's investment, precisely because it is part of a swerve in the story of secularization that clearly includes both Kafka and Beckett as well. What remains always only implicit in Adorno's approach to the modernist avant-garde of his era is the sense that beneath his concern for the ability of the work of art to embody the contradictions of a bad social totality in purely formal terms lies some undefined religious orientation toward redemption (this is particularly evident in Adorno's "Notes on Kafka").[3] Contrary to Rushdie, I want to emphasize instead that Coetzee, like Beckett and Kafka before him, is quite literally concerned with the problem of redemption, social and otherwise, and that this distortion in, this swerve away from, the purely secular accounting for human evil is the primary, if unstated, source of Rushdie's and Lukács's discomfort.

Coetzee is the author of *Elizabeth Costello* (2003), a book that seemingly returns us to questions of "religion" and "belief" (the scare quotes are necessary, at least at this point) even as its protagonist holds fast to the vocation of disinterested ironist, the secularizing detachment that the Schlegel brothers loved, Hegel hated, and the early Lukács elaborated as the dialectical signature of the novel's generic fallen-ness amid utopian promise. That Lukácsian fallen-ness, through which the novel points to "where God is to be found in a world abandoned by God," is very much the modern *saeculum*, the world of disgrace or the absence of grace, inhabited by Coetzee's characters and I think by Coetzee as well. The early Lukács imagined that Dostoevsky had shown us a way out of this impasse, and others have pointed to Kafka for the same reason. Coetzee invokes both Dostoevsky and Kafka. In *The Master of Petersburg* (1994) he provides a bio-fiction of one stage in the Russian writer's life surrounding the death of a son (something Coetzee also endured). And in *The Life and Times of Michael K* (1983) he retells the deracinated, dehumanized story of a man whose "non-white" race is so assumed by the Afrikaners in the text that it is not even mentioned, though Michael K is at one point described, correctly or not, by the police as a "CM—40" (Coetzee, *Michael K*, 70)—that is, a forty-year-old colored male, a person of the Khoisan or Bantu tribes, or of mixed, Indian, or Asian heritage. He is wandering a South Africa facing civil war as if he were on a quest for answers as inscrutable as those in Kafka's *The Castle*. It is impossible, I think, to comment on Coetzee's work without recalling Lukács's meditation on transcendental irony in the novel, and equally impossible to imagine that Coetzee, that erstwhile scholar of language and literature, did not have it in mind as well. In my remarks on his work, I hope that something about the relationship of the postcolonial novel to religion and to the "secularization thesis" that has so defined the West to itself for more than a century will begin to emerge.

Whether one thinks of Coetzee as a religious or secular novelist, it is fairly clear that the great theme of everything he has written so far is abjection, and I mean this word not only in the psychological sense but in the religious sense as well.[4] *Abjection* means "a casting out," and the closest synonym for this in the Christian world (and the Dutch-Afrikaans world from which Coetzee emerges) is "disgrace," by which I mean both the loss of grace due to particular events and the condition of a life that precludes the possibility of grace. It is surely no accident that one of Coetzee's most affecting and troubling novels (and the one most often written about) is titled *Disgrace*, and it is hard not to think, after reading that novel, that Coetzee thinks of himself—that is, Coetzee the nominally Christian Afrikaner—as someone who must, especially after apartheid, live in abjection, someone who must live in a state without grace. In one sense or another, this is what all of Coetzee's work is about; it is the great theme of his novelistic universe. In particular, *Disgrace*, like *Elizabeth Costello*, *Slow Man* (2005), *Age of Iron* (1990), and *Diary of a Bad Year* (2007), is a novel written from a point of view—an academic, disenchanted point of view in which "novels" may turn out to be largely composed of already published scholarly "essays"—that allows us to understand both the meaning of disgrace, or abjection, in all its permutations, as well as the powerful, persistent, yet permanently foreclosed human yearning for redemption from that condition. Indeed, I believe most readers would find it impossible by the end of all of Coetzee's novels to distinguish between, on the one hand, an eminently this-worldly sense of an always already foreclosed desire for release from a life of punishing psychological shame and moral guilt and, on the other hand, a theological condition of life bereft of grace, emptied of faith, and forsaken by God.

This is in no sense a condition unknown to the English novel before Coetzee. When Jude Fawley walks into a bedroom late in Hardy's *Jude the Obscure* (1895) to discover his three children hanging lifeless along the wall, the two youngest strung up by (no surprise here) the suicidal eldest child, Jude, nicknamed "Father Time," in a heinous act *"Done because we are too menny,"* abjection becomes the fate of the novel itself, at least for Hardy.[5] Hardy abandons the genre afterwards, precisely because he could no longer write a novel that was not about abjection, and his readers had become increasingly critical of that choice. Coetzee feeds on this heritage. In fact, his *Elizabeth Costello* echoes Hardy's phrase when she is explaining, in *Elizabeth Costello*, why her sympathy with what she calls masculine "primitivism" (the ritualized, agonistic killing and then eating of animals, as in Ernest Hemingway's celebration of bullfighting) can only go so far as an alternative to the mechanized slaughterhouses of modern life. In addition to having suspect political implications, such primitivism is also hopelessly impractical, since hunting with bows and arrows will not do. "We have become too many," she observes.[6] After proving helpless to stop the rape of his daughter, David Lurie, the abject antihero of Coetzee's *Disgrace*, winds up assisting someone else in the euthanizing of dogs. The displacement of direct responsibility is crucial and repeats itself in other novels, since it seems the pathetic, emotionally drained Lurie could not bear to take on the role of Hardy's Father Time directly, that is, to euthanize dogs who must be killed for no other reason than that they are also *"too menny."*

Lurie is the bystander who might have watched while Abraham demonstrated his willingness to sacrifice an Isaac whom no one could know would be rescued, and what bothers Coetzee (and his readers) to the core—it is certainly what infuriated Rushdie—is that Coetzee insists that neither he nor anyone else is, finally, any more truly innocent, any less complicit, than Lurie. When Elizabeth Costello, the character, finds herself stranded at the gates of salvation (though it could surely be damnation as well) and sees a mangled cur lying in front of her—a wretched, abandoned dog right out of the moral abyss that is Joseph Conrad's *Lord Jim*—she can only make a tired joke to herself about the dog–god anagram. It is a bad joke that will be repeated in *Slow Man*, where Elizabeth Costello the novelist reappears. Yet *Elizabeth Costello*, the novel, still ends with a letter from "Elizabeth, Lady Chandos" (another Elizabeth C.) to Francis Bacon—a letter that is a sort of spousal sequel to the argument of Hugo von Hofmannsthal's fictional "Letter" (of Lord Chandos) (1902), also written to Francis Bacon (known for his emphasis on clarity and precision in language), in which Philip, Lord Chandos, complains that he has lost the organic wholeness of his life by which the spiritual and the physical, the mental and the material, were once intimately connected. He writes that now he has lost the ability to think or speak of anything with any coherence, a disease of sorts that has progressed from philosophical and aesthetic endeavors to everyday conversation. This crisis of language—of his inability to connect his experience to language—has become debilitating, and he will write no more. It is a crisis often attributed to Hofmannsthal himself, but it would be hard not to see in it as well a prefiguration of everything Beckett found in Arnold Geulincx—that separation of mind and body, will and action, that can be obscured only by the grace of God.

Coetzee quotes a brief passage from this letter before the "post-script" of Lady Chandos's letter, in which she both affirms what her husband has written about himself and pleads her case with Bacon. "We are not meant to live thus, Sir. . . . There may come a time when such *extreme souls* as I write of may be able to bear their afflictions, but that time is not now. It will be a time, if ever it comes, when giants or angels stride the earth . . ." (Coetzee, *Elizabeth Costello*, 228–29). Faced with what she calls the "contagion" afflicting her and her husband, in which human language refuses to maintain any stability— one is "saying one thing always for another" (Coetzee, *Elizabeth Costello*, 228)—but through which, from God's perspective, "All is allegory, says my Philip" (Coetzee, *Elizabeth Costello*, 229), Lady Chandos concludes with a line, addressed to no one in particular, that reads, "Drowning, we write out of our separate fates. Save us" (Coetzee, *Elizabeth Costello*, 230). On the one hand, Coetzee seems to be alluding to Benjamin's use in his "On the Mimetic Faculty" (discussed in my introduction) of the final lines of Hofmannsthal's play, *Der Tor und der Tod*, for in both the play and Lord Chandos's letter, Hofmannsthal is referring to the human propensity (derided by the figure of Death) "to read what was never written," to long for a grander, divine, allegorical perspective when language itself yields only incoherence and finally silence. On the other hand, the "letters" of both Lord and Lady Chandos point to a predicament that is surely Coetzee's own. He is a writer who, from *Dusklands* (1974) on, writes out of his "separate" fate even as he signals constantly that he is being drowned by that fate. His language—and *Elizabeth Costello* perhaps foregrounds this problem more deliberately than any of his other novels—persistently works as if (in Lady Chandos's line, citing her husband), "Each creature is key to all other creatures," so that a dog licking itself in the sun is in the next moment "a vessel of revelation" (Coetzee, *Elizabeth Costello*, 229).

But the possibility of this "divine" perspective is precisely what makes human language so incoherent and full of holes, no matter how confident Benjamin had once been in his own ability to recover the flashes of mimetic (divine) similarity in the merely arbitrary signs of human discourse. The disturbing intimation that "all is allegory" even as human language fails is what makes human life so intolerable, and that is the contagion that is drowning Lord and Lady Chandos as well as Coetzee himself. In this way, Coetzee has reformulated the "postcolonial" novel—or at least the postcolonial novel composed by a scion of the guilty colonizer—as a deeply religious genre without (or without much) religion. It is, in effect, a prayer for grace in a world without grace, a hope for forgiveness in a world without forgiveness (despite postapartheid South Africa's earnest if, in Coetzee's eyes, flawed efforts with its Truth and Reconciliation Commission) and a deep desire for salvation in a world without salvation. It is a genre that can only be exemplified from the point of view of the disinterested—and disenchanted—scholar who is able to articulate desires that ought to be, but can no longer be, fulfilled. It is, as Samuel Beckett demonstrated in other guises, a genre in which justifying our lives can no longer go on, but does.

Coetzee's most direct statement about his own theological position might be found in *Diary of a Bad Year*, which is itself a perfectly ambiguous performance, a disorienting combination of diary, novelistic diary, and novel, each part occurring in pieces on every page, and each part, each voice, frequently commenting on one or both of the others. There Coetzee (or his narrator) expresses his lack of affinity with "intelligent design" theory while at the same time insisting that he finds "random mutation and natural selection not just unconvincing but preposterous as an account of how complex organisms come into being."[7] Instead, he seems to be working out a position close to that of Spinoza, in that "it does not seem to me philosophically retrograde to attribute intelligence to the universe as a whole . . . even if the purpose in question may for ever be beyond the grasp of the human intellect and indeed beyond the range of our idea of what might constitute purpose" (Coetzee, *Diary*, 84). This attitude, which Coetzee admits is still very far from a God who "had any interest in our thoughts about it ('him'), or a God who rewarded good deeds and punished evildoers" (Coetzee, *Diary*, 84), nevertheless comes very close to the faith of Arnold Geulincx, whose work appears at about the same time as Spinoza's in the Netherlands and provides a context that in Coetzee should be connected both to Beckett and to the Calvinism that runs throughout his writing.

■   ■   ■

My primary claim in what follows is that Coetzee's perspective is both a furious attack on and an inescapable reproduction of the Dutch Reformed Calvinism of his tribe. Superficially, this condition of mind resembles the dilemma of James Joyce and his narrative avatar Stephen Dedalus, whose consciousness seems to be "supersaturated" with the faith in which he says he disbelieves. In fact, Coetzee is nothing like Joyce. It is clear from Coetzee's comments on his own upbringing, to the extent these can be trusted, that (quite unlike Joyce) his family practiced no religion at all, and he studiously avoided Afrikaner Calvinism's religious instruction whenever possible.[8] It is as if the doctrinal and moral pull of a specific confessional worldview came about quite despite the overt absence of religious affiliations in his personal life. Yet Coetzee the author seems fully aware that he is often paradoxically rehearsing Afrikaner puritanism in his denunciation of it.

The problem of his own intractable Calvinism is confronted directly, in my view, by Coetzee's 1985 essay on the duplicity of confession in the novel.[9] Coetzee's goal in this essay is an exploration of the necessary interminability of secular confession. In a world where no authority has the divine power, the keys, to loose and bind, the problem for novelists is "how to bring the confession to an end in the spirit of whatever they take to be the secular spirit of absolution," which means, "without being self-deceived" (Coetzee, *Doubling*, 252). For Coetzee, this turns out to be a problem without solution, without end, since every time the confessing individual admits that there may be some sort of ulterior motive behind a confession, however sincerely he or she may offer it—and it seems almost impossible not to acknowledge the possibility of insincerity when, at the very least, the one confessing in novels always wants something in return for the confession—the confessant is at the same time beginning all over again the process of confession, the confession of guilt for the falsely motivated confession that has just been made. Tolstoy, Rousseau, Dostoevsky—all confront the problem of the secular confession in their own ways, and in each case Coetzee tracks down the writer's inability to bring the confession to the satisfactory end that would amount to absolution. But it is also perfectly obvious that Coetzee's problem with secular confession is also deeply Calvinist in substance. Since Calvin specifically denies the possibility that one may advance one's candidacy for salvation by earthly acts designed to please God, Calvin has also deliberately foreclosed, via the doctrine of election, the event that Coetzee considers inevitable in secular confession— that is, the likelihood, even the certainty, that one's confession will be fatally compromised by the worm of self-interest, of amour propre, rather than defined by the pure, disinterested love of God.

In a most profound way, Coetzee's major difficulty with secular confession seems to be lifted right out of Calvin's *Institutes*, from the chapter in which Calvin elaborates his stern objection to what was called "auricular" confession, heard by a priest, that the Church of Rome demands of its members in sacramental form. Calvin's objections to auricular confession amount to a thoroughgoing deconstruction—if I may be permitted so anachronistic a phrase—of the Roman sacrament, one that goes well beyond Luther's accommodation, and it is a deconstruction that Coetzee repeats in his treatment of Tolstoy, Rousseau, and Dostoevsky.[10] While it is obvious that much of Calvin's resistance to auricular confession is stimulated by the same issues compelling his resistance to the Roman Church more broadly—the presumption of divine authority by the pope, his cardinals, his bishops, and his priests, by means of the sacrament through which they exercise that authority—it is also the case that Calvin's objections are rooted, very much like Coetzee's, in what he takes to be the psychological implausibility of the good, absolutely sincere, and complete confession. And since no one in the Roman Church can finally be assured that his absolution is guaranteed unless his contrition is "just and full" (Calvin, *Institutes*, 625), which is a condition Calvin denies we can ever achieve—"For when will anyone dare assure himself that he has applied all of his powers to lament his sins?" (Calvin, *Institutes*, 625)—the confessing sinner is left in a perfectly "miserable" and "deplorable" state and is hence all the more likely to be dependent on the ecclesiastical authorities that have abused him or her in the first place. (It would not be too much, I think, to say that Calvin here discovers what the Catholic structural Marxist Louis Althusser used to call an Ideological Apparatus, not of the state, but of the Roman Church.)

Moreover, for Calvin, repentance can in no sense be considered the cause of the forgiveness of sins, but merely the psychological preparation for the sinner's invocation of (and hope for) God's merciful grace and (consequently) the increase of his faith, which is in the end the only, though always inscrutable, path to salvation. As Coetzee summarizes the crux of the matter of confession in relation to Dostoevsky, his own solution is also then perfectly Calvinist: "True confession does not come from the sterile monologue of the self or from the dialogue of the self with its own self-doubt, but (and here we go beyond Tikhon) from faith and grace" (Coetzee, *Doubling*, 291). But Coetzee's going "beyond" the monk Tikhon, in *The Possessed*, is also, intentionally or not, going well "beyond" the Orthodox Dostoevsky, that is, all the way to Calvin. Nothing in Dostoevsky implies that confession, secular or sacred, depends only on "faith and grace"— as Dostoevsky's fiction routinely demonstrates, the confessions must be "auricular," and they will also require "satisfaction" in one or another form of penance as well. The purely "secular" reading of confession that Coetzee offers, beyond the language of Dostoevsky, is also pure Calvin.

One might object that Calvin has merely replaced the miserable and deplorable condition of the sinner who can never be sure of the authenticity of his or her confession with another, equally miserable condition—that is, the condition Max Weber called the "unprecedented inner loneliness" of the Puritan unable to do anything to promote his or her own salvation (Weber, *Protestant Ethic*, 60). But for Calvin, the miserable logic of putting assurance out of reach once and for all handily trumped the even more miserable logic of having that assurance constantly offered up by a priest in ways that doctrinally only caused terrible and recurring abysses of self-suspicion. And this is very much Coetzee's point about secular confession in the novel. Writing of Tolstoy's presentation of Pozdnyshev's confession in *The Kreutzer Sonata* (1889), for example, Coetzee observes, "To a writer to whom the psychology of self-deception is a not unlimited field that has for all practical purposes already been conquered, to whom self-doubt in and of itself has proved merely an endless treadmill, what potential for the attainment of truth can there be in the self-interrogation of a confessing consciousness?" (Coetzee, *Doubling*, 293). Calvin agreed wholeheartedly and put the matter in even starker terms in the mid-sixteenth century. In Calvin's view, the forgiveness of priestly confession "depends upon the judgment of the priest, and unless he wisely discerns who deserve pardon, his whole action is null and void. In a word, the power of which they speak is a jurisdiction connected with examination, to which pardon and absolution are confined. On this point one finds no firm ground. Indeed there is a bottomless pit" (Calvin, *Institutes*, 648). The deconstructive mise en abîme that yawns here beneath the confessional is Coetzee's as well. It is little wonder he voiced such skepticism toward the postapartheid Truth and Reconciliation Commission that was set up as a path toward political harmony.

Yet Coetzee's hatred of the Boer, as well as of the devout Calvinist who lives within the Boer, is everywhere legible in his novels—nowhere more evident, perhaps, than in a brief passage from *Age of Iron*, a novel in which *Boer* is also written as *Boar*, that is, the boar that devours its offspring, not unlike Joyce's Irish Catholic Church.[11] The narrator, Elizabeth Curren, a professor of classics (mostly Latin), writing a novel-length letter to a daughter who has immigrated to the United States, finds herself diseased with bone cancer, at the end of her life, living alone in Cape Town, and confronted with a beggar named Vercueil who has taken up residence in her garage. Vercueil's name has been seen as a derivative of Afrikaans, such as *verskuil* ("hidden") or *verkul* ("deceived").[12] But it is perhaps better understood (given the spelling) as derived from French, where it most literally means "worm-gatherer" (*ver* [worm] + *cueillir* [to gather]), signifying that Vercueil is either the envoy of the grave or the collector of the worm of guilt that, no less than her cancer, eats away at

Curren. Vercueil is both the realistic figuration of South Africa's black underclass and the allegorical figuration of a death and a release from shame long desired by the deteriorating narrator—Vercueil shows up in his rags and boxes in the alley adjacent to Curren's house on the same day she receives her diagnosis.[13] At the end of the novel, Vercueil embraces our narrator "so that the breath went out of me in a rush. From that embrace there was no warmth to be had" (Coetzee, *Age*, 198). But long before that well-foretold "death" occurs (the scare quotes are needed, if only because—outside of Beckett—narrators generally do not narrate their own deaths), the ironic, academic narrator vents her spleen to her daughter on the utter catastrophe that is Afrikaner South Africa during the last days of apartheid.

> Are there not still white zealots preaching the old regime of discipline, work, obedience, self-sacrifice, a regime of death, to children some too young to tie their own shoelaces? What a nightmare from beginning to end! The spirit of Geneva triumphant in Africa. Calvin, black-robed, thin-blooded, forever cold, rubbing his hands in the after-world, smiling his wintry smile. Calvin victorious, reborn in the dogmatists and witch-hunters of both armies. How fortunate you are to have put all this behind you! (Coetzee, *Age*, 51)

A more unequivocal repudiation of Afrikaner Calvinism could hardly be expected.

Coetzee's rejection of Afrikaner faith is equally direct in the three memoirs of his boyhood collected in *Scenes from Provincial Life* (2012), where he writes, "the great secret of school life, the secret he tells no one at home, is that he has become a Roman Catholic, that for all practical purposes he 'is' a Roman Catholic" (Coetzee, *Scenes*, 16). The reason for the scare quotes around "is" in this statement soon becomes clear: Coetzee as a boy is already so deeply ashamed of his Afrikaans-speaking schoolmates that he falsely declares his allegiance to the papacy, which means that he can be sent out to the yard to play with the Jews when services are held inside the school's chapel. Coetzee's immediate family is overtly secular, though his mother is also overtly racist and anti-Semitic. Moreover, his is a family that speaks English at home, even if the young Coetzee is expected to speak his native Afrikaans elsewhere. The affiliation to English extends to an affiliation with the British elements of South African life (rooted in the southeast) and outward from there to London, the United States, and Australia. But the intrinsic blood relation, so to speak, of J. M. Coetzee to Afrikaner history is inescapable. In Coetzee's first published novel, *Dusklands*, in the second half, titled "The Narrative of Jacobus Coetzee," the Afrikaner—and more specifically Boer—identity is made explicit: the further north Jacobus Coetzee travels, away from the administrative "Castle" in Cape Town, the more authentically Afrikaner he becomes. (We should perhaps remember that the Hebrew roots of *Jacob* contain the suggestion of both one who follows behind and one who supplants.) Jacobus's "Narrative" is then followed by a piece of self-serving Afrikaner historiography written by one Dr. S. J. Coetzee (the supposed father of our narrator) in a parodic "Afterword," which is followed in turn by Jacobus Coetzee's even more self-serving official "Deposition" of 1760. Coetzee writes himself into Afrikaner life even as—and one might say, every time— he appears to escape it. When Elizabeth Curren, the narrator of *Age of Iron*, tells her daughter that she is "fortunate to have put all this behind you," she is no doubt speaking for Coetzee, who has obviously been able to forget about none of it.

In *Diary of a Bad Year*, Coetzee expands a bit on this inability to put his South African heritage behind him.

The generation of white South Africans to which I belong, and the next generation, and perhaps the one after that too, will go bowed under the shame of the crimes that were committed in their name. Those among them who endeavor to salvage personal pride by pointedly refusing to bow before the judgment of the world suffer from a burning resentment, a bristling anger at being condemned without adequate hearing, that in psychic terms may turn out to be an equally heavy burden. Such people might learn a trick or two from the British about managing collective guilt. The British have simply declared their independence from their imperial forbears. The Empire was long ago abolished, they say, so what is there for us to feel responsible for? And anyway, the people who ran the Empire were Victorians, dour, stiff folk in dark clothes, nothing like us. (Coetzee, *Diary*, 44)

One wonders, in passages like these, just how much Coetzee blames the same Dutch Calvinism he repudiates for the sense of responsibility he feels, and which he suggests the British have too easily, or thoughtlessly, put aside.[14]

And so we are left with an interesting conundrum. If we go by the evidence of his novels, his treatise on confession, and miscellaneous statements (albeit almost always made via a fictional persona) about himself and his beliefs, Coetzee indeed seems in some way consumed by characteristics of a religion he repudiates, a Calvinism that he nevertheless holds responsible in part for the horror that became South Africa under apartheid. Even Coetzee's understanding of his personality as a published writer—a public figure—is more than a little bit puritan: "The truth is, I was never a bohemian, not then and not now. At heart I have always been a sobrietarian, if such a word exists, and moreover a believer in order, in orderliness" (Coetzee, *Diary*, 191).[15] In *Summertime* (2009), the third volume of Coetzee's rather unorthodox memoir, the reader confronts a putative biography of Coetzee organized, *Rashomon*-like, by a third-person narrator, made up of putative snippets from Coetzee's notebooks and putative interviews with past friends, lovers, and colleagues. In the interview with "Sophie Denoël," a onetime fellow teacher and lover of "John Coetzee," the French Denoël is asked whether Coetzee's politics were "unrealistic" if, as she has suggested, they were also so Utopian. "He looked forward," she replies, "to the day when politics and state would wither away. I would call that Utopian. On the other hand, he did not invest a great deal of himself in these Utopian longings. He was too much of a Calvinist for that" (Coetzee, *Scenes*, 456). On the one hand, "Denoël" (or Coetzee himself) implies, we find a non-Marxian, quasi-Luddite romantic, one for whom even a successful black African nationalism was of little interest, one for whom the only true Utopia would mean "The closing down of the mines. The ploughing under of the vineyards. The disbanding of the armed forces. The abolition of the automobile. Universal vegetarianism. Poetry in the streets. That sort of thing" (Coetzee, *Scenes*, 457). On the other hand, we confront an "anti-political" man, a "fatalist" for whom "there is no point in being hostile to the course that history takes, however much you may regret it. To the fatalist, history is fate" (Coetzee, *Scenes*, 456–57). I want to trace out the nature and implications of this tension in some of Coetzee's novels, a tension that includes not only a deeply Calvinist sense of the loss of grace in a world where only grace (and not "good works") would be efficacious, as well as a quite puritanical ethical logic that is capable of comparing human carnivorousness to the Jewish Holocaust (as in *Elizabeth Costello*), but also a lively embrace of the occasionalist discrepancy between mind and body that reveals Coetzee's larger debts to Samuel Beckett, Arnold Geulincx, and finally Calvin himself.

▪   ▪   ▪

Coetzee's evocation of Beckett's prose runs throughout his work, though it is perhaps most striking in the first half of *Dusklands*.[16] "The Vietnam Project" is built around a Beckett-like narrator, Eugene Dawn, who has been asked to revise his "report" for his supervisor, named Coetzee, in the psychological warfare section of the U.S. intelligence services—a situation that deliberately parallels that of Beckett's *Molloy.* Coetzee's strategy here, as in so many of the novels that follow, is to put a kind of realist social flesh on the skeletal and contextually evacuated situations that Beckett favored. Where Beckett's insistence on a zero degree of writing became what I earlier called a paradoxical "secularization" of writing that turned back on itself to reveal a Geulincxian Calvinism at work, Coetzee would seem instead to have reconstituted the sort of social and historical specificity that Beckett strenuously avoided. Most striking of all, for my purposes, Coetzee also seems to have put legible flesh on the bare bones of Beckett's tragicomic Calvinism even as he maintains the Geulincxian occasionalist logic of thought and action that one finds in Beckett.

Coetzee's opposition to Dutch Calvinism's social and historical legacy in Afrikaner history is thus always in subtle conflict with the Geulincxian Calvinism of his prose, which time and again reminds us that the "disgrace" haunting so many of Coetzee's characters, the shameful discrepancy between what they think and what they do, what they believe and the lives they actually live, is perhaps more intractable, more irreducible, than mere sociohistorical explanation could possibly suggest. "We are all more or less guilty," Eugene Dawn remarks, "the offense is less significant than the sin."[17] The war that Dawn analyzes only through disturbing photographs belongs to "an irredeemable Vietnam in the world which only embarrasses me and alienates me" (Coetzee, *Dusklands*, 16). But as Coetzee's writing unfolds in subsequent novels, it becomes clear that Vietnam is no more "irredeemable" than any other place that Coetzee represents in his writing, and that the embarrassment and alienation that Eugene Dawn experiences in viewing the pornography of war is the embarrassment and alienation that Coetzee discovers, like the dark side of Wordsworth's great soul, running through all things. Everything happens in Coetzee's writing as if he had discovered in Beckett a sort of prose algorithm that could be perfectly adapted to map out the shame of life on this planet today, as Coetzee finds himself living it. On the one hand, Dawn's argument to Coetzee, his superior, is that the Vietnamese villagers must be Calvinized: "If we had rather compelled the village, the guerilla band, the individual subject to conceive himself the village, the band, the subject elected for especial punishment, for reasons never to be known, then while his first gesture might have been to strike back in anger, the worm of guilt would inevitably, as punishment continued, have sprouted in the bowels and drawn from him the cry, 'I am punished therefore I am guilty.' He who utters these words is vanquished" (Coetzee, *Dusklands*, 24). On the other hand, we modern subjects are always already guilty and hence always already vanquished. When Dawn is institutionalized after attacking his son Martin with a knife (rather like a deranged Abraham), his "true ideal (I really believe this) is of an endless discourse of character, the self reading the self to the self in all infinity" (Coetzee, *Dusklands*, 38), which is precisely the interminable hell of secular confession that

Coetzee indicts in his essay on Tolstoy, Rousseau, and Dostoevsky, and that Calvin rejects in the *Institutes.*

Coetzee's second novel, *In the Heart of the Country* (1977) is narrated in an eerily Faulknerian tone by an unmarried woman, still living at home in the rural expanse of South Africa, who kills her widowed father when he appropriates the new young wife of one of his black farm workers, Hendrik (the big Faulknerian theme of miscegenation thus appears as well). Afterwards, she asks herself why she has done so, in terms that are overtly Geulincxian: "Am I, I wonder, a thing among things, a body propelled along a track by sinews and bony levers, or am I a monologue moving through time, approximately five feet above the ground, if the ground does not turn out to be just another word, in which case I am indeed lost?"[18] And once she has been sexually assaulted and appropriated in turn by Hendrik, our narrator deteriorates in a most Beckettian and Calvinist way: she hears the voices of flying machines that speak to her in "pure meaning" and in Spanish (Coetzee, *Heart*, 126), as if "from gods" or from "another world" (Coetzee, *Heart*, 127), and wonders, "Perhaps their words are meant only for Spaniards, because unknown to me it has been decreed that Spaniards are the elect" (Coetzee, *Heart*, 129). The novel ends with her acknowledgment that she is "corrupted to the bone," living in a "forsaken" world (Coetzee, *Heart*, 139), a remark that rehearses a conceit that worries her at the novel's start, when incest is imagined to be inextricably rooted in Adam's sin: "Original sin, degeneracy of the line: there are two fine, bold hypotheses for my ugly face and my dark desires . . ." (Coetzee, *Heart*, 23). As in Faulkner, Coetzee's Calvinism is a religion of the body as well as the mind, and the disgrace it names is ultimately both palpable and inescapable.

In emphasizing the Dutch Calvinism that bubbles to the surface in the characters of Coetzee's early fiction, I do not mean to neglect the startling realism of his work, especially in his subsequent *Waiting for the Barbarians* (1980), the novel that initially put Coetzee on the map of what certain superficial critics these days like to call "world literature." The spare but telling details of the garrison town's existence, from its insularity and complacency to its brothels, and the graphic nature of Coetzee's scenes of torture—the burning of the eyes of the barbarian girl and her father, the hanging and the strappado inflicted on the magistrate—emerge in a mundane, at times affectless, verisimilitude in which there is no trace of the magical, the wondrous, or the exotic that had become a defining characteristic of postcolonial fiction after Jorge Luis Borges and Gabriel García Márquez. In this novel, Coetzee's characteristic narrative restraint is put to historically resonant and disturbing use as the tortured consciousness of the magistrate who narrates the tale, from what Conrad would have ironically called an "outpost of progress" on the frontier of a repressive land empire, soon finds itself locked within a brutally tortured body, at the mercy (again as in Conrad) of a perfectly hollow yet vicious colonel, morally blind behind his new sunglasses. Coetzee makes it explicit, in ways Conrad generally does not, that the magistrate's descent into "disgrace" is something like a set of nested matryoshka dolls, each level more piercing than the previous one. The merely unpleasant embarrassment of serving an empire whose methods he questions gives way to the shame of taking care of a tortured "barbarian" girl who simultaneously excites and alienates him, and this shame gives way in turn to the utter humiliation of being arrested and tortured by his own superior, which gives way finally, as the barbarians approach, to the existential shame of realizing that his mistake was his desire "to live outside history. I wanted to live outside the history that Empire imposes on its subjects, even its lost subjects."[19] And to make sure the political lesson is not lost on the reader, Coetzee allows the magistrate to confess his "bad faith" directly: "For I was not, as I liked to think, the indulgent pleasure-loving opposite of the cold rigid Colonel. I was the lie that Empire tells itself when times are easy, he the truth that Empire tells when harsh winds blow. Two sides of imperial rule, no more, no less. But I temporized . . ." (Coetzee, *Waiting*, 135). Though the message about the truth and the lie of empire is largely Conrad's, it now emerges without the obscuring yet meaningful penumbra of ambiguity that Conrad was expert in producing around the events of his tales.

But even here, Coetzee's realism is wrapped in the endlessly ramifying implications of Kafka's unanchored allegories. The empire in *Waiting for the Barbarians* points most obviously to the South African apartheid regime in what would turn out to be its last decade, but it points just as effectively as allegory to the Roman Empire just before being overrun by the original Germanic "barbarians," to the British in the last days of the Raj, to the French in North Africa, the Belgians in the Congo, the Japanese in China, the Spanish in Mexico, the Germans and the Russians in Eastern Europe, the Italians in Ethiopia, the Israelis in the West Bank, and so on. The U.S. citizen may be tempted to take illusory comfort in feeling that all of this barbaric history belongs to old Europe, until he or she realizes that the only reason the United States escaped the fate of the major European empires is that it was one of the only empires to have been completely successful in eradicating its indigenous "barbarians," at least for all political purposes—Coetzee's barbarians are indistinguishable from the Amerindians of the New World. While Coetzee's reading of empire in this novel is Kafkaesque allegory, it diverges from Kafka's in one important respect: it is the allegory that would be written by a guilty, disgraced man, a writer for whom the choice of allegory as a vehicle becomes in itself one more source and sign of his shame, as if the ultimate disgrace was the disgrace that arises from acknowledging that, as a writer, disgrace as a literary theme becomes the vehicle of working through the terms of his own moral and political complicity, a strategy that, in turn, can only guarantee more shame. This is a narrative rabbit hole, as it were, with no possibility of escape—a rabbit hole, as I noted earlier, that Coetzee explored in terms of the interminability of "secular confession," which is, in some sense, all that Coetzee has ever written.

Hence, Coetzee's realism is always shadowed by allegories that he seems compelled to produce, yet about which he remains deeply ambivalent—not unlike those slips of wood, inscribed with an unknown script, that the archeologically inclined magistrate has dug up in the lands surrounding the town. What Colonel Joll dismisses as likely no more than "gambling-sticks," the magistrate translates as arcana that bear a certain resemblance to both Kafka's prose and Coetzee's: "They form an allegory. They can be read in many orders. Further, they can be read in many ways," not least as a history of a previous and now fallen empire (Coetzee, *Waiting*, 112) and as an object lesson for Colonel Joll. But the magistrate actually has no sense of what the wooden slips mean—Joll, after all, could be right—and his allegory is simply an interpretation imposed on them to fit present circumstances. The magistrate's dreams, haunted by the figure of the barbarian girl, are likewise densely allegorical, like all dreams perhaps: when he dreams of the girl building a replica of the town in snow, one absent of people, he remarks to himself, "So this is what it is to see!" (Coetzee, *Waiting*, 53). Yet the dreams dissolve into real children building a snowman in the square at the novel's end, blissfully ignorant of the catastrophe to come, as if all the dream-work in the world would be unable to forestall it.

The nameless magistrate's attentions to the tortured barbarian girl he takes in are both startlingly realistic and grandly allegorical. He bathes and oils the broken ankles of the equally nameless barbarian girl in a crude aura of erotic satisfaction that reveals just how intimately related are the pleasures of torture and the pleasures of sex: for her, the magistrate's caresses are part of the larger expression of colonial power, something she has experienced many times before at the hands of the soldiers and that she expects in turn from him, while for him they suggest a deeper connection between the bones broken by the torturer and the rudiments of masculine sexual pleasure. Though she is initially confused by the magistrate's reluctance to take her as a lover, her expectations are eventually met. And yet it is obvious that a religious allegory has been fastened onto this realistic, politico-psychological drama. The magistrate's bathing of the barbarian girl's feet is clearly an evocation of Christlike humility: it is an attempt at atonement, at reparation for a life lived at the service of injustice, though it is at best an ambiguous and ultimately futile attempt at redemption. The futility of the magistrate's efforts is in no way lost on the barbarian girl. When he tells her of his attempt and failure to kill a waterbuck, she responds with a most un-Geulincxian, un-Calvinist, reproach. "'If you want to do something, you do it,' she says very firmly. She is making an effort to be clear; but perhaps she intends, 'If you had wanted to do it you would have done it.' In the makeshift language we share there are no nuances" (Coetzee, *Waiting*, 40). This

is, quite precisely in fact, the opposite of Geulincx's ethical maxim—
"Quod nescis quomodo fiat, non facis," that is, "What you do not
know how to do, you do not do" (Geulincx, *Ethics*, 227). It is also a
complete reversal of all that fits under the heading of Beckett's "velleity": as the narrator of *The Unnamable* explains, "I don't know
how to want to, I want to in vain" (Beckett, *Selected Works*, 2:343).
The barbarian girl's reproach is thus generalizable: the magistrate,
right to the end of the novel, still searches for ways to absolve his
complicity, and Geulincxian occasionalism is one way to do it.

Yet, no doubt to the great frustration of those readers of Coetzee
who long for some kind of moral certainty, or even firm ground, in
his fictional worlds, Coetzee's novels refuse, over and over again, to
sympathize with the barbarian girl's purely volitional metaphysics
and morality. First, if she were correct, the world would likely be a far
more violent place than it already is: there would be no restraint at all
on what Freud simply called our aggressive instincts, as there apparently was in the case of the magistrate's refusal to kill the waterbuck,
wherever that restraint (a most Conradian term) originated. Second,
at least in Coetzee's world, there would be no space for ethics at all,
since the ethical in his novels is indistinguishable from the guilt,
shame, and disgrace that, in sufficient quantities, eventually debilitate
the will. And because, as we learn in both "Confession and Double
Thoughts" and many of the novels, there is no possible recourse to
secular confession, there is also no real possibility of full atonement
or redemption: complicity with evil metastasizes, like Curren's cancer
in *Age of Iron*, or like Lady Chandos's "contagion," to the point
where it becomes the general condition of sublunary life, which is no
different from what Augustine had claimed about Adam's fall centuries ago.

Contemplating the final victory of the barbarians over the town,
the magistrate thinks, "To the last we will have learned nothing. In all
of us, deep down, there seems to be something granite and unteach-
able" (Coetzee, *Waiting*, 143). In his parting words to Colonel Joll,
defeated and on the run, no longer protected by his dark lenses, the
magistrate admonishes him: "'The crime that is latent in us we must
inflict on ourselves,' I say. I nod and nod, driving the point home.

'Not on others,' I say: I repeat the words, pointing at my chest, pointing at his" (Coetzee, *Waiting*, 146). The wording here is significant. The magistrate explicitly does *not* say that the crime we have inflicted on others we must inflict on ourselves, as if some sort of moral reckoning would thus be possible. Instead, he refers to "the crime that is latent in us," as if the crime is innate, always already present, so that the only "moral" response is, in fact, ineradicable guilt and shame, a conclusion Calvin heartily embraced. Just before he himself leaves the town, "feeling stupid" and lost, on a road "that may lead nowhere" (Coetzee, *Waiting*, 156), the magistrate acknowledges an illness that he has, in a sense, contracted from the barbarian girl, whose vision, partially destroyed by Colonel Joll's torturers, had been reduced to its peripheries, its center field being scarred into opacity. The magistrate's blindness is a kind of moral macular degeneration: "I think: 'There has been something staring me in the face, and still I do not see it'" (Coetzee, *Waiting*, 155). And yet there is nothing in this novel, nor in any of the novels that follow, that would allow us to say what, exactly, the magistrate does not see, since were the reader to be offered the keys to the magistrate's complicity—that is, a vision of things that demonstrates exactly how, as the magistrate says, "I seduced myself, taking one of the many wrong turnings I have taken on a road that looks true but has delivered me into the heart of a labyrinth" (Coetzee, *Waiting*, 136)—that reader would also have precisely what Coetzee denies anyone (any longer) has: the keys to loose and bind absolutely, the keys to atonement and forgiveness, the keys finally to justice and the kingdom of heaven. Were such keys available, Coetzee's novels would not exist.

▪   ▪   ▪

The endless rabbit hole, the moral labyrinth, of Coetzee's attitude toward confession is central to both *Disgrace* (1999) and *Elizabeth Costello* (2003), novels that put the disgraced (or at least ashamed) writer at the center of their moral agonistics, and it is not surprising that the latter ends with the writer in front of Kafka's gates, "Before the Law" as it were, struggling to explain why narratively explaining moral dilemmas (as in *Waiting for the Barbarians*) should be enough to provide redemption to a writer, all the while knowing, and being explicitly told, that it is not enough. Kafka's parable, itself part Calvinist in tone—the man from the country repeatedly tries to "bribe" the doorkeeper with the "black Tartar beard" but is never granted admission to the Law, and hence the right to plead his case, since admission does not depend on anything the man from the country does—is an implicit commentary on Elizabeth Costello's predicament, for what she cannot produce is a statement of *"belief"* (that is, a confession, not of sins, but of faith), a statement of *"fidelities,"* which "she recognizes as the word on which all hinges" (Coetzee, *Elizabeth Costello*, 222, 224).[20] Here Coetzee's work also invokes Beckett, for it is finally Beckett's writings, along with Geulincx's Calvinism, that suggest the only form of narrative resolution possible in a world of interminable secular confession—and we should remember that not knowing how to get to the "end of the chapter" is precisely the difficulty Coetzee found rehearsed over and over in Tolstoy, Rousseau, and Dostoevsky (Coetzee, *Doubling*, 253).

The idea that it is Coetzee, the writer, who saves the "unnamable" figures of empire from oblivion, all the while taking on the disgrace of their condition, is clearly implied in *The Life and Times of Michael K* (1983). It is a condition already half-recognized by the magistrate of *Waiting for the Barbarians* when he observes to himself, without consolation, that "When some men suffer unjustly . . . it is the fate of those who witness their suffering to suffer the shame of it" (Coetzee, *Waiting*, 139). The narrator of part 2 of *The Life and Times of Michael K*, the pharmacist-turned-medical officer of the rehabilitation camp in which Michael K is interned for a time, pleads to his superior, Noël, for leniency toward Michael K (whose name has also been abused and pluralized by this time) so that he will not be interrogated, so that he might be released. In all this, the medical officer is very much like the magistrate of *Waiting for the Barbarians*: he is obsessed with the abject, harelipped figure of "Michaels," who has become for him something of an Adamic-redemptive figure: "I am the only one who sees you for the original soul you are."[21] On the one hand, Michael K is figured in the medical officer's imagination as a being *so* original, having tended his makeshift garden of pumpkins in an abandoned yet Edenic *veld* before his arrest, that "Michaels" becomes a parable of autochthony. "With Michaels it always seemed to me that someone had scuffled together a handful of dust, spat on it, and patted it into the shape of a rudimentary man, making one or two mistakes (the mouth, and without a doubt the contents of the head), omitting one or two details (the sex), but coming up nevertheless in the end with a genuine little man of earth . . ." (Coetzee, *Michael K*, 161). On the other hand, Michael K is a bit of a Dostoevskian holy fool, a man buffeted by the winds of civil war, misrecognized time and again, and constantly driven by forces beyond his control or comprehension. Eventually he is portrayed as a Christ figure by the medical officer, who in considering that he might just follow his patient's example after Michael K has escaped from the camp, observes, "I would have said: 'Michaels, forgive me for the way I treated you, I did not appreciate who you were till the last days. . . . Therefore I have chosen you to show me the way'" (Coetzee, *Michael K*, 162–63).

But the medical officer's allegorical figuration of Michael K becomes a problem for the novel in turn. As the medical officer observes toward the end of his part of the narrative, when he warns Michael K against attempting escape, "So I would have to run after you, ploughing as if through water through the thick grey sand, dodging the branches, calling out: 'Your stay in the camp was merely an allegory if you know that word. It was an allegory—speaking at the highest level—of how scandalously, how outrageously a meaning can take up residence in a system without becoming a term in it'" (Coetzee, *Michael K*, 166). The novel indeed unfolds as if Michael K takes up residence within it as an allegorized Christ figure, but only in scandalous, outrageous fashion, as if this narrative transformation of Michael K—the nearly mute, half-conscious embodiment of abjection at the novel's center—into the Adamic yet Christlike Michaels takes place quite despite Coetzee's better judgment, indeed perhaps despite his initial intentions in writing the novel. In effect, Coetzee is both responsible for that scandalous transformation and deeply ashamed of it. After all, it is the medical officer himself, behaving as if he were a novelist with a guilty conscience, who thinks to himself, "So, Michaels, the long and the short of it is that by my eloquence I saved you" (Coetzee, *Michael K*, 142). But if that is true of the medical officer, it is all the more true of Coetzee, whose shameful, novelistic attempt at self-exculpation via allegory suddenly appears to be an even greater scandal than that described by the medical officer. Coetzee becomes the allegorizing novelist who turns abjection into dramatic (and ultimately prizewinning) moral tales in order to soothe his own disgrace, and yet feels, even as he is doing it, all the more ashamed for having done so.

It is not until Coetzee's *Age of Iron*—a novel written during and reflecting the state of emergency imposed by the South African government between 1986 and 1990—that the "no exit" condition of Coetzee's allegorizing of disgrace turns explicitly to Beckett and Geulincx's occasionalism to find a resolution of sorts.[22] Trapped in her "pit of disgrace" (Coetzee, *Age*, 117)—a disgrace that is almost in equal parts moral, political, and physical—and staring out over the real "False Bay," which is also the "bay of false hope" (Coetzee, *Age*, 118), Coetzee's dying narrator Mrs. Curren wants desperately to redeem herself but is "full of confusion about how to do it" (Coetzee, *Age*, 117), and in response she arrives at one of Beckett's great themes: "There seems to be no limit to the shame a human being can feel" (Coetzee, *Age*, 119). But her sentiments on suicide point beyond Beckett to Geulincx and ultimately to Calvin: "But how hard it is to kill oneself! One clings so tight to life! It seems to me that something other than the will must come into play at the last instant, something foreign, something thoughtless, to sweep you over the brink. You have to become someone other than yourself. But who? Who is it that waits for me to step into his shadow? Where do I find him?" (Coetzee, *Age*, 119). In the event, that "other" will be Vercueil, the worm-gatherer, who has been slowly nudging Curren toward death all along, and who finally helps her embrace it by physically embracing her.

Her observation that "something foreign," something beyond her own will, must come into play at the final moments is the more severe Calvinism of Geulincx, for whom even our attempt at suicide would still depend for its success or failure, at the last instant, on the will of God. In *The Master of Petersburg*, Coetzee allows Dostoevsky to invoke rather directly Geulincx's argument that the Stoic (and later existentialist) belief in suicide as a final expression of human will is groundless. Explaining to the child Matryosha why he does not believe his son Pavel committed suicide, Dostoevsky observes, "No one kills himself, Matryosha. You can put your life in danger but you cannot actually kill yourself. It is more likely that Pavel put himself at risk, to see whether God loved him enough to save him. He asked God a question—Will you save me?—and God gave him an answer. God said: No. God said: Die."[23] When Matryosha then asks why God allowed it, Dostoevsky replies, "Perhaps God does not like to be tempted" (Coetzee, *Master*, 75). Since human will is itself always dependent, as Augustine had already observed, on the immediate priority of God's will, Dostoevsky is only making explicit here what Curren, in her despair, acknowledges: that her death, like her life, and no matter what her intentions, in the end seems to be what Geulincx calls "someone else's affair" (Geulincx, *Ethics*, 34).

In fact, everyone in *Age of Iron* slowly comes to reproduce the puritanism of the ruling Boers. Even the black students who throw rocks at the white soldiers and police "have ceased being children," she tells Vercueil, "but what have they become? Dour little puritans, despising laughter, despising play" (Coetzee, *Age*, 125). And just like the puritan Elizabeth Curren is (or has become) quite in spite of her anti-Calvinism, she cannot shake the fear that she has been transcendentally abandoned. "Why do I not call for help, call to God? Because God cannot help me. God is looking for me but he cannot reach me. God is another dog in another maze" (Coetzee, *Age*, 137–38). The cause of this forsakenness is a "crime committed long ago. How long ago? I do not know. But longer ago than 1916, certainly. So long ago that I was born into it. It is part of my inheritance. It is part of me, I am part of it" (Coetzee, *Age*, 164). That it is impossible to stop the slippage from the year of our narrator's birth toward some far more primal scene of disgrace, or to tell finally which "inheritance"— white European dominion in Africa or original sin—is being invoked here, all this is central to Coetzee's larger elaboration of what we could call (given Curren's cancer) the incurable growth of shame in this novel. In *Diary of a Bad Year*, political shame is itself something that occurs as if by divine election: "Dishonour is no respecter of fine distinctions. Dishonour descends upon one's shoulders, and once it had descended no amount of clever pleading will dispel it" (Coetzee, *Diary*, 40). Later in *Diary of a Bad Year*, Coetzee writes, "If I were pressed to give my brand of political thought a label, I would call it pessimistic anarchistic quietism . . . anarchism because experience tells me that what is wrong with politics is power itself; quietism because I have my doubts about the will to set about changing the world, a will infected with the drive to power; and pessimism because I am skeptical that, in a fundamental way, things can be changed. (Pessimism of this kind is cousin and perhaps even sister to belief in original sin, that is, to the conviction that humankind is imperfectible)" (Coetzee, *Diary*, 203). I would argue that pessimistic anarchistic quietism is a splendid description of Calvinism in its most authentic, most radical form.

Curren nevertheless feels and examines the strong temptation of clever pleading. "Though it was not a crime I asked to be committed, it was committed in my name. I raged at times against the men who did the dirty work . . . but I accepted too that, in a sense, they lived inside me," she confesses to Vercueil (Coetzee, *Age*, 164). Like Coetzee in his essay on literary confessions, she recognizes that there is a pleasure in her "confession," a confession she makes to Vercueil to show him that she is a "good person," but that this pleasure is also in itself a "shameful pleasure; it never ceased to gnaw me. I was not proud of it, I was ashamed of it. My shame, my own" (Coetzee, *Age*, 165). That is, just to be clear, Curren confesses because she is ashamed of the crimes done in her name; she feels a pleasure, a release, in her auricular confession to Vercueil, to the dark figure of oppression and mortality itself; but she then also feels ashamed at the pleasure she earns from the confession—confessing is a shameful pleasure; and thus the shameful pleasure of confession immediately becomes fit material for a new confession in turn—ad infinitum. It is no wonder that she concludes, "what times these are when to be a good person is not enough!" (Coetzee, *Age*, 165). And suddenly, behind Elizabeth

Curren, the reader may glimpse in his or her imagination the "black-robed, thin-blooded, forever cold" figure of John Calvin (Coetzee, *Age*, 51)—who is remarkably akin to Vercueil himself—whispering softly, "When was being a good person *ever* enough? Do you, Mrs. Curren, now understand what election really means?" Like the cancer lodged deep within her bones, Curren's disgrace is not something she ever had the ability to escape.

Age of Iron ends with Curren telling Vercueil that she feels that she is "standing on the riverbank awaiting my turn. I am waiting for someone to show me the way across" (Coetzee, *Age*, 179). It is a position that at once recalls Virgil's description of the underworld, the Puritan hope for deliverance, and Beckett's *en attendant*—and the ferryman in this case will be Vercueil (who had worked for a time, we learn, on a Russian trawler), a "man who came without being invited" (Coetzee, *Age*, 179). But before Vercueil finally enfolds her in his deathly embrace, Curren has an eschatological revelation of sorts about him, that is, a revelation that is in my reading ambiguously yet appropriately Calvinist: "When it comes to last things, I no longer doubt him in any way. There has always been in him a certain hovering if undependable solicitude for me, a solicitude he knows no way of expressing. I have fallen and he has caught me. It is not he who fell under my care when he arrived, I now understand, nor I who fell under his: we fell under each other, and have tumbled and risen since then in the flights and swoops of that mutual election" (Coetzee, *Age*, 196). Coetzee has here superimposed three kinds of election—the immediate affinity of Curren with Vercueil, the willed or elective or "mutual" quality of which is impossible to distinguish from its predestined nature; the broader, but perhaps also in some sense historically determined, tragically asymmetric entwinement of white Afrikaners and black Africans; and finally the gnawing, cancerous sense of "election" concerning "last things" within Curren herself, a woman utterly dependent on the grace of a redemption she knows in advance she cannot earn.

Perhaps Coetzee's most intriguing novel, in relation to my earlier invocations of Beckett, Geulincxian occasionalism, and Calvin's legacy, is *Slow Man* (2005). It is one of Coetzee's most personal novels, in a career filled with one personal novel after another, and is set in Australia, to which Coetzee moved soon after the African National Congress came to power. Like his previous novels, this one is structured as allegory, in this case the story of Saint Paul's conversion. Paul Rayment is aptly named—that is, phonetically, he is also Paul *Remonte*, Paul who will rise again. "St. Paul his namesake, name-saint," Rayment thinks at one point.[24] He is a rather fastidious, acerbic, French Catholic (though with a hated Dutch Calvinist stepfather), retired, immigrant photographer, in possession of a collection of vintage photographs from Australia's earlier days that will be donated to a museum on his death. He is thrown from his mount—the mount being a bicycle, à la Beckett—when struck by a car on Magill Road in Adelaide. The accident forces the amputation of one of his legs, an event that renders him all the more akin to Beckett's damaged characters—the narrator of *The Unnamable* tells us, "This time I am short of a leg" (Beckett, *Unnamable*, 309)—but that also begins the tortuous unfolding of Rayment's Pauline moral reevaluation. It is a reevaluation that implies repentance, though when he imagines being asked at heaven's gate what he has to repent, he realizes, not unlike Elizabeth Costello before him, that all he can finally confess is his stupidity in having wasted his life. Much of the novel concerns his unrequited lust for one of his physical therapists—a Croatian immigrant named Marijana—and his hapless attempt to display a self-serving generosity toward her teenage son, Drago (self-serving generosity being the penitent counterpart, in this novel, to self-serving confession in *Age of Iron*).

The most significant turn in the narrative is the entrance of Elizabeth Costello, herself an immigrant of sorts from Coetzee's earlier novel about her, who reappears here as the writer of Paul's story in order to express her dissatisfaction with the way Paul is developing as a character in the plot she has constructed for him. (At one point, Paul reads Elizabeth Costello's notes for his character from her diary, and his ears burn with the shame of realizing he has never been more than a rat in a cage [Coetzee, *Slow*, 122], a puppet with a life determined by a "celestial typewriter" [Coetzee, *Slow*, 123].) It is as if one of Thackeray's puppets—"Come children, let us shut up the box and the puppets, for our play is played out"—had suddenly realized his true nature.[25] There follow several fitful experiments devised by Elizabeth Costello to get Paul into a more compelling narrative track. His "author" wants him to be a man of action, to "live like a hero. That is what the classics teach us. Be a main character" (Coetzee, *Slow*, 229). These failed authorial efforts include finding him a more suitable handicapped lover and extricating him from the increasingly shameful and embarrassing pursuit of Marijana and her family. (At one point, Rayment imagines he might just live with her family as a kindly, one-legged godfather.) By the novel's end, Paul decides to part with Elizabeth Costello altogether, in an act of self-liberation that is perhaps Coetzee's most satiric and biting attack on the shamefulness of his chosen profession.

Like Beckett's earlier dismantling of the writer's art—"He gives me money and takes away the pages. So many pages, so much money," Molloy tells us on the first page of his narrative (Beckett, *Molloy*, 3)— Coetzee's satire is at once terribly funny and terribly dark. For it reflects Coetzee's own larger sense that, as he notes in *Diary of a Bad Year*, he may not really be a novelist, an "author" per se, in any case: "But now the critics voice a new refrain. At heart he is not a novelist after all, they say, but a pedant who dabbles in fiction. And I have reached a stage in my life when I begin to wonder whether they are not right—whether, all the time I thought I was going about in disguise, I was in fact naked. . . . I was never much good at evocation of the real, and have even less stomach for the task now" (Coetzee, *Diary*, 191–92). And this self-parody brings us at various points in *Slow Man* to a central problem in Beckett, Geulincx, Calvin, Augustine, and Saint Paul alike: that Paul Rayment is, in the end, always a character in someone else's narrative, that his actions are, no matter his intentions, always someone's else's affair, and that—as the sudden change in his fortunes triggered by the bicycle accident demonstrates— he has never really been in control of things. Like Beckett's unnamable, Paul tells Elizabeth Costello, "Privately, I have always felt myself to be a kind of ventriloquist's dummy. It is not I who speak the language, it is the language that is spoken through me" (Coetzee, *Slow*, 198). In many ways, Paul's anxiety is peculiar neither to him nor to Coetzee and Beckett. It is finally part of much older questions, surfacing in the modernism of Flaubert and Joyce, but rooted in the long history of theology, and it emerges once again in the later Heidegger's *Verwindung* of that history.

Rayment's concern about language, expressed in far grander terms and without the pejorative sense of being a mere dummy for a ventriloquist, can be found in Heidegger's late essay "Language," a lecture originally delivered in 1950 but not published (in German) until 1959: "Language speaks. . . . Mortals speak insofar as they listen."[26] That Heidegger would have known of Beckett's *The Unnamable*, written prior to Heidegger's lecture but not published (in French) until 1953, is very unlikely. The sheer coincidence of these views of language and speech, across languages, nations, and disciplines, is for me instead one of the signature events in modern intellectual history, an event that, perhaps, proves precisely the point that Beckett and Heidegger wish to make: it is language that all along has been speaking the truth about itself, which is that it has been speaking through them, quite apart from their awareness of one another's ideas, instead of being spoken by them. Geulincx would have been in full agreement.

In *Diary of a Bad Year*, Coetzee makes it plain that Paul Rayment's self-understanding in relationship to Elizabeth Costello, the fictional "author," is finally not that different from Coetzee's own, in the sense that the English language has always seemed to come from somewhere else for J. M. Coetzee, the Afrikaner malgré lui. "For at times, as I listen to the words of English that emerge from my mouth, I have a disquieting sense that the one I hear is not the one I call *myself*. Rather, it is as though some other person (but who?) were being imitated, followed, even mimicked. *Larvatus prodeo* ['I go forward as a ghost' or 'I go forward masked, as if on a stage']" (Coetzee, *Diary*, 195). As in Beckett and Geulincx, Paul Rayment's thoughts and his physical life run along two different tracks, a fact his accident has now made obvious. Coetzee's thoughts, at least those in English, seem to run along a track that is someone else's affair as well.

This revelation, the helplessness Rayment feels as a figure in a narrative that someone else will—or is at least trying to—shape, is not merely the existential, metafictional dilemma of the character who finds himself in the wrong plot, a dilemma Lionel Abel once found best exemplified in "metatheater," a genre stretching for him from Shakespeare to Shaw, Genet, Pirandello, Brecht, and Beckett, a genre that equally includes so much of the early postmodern fiction of writers such as John Barth, Vladimir Nabokov, and Alain Robbe-Grillet. Coetzee also makes explicit what I have tried in earlier chapters to describe as the peripatetic return of this eminently secular moment back upon those theological roots that are more faintly legible in Beckett's fiction. Rayment himself, as he muses not only on his new lack of control over his body but also on his inability to manage his perfectly ineffectual desire for Marijana as she bathes and massages him, puts it in terms that resonate quite powerfully, I think, with themes addressed earlier in Beckett and Mann.

> Before the Fall, said Augustine, all motions of the body were under the direction of the soul, which partakes of God's essence. Therefore if today we find ourselves at the mercy of whimsical motions of bodily parts, that is a consequence of a fallen nature, fallen away from God. But was the blessed Augustine right? Are the motions of his own bodily parts merely whimsical? It all feels one to him, one movement: the swelling of the soul, the swelling of the heart, the swelling of desire. He cannot imagine loving God more than he loves Marijana at this moment. (Coetzee, *Slow*, 186)

And yet, in the letter Rayment subsequently writes to Miroslav, Marijana's husband, telling him he does not wish to break up Miroslav's family but rather to join it as a "godfather," he explains what he means in terms that he hopes the Catholic Miroslav will grasp, terms that once again illustrate his desire *not* to be the active hero of his own life, but rather to be, precisely, *en attendant*, just off to the side of the main events, one who is thus perhaps beyond disgrace, shame, and guilt, if only because he is beyond the body altogether. "*As the priest in the ritual of baptism is the personification of the Son and intercessor, and the father is of course the Father, so the godfather is the personification of the Holy Ghost. At least that is how I conceive of it. A figure without substance, ghostly, beyond anger and desire"* (Coetzee, *Slow*, 224; Coetzee's italics), in, but not of, the world.

In the end, Rayment refuses the conversion that turns the imperial bureaucrat Saul of Tarsus into the disgraced, reformed, and then heroic Saint Paul—the conversion Elizabeth Costello wants him to accept. "Are you trying to tell me that God had some plan in mind when he struck me down on Magill Road and turned me into a hobbler?" (Coetzee, *Slow*, 198). But in doing so, Rayment reinserts himself into a series of new and largely theological problems. First, accepting Costello's offer is impossible, not only because he is now aware of his prescribed—his predestined—status in the narrative she wishes to conclude, but because Elizabeth Costello, the writer, is no better off, imaginatively speaking, than he is. When Paul asks her, "What am I to you?" as if to ascertain the true nature of his existence—a question very much like the one Vercueil puts to Curren in *Age of Iron*, that is, "Who am I?"—Costello responds, "You came to me" (which is similar to Curren's reply to Vercueil: "Just a man. A man who came without being invited" [Coetzee, *Age*, 179]). To Rayment, Costello continues, "In certain respects I am not in command of what comes to me. You came, along with the pallor and the stoop and the crutches and the flat that you hold on to so doggedly and the photograph collection and all the rest" (Coetzee, *Slow*, 81). Second, Rayment also has come to believe in the fortunate fall, the *"Felix lapsus"* (Coetzee, *Slow*, 187) as he puts it. Had he never been struck by the car of the aptly named Wayne Blight, had he never lost his leg, he would never have met Marijana and Costello, he would never have realized his humiliating—but also, per Geulincx and Beckett, morally humbling—role as a figure in someone else's affairs. Third, and most important from my perspective, in accepting that he is inevitably the affair of "someone else," whether of Costello or the Holy Ghost or something irreducibly unnamable, he also acknowledges that even his impossible love for Marijana is out of his hands and that the reassertion of will, whether Costello's or his own (whatever that may mean), is, as Geulincx taught, perfectly outside of his own willpower, however things may appear to him. In refusing to please Costello, his "author," at the novel's end—in refusing, that is, to be one of her good narrative subjects—Rayment tells her, "No . . . that is not love. This is something else. Something less" (Coetzee, *Slow* 263). But in doing so, Rayment is also, in a spectacularly Calvinist way, refusing to assume that pleasing his maker by acting out a plot that she admires will assure any sort of redemption. In what is for me a profound nod to the Dutch Reformed Protestant within him, Coetzee leaves us with an individual who accepts that he cannot know or determine what God, or the gods, have in store for him; that he must live with the indelible shame of his own uncontrollable desires; that there is no possibility of a life story, a heroic plot, that would eliminate his dependency, his impotence, his permanently damaged life; and that adopting a position of utter humility in relation to his own primordial humiliation is finally all that he can do. Whether this can ever amount to a kind of redemption in its own right is the inscrutable question that all of Coetzee's fiction winds up asking.

▪   ▪   ▪

I will devote the last half of this chapter to remarks about Coetzee's most recent work, *The Childhood of Jesus* (2013), a novel that seems, at least in superficial ways, to point in some rather new directions. It is, perhaps, the first of Coetzee's novels to suggest that there may be ways of thinking about shame and guilt that are not resolutely Calvinist, or that at least do not depend completely on an ethical stance in which, however free we may be to choose between good and evil, no such choice can be made with an eye to redemption, either in this world or the next. This is not to say that Coetzee has abandoned the deeper puritanism of his outlook: there is no more possibility of efficacious auricular confession, for example, in *The Childhood of Jesus* than there is in *Disgrace*, and there is no greater understanding of what redemption would mean in the mind of Simón, the protagonist of *The Childhood of Jesus*, than there is in the mind of Elizabeth Costello, interminably delayed before the gates of the law. Yet, for the first time, Coetzee seems to provide a glimpse of how one might manage to climb out of the pit of abjection, the slough of despond, and unsurprisingly, perhaps, he suggests that it is by means of a polysemous ladder—Plato's ladder and finally Jacob's ladder, as we shall see. In *The Childhood of Jesus*, that ladder is both a figure of rising interpretive possibilities, that is, of meanings simultaneously literal, allegorical, moral, and anagogical, as well as the key symbol of the anagogical or redemptive promise of the story itself. In that sense, Coetzee has now provided, not inappropriately given his career-long obsession with allegory, the most complete example in the postmodern novel of the fourfold understanding of allegory once developed by Aquinas and Dante.[27] That it lies at the center of a book titled *The Childhood of Jesus* is in many ways, however, central to what Coetzee's writing has been about for some time.

To appreciate the workings of the novel, it might be useful to provide a glimpse of a particular political context about which most readers outside of Australia will likely be unaware, and a context that even the Australian reviews of the book have so far largely neglected. In terms of any "historical" realism, the early reception of the book has focused naturally enough on the fact that the setting is a Spanish-speaking place called Novilla. (The word *novilla* in Spanish means "heifer," which is an animal found by religious convention in stables where traveling mothers may give birth to divine infants. But as some reviewers have noted, the word also hints at the idea that this new place is not just a "novel" land; it is also a land of the novel as genre, and a "nowhere" city, a no-villa.) Simón and David, a man in his forties and a child of perhaps five who are the paired but unrelated seaborne refugees at the heart of the story, struggle to master a Spanish that is not their native tongue, and at the end decide to head north, away from Novilla, with a small band of followers, to a place called Estrellita del Norte. The inference that this is a parable set vaguely in South America, or perhaps Mexico, is hard to resist, especially since "el norte" is a fairly common name for the United States among Spanish-speaking immigrants making their way there. After all, that David, the Jesus figure of the novel, would turn out to be something like an "illegal alien" trying to pursue his mission in the United States would not be an implausible plot device for Coetzee, who has had a prickly relationship with U.S. policies ever since he was forced to leave the country after joining protests against the war in Vietnam.

But the more interesting analogy—the second level of the four-fold hermeneutic, which is "allegory" proper (above the first or "literal" level), in which people and events in the book become figures for people and events elsewhere—may be to something much closer to Coetzee's current adopted homeland: the "immigration detention facilities" now run by a British company, Serco, under contract to the Australian government, that process the thousands of "unauthorized" immigrants who attempt, and usually fail, to get into Australia without visas or passports.[28] Such refugees, in many cases coming from across Southeast Asia, some from as far away as Iraq and Afghanistan, often depart from an Indonesian port and are, like Simón and David, boat people who generally arrive with nothing, are given clothes, food, and shelter, and who—again like Simón and David— make their way, if lucky, through a series of detention centers, residential housing centers (which allow something like normal life while under detention), transit accommodation centers (for the short-term detention of those deemed to pose little risk), and alternative places of detention, including hospitals, schools for children, and even rental housing. Late in *The Childhood of Jesus*, civil servants argue about the veracity of David's claim that barbed wire surrounds the government school from which he has escaped. While simpler versions of this model have been in effect in Australia since the Migration Act of 1958 and have allowed some who arrive without visas eventually to obtain the proper authorization to enter Australia, many also languish for extended periods of time as essentially stateless persons (the longest detention since 1996 seems to have been for seven years), and the system of seemingly endless detention without legal rights has been denounced by independent organizations such as Amnesty International, Human Rights Watch, the United Nations, and even the Australian Human Rights Commission.

Indeed, because of the hazards (and obvious political headaches for Australia) encountered when people without visas seek political asylum via overcrowded and unfit vessels, the Australian government declared in July 2013 that refugees arriving by sea would be turned away, sent as part of a "Pacific Solution" to neighboring islands or to Papua New Guinea. As I write, a boatload of people has just sunk in the Indian Ocean, 140 miles north of Christmas Island, where Australia runs one of its last off-mainland detention centers (most of those on board seem to have been rescued by the Australian navy). In *The Childhood of Jesus*, the detention center from which David and Simón have come to Novilla is called Belstar, a name producing the vague echo of a Nazi concentration camp (Bergen-Belsen). It is not difficult to see why the somewhat Kafkaesque arrangement of detention centers that masquerade as "real life" villages would appeal to Coetzee, who witnessed far harsher versions of such administrative chicanery in the racially segregated "homelands" of South Africa, nor is it hard to understand how something that the boy David insists upon in *The Childhood of Jesus*—that, contrary to Simón's common-sense view, people really do "fall down cracks and you can't see them any more because they can't get out," a fear that haunts David throughout the novel—finds a real-world application in the case of Australia's supposedly humane chain of detention facilities.[29]

In the end, however, as in *Waiting for the Barbarians*, there is no reason to assume that Coetzee has only one version of a detention center in mind. They exist for "illegal immigrants" crossing into the United States from Mexico, and they exist, in a variety of related forms, all over the world, wherever those trying to escape poverty or oppression, or often both, try to find their way "to the new life" in a more prosperous and promising land, as David observes on the way to Estrellita del Norte (Coetzee, *Childhood*, 276). During World War II they existed in Manzanar's "Relocation" center for Japanese citizens, and such places are not unlike the Indian reservations created in the United States during the westward expansion of British and European settlers—though the latter case is more akin to the apartheid quarantining of the indigenous peoples of South Africa. Coetzee's sleight of hand with language in the novel is designed to emphasize both the ubiquity and the arbitrariness of detention, of "falling through the cracks," an arbitrariness not unlike that of language itself. It is an arbitrariness well captured by Giorgio Agamben's notion of "bare life," that is, human being reduced to its most basic conditions for survival, even if Novilla is clearly far more anodyne than what Agamben has in mind.[30] Simón and David apparently try to speak Spanish throughout the novel, which is peppered with Spanish phrases, yet given the language of the novel it is English they actually speak. David, taking music lessons from Elena, who has become Simón's terribly unenthusiastic lover, learns to sing a musical setting of Goethe's poem "Erlkönig" (the Erlking or Elf King), a Danish folktale retold before Goethe by Johann Gottfried Herder, about a child whose father cannot protect him from the king of the Elves during a stormy ride on horseback through the forest. David sings in German but assumes the language is English. When he asks for a translation, Simón simply says, "I don't know. I don't speak English" (Coetzee, *Childhood*, 67). A version of the Erlking himself has shown up earlier in the novel—a "walnut"-tanned tempter-magician named Daga (or "knife") (Coetzee, *Childhood*, 44), whose coloring is a glancing reference to the Danish alder tree that may have been a source for the forest legend. Daga is prone to violence, has an alluring female assistant (not unlike the Erlking's daughters), owns a television that airs cartoons of Mickey Mouse with his dog "Plato," in David's account, and is the cause of a near-death experience for David, when late in the novel the boy dons a magician's cloak and ignites some magic (magnesium) powder, given to him by Daga, in an effort to become invisible, that is, something like pure spirit.

Goethe's poem has an obvious relevance to David's possibly divine mission—the Erlking tempts the boy with worldly delights, and his father grasps him all the tighter, but the boy has died by the time they reach home—yet it also allows Coetzee to muddle the linguistic waters, as if the names of languages were as interchangeable as detention centers themselves. All the same, the facts that David and Simón arrive in Belstar after an onboard accident in which David loses documents indicating the name of his mother, that they do not suffer much physically even as they are socially degraded to refugee status, and that their hosts once in Novilla are consistently "so bloodless. Everyone . . . is so decent, so kindly, so well-intentioned" (Coetzee, *Childhood*, 30), are perhaps Coetzee's way of suggesting the banality of evil in the relatively humane but numbing bureaucratic maze of Australia's detention facilities in particular.

When Simón tries to convince Ana, the civil servant at the Centro de Reubicación Novilla, to allow him to look through the center's records in hope of finding David's mother, he pleads, "The child is motherless. He is lost. You must have seen how lost he is. He is in limbo." Curiously, Ana replies, "In limbo. I don't know what that means" (Coetzee, *Childhood*, 19). That Ana is unfamiliar with the concept of limbo can only be explained on other levels of Coetzee's allegorical structure, but that Simón knows the term (without giving any indication he recalls its religious significance) reinforces the arbitrariness of language in this novel. Just as German is called English, and the English spoken by the characters is called Spanish, so one character may have a dim memory of concepts that would seem to be meaningless to everyone else. Like a disoriented refugee with a fading past encoded in another language, Simón's mind is filled with recollections—of meat, of sex, of news, of political debate, of salt, and most of all, of irony—that no longer exist in the flavorless world of his "new life." "Things do not have weight here," he wants to say to Elena, his passionless but sympathetic lover. Music, lovemaking, their diet of bread and bean paste, all of it "lacks weight . . . lacks the substantiality of animal flesh, with all the gravity of bloodletting and sacrifice behind it. Our very words lack weight, these Spanish words that do not come from our heart" (Coetzee, *Childhood*, 64–65). It is a version of limbo indeed, complete with the lack of any sacrificial lamb that would provide some sort of salvation. In Novilla, one might say, no word has ever been, or could ever be, made flesh. In the midst of his tedium, Simón stubbornly holds on to the mere shadows of his memories, he "suffers" from them, but willingly, gladly (Coetzee, *Childhood*, 65). They are all he has as a bulwark against the meaninglessness of his deracinated "new life" and "new name" in Novilla, where, as Ana tells him early on, "people . . . have washed themselves clean of old ties" (Coetzee, *Childhood*, 18 and 20). But what, finally, does it mean to be "washed clean" in a "new life," especially one as vacuous as that provided by Novilla? To answer that question we will need to move up the hermeneutic ladder, so to speak, to the third, or moral, level.

In Aquinas, the moral level is guided by the example of Christ and refers to what we ought to do. That is, it is about good and evil, right and wrong, even about how to live the "good" life in the most expansive sense of that term. On this level, Novilla is not so much a Center for the Relocation of Refugees, who will find it easier to adapt if they are washed clean of their past, as it is a figure for pre-Christian Greek and Roman stoicism. Ironically, Novilla appears related to the sort of society of which Coetzee's Elizabeth Costello might have approved, and perhaps even closer to the one "Sophie Denoël," in *Summertime*, suggests Coetzee himself considered utopian: no mines or machinery, no vineyards, no armed forces, (almost) no automobiles, no meat-eating. But it is the overriding stoicism of Novilla's inhabitants—they are all satisfied with what they have, they get upset about nothing, they are almost all perfectly well-intentioned toward one another, they are devoted to their occupations and duties without coercion or guilt or police, they reveal no desire for progress or change, they have no longing for any other world nor for any more elevated purpose in this one, and they seem not even to recognize any discrepancy between what is the case around them and what they might imagine the case could be (there is no irony in Novilla)—that is the most painful part of Simón's "relocation." Throughout the first part of the novel, that is, Simón argues against everything that the more puritanical and fatalistic Coetzee would seem to stand for. There is also no poetry in the streets of Novilla, and while Simón's initial hunger is for flesh, both the kind one caresses and the kind one eats, and for salt, and argument, and irony, it soon becomes apparent that his larger problem is, on a very basic level, precisely the lack of poetry in the streets: Novilla is, quite simply, a place without imagination of any sort, without even the sense that anything is missing. One cannot escape the conclusion that Novilla is also Coetzee's gimlet-eyed take on the realities of life under communism as the twentieth century has known it, perhaps especially in Cuba: Elena's son is named Fidel, and his future mother has a dog named Bolívar. Replying to Simón's complaint that life in Novilla lacks all passion, Elena responds in the fairly harsh terms of a minister of reeducation: "This endless dissatisfaction, this yearning for the something-more that is missing, is a way of thinking we are well rid of, in my opinion. *Nothing is missing.* The nothing that you think is missing is an illusion. You are living by an illusion" (Coetzee, *Childhood*, 63). And yet it is clear that what Coetzee has in mind goes far beyond the materialist conquest of the imagination that one might find in the false utopia of a coercively socialist state.

After Simón is invited by his coworkers to attend a sort of adult education program called the Institute one evening, he discovers that Spanish language courses are taught, but no Spanish literature; calculus and engineering are taught, but no number theory; philosophy is taught, including the Philosophy of Labor and the most rudimentary, pragmatic version of Plato's theory of ideal forms, but nothing concerning morality, politics, religion, or cosmology; and the most popular course is Life Drawing, for which Ana is a model, though the students seem uninterested in her sexual charms and disinterestedly focused, as in Kantian aesthetics, only on learning about the formal beauty of the human body. In the chapter just preceding this, Simón is clear about what bothers him in the view of life encoded in such education, and he does so in the context of an argument with his fellow stevedores on the grain dock about their lack of interest in any sort of technical improvements (such as using a crane or regulating inventory so that less grain is lost to the rats, in order to free them for less utilitarian pursuits). It is not that the men deny change; they simply regard it as outside their control. As the foreman, Álvaro, observes, "Change is like the rising tide" (Coetzee, *Childhood*, 114). Simón's response is not a pragmatic one, however. It is frankly moral and metaphysical, and on a basic level it is about the persistence of certain ideas, about the persistence of *his* ideas, from before his arrival in stoic Novilla, that is, ideas quite apart from purely material life, ideas that seem to have no place here.

> Ideas cannot be washed out of us, not even by time. Ideas are everywhere. The universe is instinct with them. Without them, there would be no universe, for there would be no being.
>
> The idea of justice, for instance. We desire to live under a just dispensation, a dispensation in which honest toil brings due

reward; and that is a good desire, good and admirable. But what we are doing here at the docks will not help to bring about that dispensation. What we do here amounts to no more than a pageant of heroic labor. (Coetzee, *Childhood*, 114)

Simón's fellow stevedores do not agree—there is no sense for them in which something called "history" can reach into their individual, physical lives, the way laziness or duty can, just as for the pre-Socratics, as well as for Plato and Aristotle, there is no sense in which something called "history" could constitute knowledge per se. Hence there is no way that Simón's larger appeal to some historical idea of "justice"—something that is the consequence of a collective endeavor over time—can have any meaning for them.

The idea of justice that Simón wants to entertain in this argument would require an entirely different understanding of time and human history, one that would be *eschatological*, in the language of the theologians, which is to say that it would be concerned, at some level, with final or ultimate things, including the possibility of achieved justice and perhaps some sort of last judgment. It is a vision of the individual human life as something inextricably connected to the entire history of human life, a vision that for earlier critics, such as Erich Auerbach, begins with the story of Abraham and Isaac and finds its model in the life of Jesus. Auerbach's now-famous account of the representation of reality in Western literature that culminates in the rise of the novel, invoked in my introduction, is part and parcel of this sense of history incarnated in each individual, and it is for him—as it is, I think, for Coetzee—the very antithesis of the cyclical, self-contained, and decidedly non-teleological worldview of Greek stoicism. For Auerbach and Coetzee alike, I believe, civilization divides itself between the decline of the Stoic Greeks and the coming of Christianity, and that is why Coetzee is so careful to set this tale of the "childhood" of a lost, badly misunderstood Jesus and his frustrated godfather in the midst of a complacent stoicism that is, unknown to itself, at the beginning of its end. Simón's hunger in the novel evolves from a longing for flesh in itself, in all its glory and degradation, into a longing for the word *made* flesh. Late in the novel, Simón argues with Señor León, a teacher at David's school, about David's supposed inability to read and write, or to follow rules of any kind. (In fact, as we learn, he reads and writes quite well.) "'Now show us how you write. Write, *Conviene que yo diga la verdad*, I must tell the truth.' . . . Writing from left to right, forming the letters clearly if slowly, the boy writes: *Yo soy la verdad*, I am the truth" (Coetzee, *Childhood*, 225). The shift to a hunger for the word made flesh marks a crucial difference, since it is David, his unrelated "son," or "godson" (as in *Slow Man*, Coetzee seems to have a fondness for the role of godfather, for the one who is off to one side, a father in spirit only), who offers the most obvious possibility of actually *being* that word made flesh.

As the early reviews have stressed, *The Childhood of Jesus* is filled with biblical allusions to the Gospel stories, and though Scripture has very little to say about the childhood of Jesus himself, there is a long tradition of speculation, much of it concerning the precocity of the young child-god (or, for Simón, godchild). Coetzee's version of this tradition focuses on Simón's efforts to find the mother of David (who bears the name of his biblical paternal House of David as the name given him by the authorities at Belstar), that is, not so much his birth mother, and not just any woman who might fit the bill, but rather someone Simón is sure he will recognize as the right woman when he finds her. He regards himself as something like a messenger, and while the angel Gabriel, agent of the annunciation, the paternal stand-in Joseph, and Simon Peter, the apostle and first pope, come to mind, the most obvious parallel, given Simón's labor in the novel as a load-bearing stevedore, is Simon the Cyrenian, who is commanded to bear Christ's cross in all the synoptic Gospels (Matt. 27:32; Mark 15:21; Luke 23:26). Simón locates this mother-elect, named Inés (the Spanish version of Agnes, the chaste one), in La Residencia, which is something like the down-at-heel old-money part of Novilla, complete with tennis courts, a proper concierge, and an automobile driven mainly by Inés's very protective brothers. Simón is initially rebuffed. Yet he assures David that the word really can be made flesh: "Of course she wants you. . . . We have planted the seed in her mind; now we must be patient and let it grow" (Coetzee, *Childhood*, 76). When Simón makes his case to Inés, he stresses that the child is lost, separated from his mother: "His father is a different matter" (Coetzee, *Child-hood*, 74), a deliberate contrast to Daga's tempting "magical" claims that he will give her a child instead. Simón begs Inés to accept his intuition that she is the designated mother for David: "Please believe me—please take it on faith—this is not a simple matter" (Coetzee, *Childhood*, 75). Throughout the novel, Coetzee plays with language in this fashion. Like the idea of "limbo," or "falling" through the cracks, or finding a "new life" as a refugee in a new land, or taking what someone says "on faith," Coetzee is constantly excavating the religious resonances behind ordinary language, as if language itself were not so much metaphorical, which we all seem to recognize now, but actually *allegorical* as well. We are constantly in the process of telling each other stories that seem vaguely to be allegories of our predicament, second-order narratives (as Freud also understood—compare his use of the story of Oedipus—on different grounds) that dimly refer to other stories already written down somewhere else. This is a peculiarity about narrative that Kafka and Beckett understood intimately, even if neither was as forthright as Coetzee in signaling and then complicating the allegorical referent. (In a reading from the novel given in South Africa, Coetzee observed that he had initially wanted a bit more obscurity for the reader than he got concerning the allegorical dimensions of *The Childhood of Jesus*: he had asked the press to publish the novel without a title on its cover, a title to be revealed only at the end, but was turned down.)

One of the most interesting ways in which Coetzee seems to be playing with the central thesis of Auerbach's book is through his use of Cervantes' *Don Quixote*. Auerbach's main thesis—like the idea of a hidden title in Coetzee, a thesis revealed fully only in his epilogue—is that the story of Christ becomes the turning point in the representation of reality in the West, for it is only with the story of the incarnation of pure spirit in worldly flesh, of a God made man and then situated among the meek and humbled, the wretched of the earth, who in theological terms actually live lives more elevated and potentially more tragic than the most elevated of worldly princes, that literature learns how to overcome the classical principle of decorum. That principle stressed the need to observe the rule that serious matters, such as the tragedy that brings godlike men to ruin, should be represented in a similarly serious high style, appropriate not only to the elevated social station of the protagonists but also to the elevated nature of the action; and that trivial matters, involving persons from the lower social orders and events that are similarly of little or no consequence, should be represented in a low or comic style suited to their nature. For Auerbach, the Christian legend is the crucial intervention that begins to upset this neat hierarchy of styles, social roles, and typical actions, though he is careful to note that the story of Abraham and Isaac already challenges classical decorum in central ways. Moreover, it becomes clear in the course of Auerbach's account that the novel plays a crucial role in this ever-more-democratic mixing of styles, to the point where the modern novel becomes quite deliberately a hodgepodge of voices, genres, classes, actions, and styles. The book that becomes for Auerbach the beginning of the novel's onslaught on decorum, not surprisingly, is *Don Quixote*—it is the first novel he treats, in chapter 14, "The Enchanted Dulcinea"— and I believe it occupies much the same position for Coetzee, the onetime doctoral student in literature.

In the world of Novilla, novels do not exist. Looking for something with which to teach David how to read, Simón finds in the "tiny library of the East Blocks community center" where he and David live merely an abused copy of *An Illustrated Children's Don Quixote*, from which the cover has been removed, as if things like novels were no more than childish toys. There are other peculiarities about the book. While it is printed in the original Spanish, Simón may or may not have read it before coming to Novilla—it may be some part of his not-quite-washed-clean memory bank. But he seems to have no knowledge of Cervantes, whose name would have appeared on the now-detached binding. He tells David simply that "a man named Benengeli" wrote the book. Cide Hamete Benengeli is the "Arab historian" who records in Arabic the tale Cervantes ironically pretends to be retelling to his readers[31]—so that in this instance Simón and David are caught up in the same earnestness, the same lack of irony, the same inability to think on two levels at once, here reduced to the literal and the figurative, that afflicts everyone else in Novilla (Coetzee, *Childhood*, 154).[32] While Simón comprehends the dramatic irony of the tale itself—he tries to explain to David that the book "presents the world to us through two pairs of eyes, Don Quixote's eyes and Sancho's eyes," and that most readers will agree with Sancho's more realistic vision—David is insistent that Don Quixote is not a fictional personage and that what he experiences is in fact real. After Señor León tries to convince David of the unreality of his hero, the boy insists to Simón, "There is a Don Quixote. He is in the book. He saves people" (Coetzee, *Childhood*, 226). Simón's response is a complex one. He admits that Quixote is real and saves people, but that "some of the people he saves don't really want to be saved. . . . They say he doesn't know what he is doing, he is upsetting the social order. Señor Leon likes order, David" (Coetzee, *Childhood*, 226). Moreover, the passage from Cervantes that Coetzee quotes and explicates at some length is the overtly allegorical episode of Don Quixote's descent into the Cave of Montesinos and his subsequent account of the dream, or revelation, he has there, contained in part 2, chapters 22 and 23.

In the truncated version provided by Coetzee, however, the essential elements of Cervantes' episode are only apparently produced faithfully. Don Quixote, having heard of the wondrous and enchanting Cave of Montesinos, persuades Sancho and a "scholar" to lower him into the cave on a rope. After about an hour they pull him out, and he regales them with all that he has seen. Most important is a meeting in the cave with the Enchanted Dulcinea, Quixote's muse and the generically appropriate distant object of his courtly love, who rides a "white steed with a jewel-encrusted bridle" (Coetzee, *Childhood*, 163). In Cervantes, Sancho Panza's disbelief in his master's account is only intensified when Quixote cites details of Dulcinea's enchantment that Sancho himself had earlier invented to feed Quixote's obsession. But the crucial point for Coetzee is the discrepancy between Sancho Panza's sense of time—Quixote was in the cave for no more than an hour, he believes—and Quixote's claim that he had been there for three days and three nights. The entire episode is so fantastic that Cervantes, in chapter 24, relates how Benengeli himself had so many doubts that he regarded the entire episode as possibly "apocryphal" (Cervantes, *Don Quixote*, 558). With irony fast piling upon irony in Cervantes' own version, what remains indisputable is the numerological parallel to Christ's harrowing of hell for three days and nights between his death and resurrection. And for Coetzee, this parallel becomes the focus, as Sancho Panza's skepticism is directly related to the temporal discrepancy. *"Oh friend of little faith, when will you learn, when will you learn?"* Don Quixote tells him. When Sancho Panza asks for even the smallest token of proof of what his master has said, Quixote replies, *"And if I were to show you such a ruby or sapphire, Sancho, what then?"* Sancho Panza responds, *"Then I would fall to my knees, your honor, and kiss your hand, and beg your pardon for ever doubting you. And I would be your faithful servant to the end of time"* (Coetzee, *Childhood*, 164; Coetzee's emphasis). Cervantes' Sancho is worried that his master has fallen victim to enchanters—to magicians like Coetzee's Daga—and begs him to reconsider what he believes to be true.

The only problem here is that the passage Coetzee apparently quotes from the *Illustrated Children's Don Quixote* does not actually occur in Cervantes. Like Cervantes himself, and later Borges, Coetzee has rather slyly turned a text from which he seems to be quoting into an invention of his own, but an invention that is, after all, very much in the spirit of the original. For just as Cervantes has invented the entirety of his own tale as the tale of the fictional Benengeli—who has, given the absence of irony in Novilla, including that of authors who pretend to be editors, become the actual author for Simón and David—so the scholar who assists with lowering Quixote into the cave is himself a kind of counterfeiter. Cervantes' scholar is a "humanist" whose first book, *The Book of Liveries*, presents for wealthy gentlemen and ladies seven hundred and three liveries, or costumes, complete with emblematic references to their love affairs (such catalogues actually did exist in Cervantes' day). As he explains, he is a writer who has determined "to give the jealous, the rejected, the forgotten, the absent, what will suit them and fit them without fail" (Cervantes, *Don Quixote*, 546). He is also at work on a burlesque of

Ovid's *Metamorphoses*, in which he will reveal the various allegories of Spanish history contained within Ovid's tales (Ovid's collection itself having long been the object of allegorical interpretation of various sorts). Finally, he is preparing what he calls the *Supplement to Polydore Vergil*, which "deals with the invention of things" (Cervantes, *Don Quixote*, 546). Working from classical sources, Polydore Vergil, an Italian historian of the late fifteenth and early sixteenth centuries, catalogued the origins of various objects and practices in the arts and sciences, in religion and law.

When the humanist hears Quixote's tale of what he has seen in the cave, including the early use of playing cards, he is delighted to have found what he believes is an account of the origins of card playing. "This demonstration is the very thing I need for the other book I am writing, the *Supplement to Polydore Vergil on the Invention of Antiquities*. I believe he never thought of inserting the invention of cards in his book, as I mean to do this in mine" (Cervantes, *Don Quixote*, 559). The line distinguishing the humanist scholar from the victim of enchantment suddenly disappears. It is as if Cervantes were demonstrating, in his inimitable way, not only the ridiculousness of Quixote's fantasies, fueled by the mischievous but quite real Sancho, but also the inevitable conclusion that the erudition of the historian is no less fantastical than is Quixote's (which is of course Cervantes' own) imagination, and indeed, that such erudition depends on precisely the fantasies of the enchanted for the evidence needed to please the worldly *disenchanted*—"the jealous, the rejected, the forgotten, the absent"—with putatively empirical accounts of the origins of things. Coetzee is in effect providing us with a version of *Don Quixote*, unreliable as it is in its redaction for children, that functions exactly as Scripture does for the jealous, rejected, forgotten, and absent, but then perhaps also for the wretched and disappeared of the refugee camps. But he is demonstrating in addition, via the embedded tale of the humanist scholar in Cervantes, that the empirical or material account of the origins and presumably ends of things, that is, the sort of account that one might find in Novilla's Institute, were such a discipline as history even to appear on the schedule of classes (it does not), is ultimately no more reliable than the inventions of the fabulists.

Cervantes' novel becomes, within Coetzee's novel, the "scripture" that reveals this truth—if only after considerable interpretation.

Coetzee produces a counterfeit version of Cervantes, inventing the evidence of the Doubting Thomas within Sancho Panza, rewriting what has long been read as an allegorical episode in Cervantes as itself an allegory of Coetzee's own approach to allegory—that is, what allegory ultimately reveals is the allegorical nature of all that we presume to be nonallegorical. The Cervantean allegory of Quixote as Christ harrowing hell becomes the Coetzeean allegory of David as Jesus harrowing the hell, or rather the "limbo," of Belstar and Novilla. It is thus no wonder that David insists with such vehemence not only on the "reality" of Quixote's vision, for that vision is very much David's own, but also on the fact that, unless he reads very quickly, "a hole will open up between the pages" (Coetzee, *Childhood*, 166). This is the same hole, I think, that Samuel Beckett, in the letter to Axel Kaun discussed in chapter 1, said he wanted to drill into language in his writing "until that which lurks behind, be it something or nothing, starts seeping through" (Beckett, *Letters*, 518). What is at stake for Beckett and, I believe, for Coetzee too, is the complete disenchantment of narrative language, but it is a disenchantment that is clearly a theologically Janus-faced project.[33] As Theodor Adorno might have said, the antidote to the falsely disenchanted world of Novilla, the "bad totality" in which Simón and David find themselves marooned, can be nothing less than the disenchantment of that disenchantment. But in the end that second disenchantment cannot preserve itself from theological possibilities, and in any case it is no different than what Cervantes was doing, many centuries earlier, in his outrageous parody of secular Renaissance humanism.

Not unlike Quixote's idealization of Dulcinea, the essential *moral* problem of the novel thus concerns the seemingly inhuman idea of perfection and the proper human attitude toward it, a problem generated by the conflicting views of history expressed by Simón and his coworkers. One could say that this means that the central moral problem of the novel also concerns Stendhal's *promesse du bonheur*, that promise of earthly happiness via the aesthetic that seems everlastingly deferred, but also the utopian promise that Lukács claimed could only point, ironically, to where God could be found in a world abandoned by God. Neither Luther nor Calvin imagined that human perfection was possible, and both actively sought to prevent people from believing that if they could only attain it, eternal salvation would be theirs. The pre-Reformation distinction, as Max Weber pointed out, between *præcepta* (the laws of God) and *consilia* (the counsel of the church, which invited people to do more, "to surpass worldly morality in monastic asceticism"), Luther regarded as pernicious (Weber, *Protestant Ethic*, 40). Indeed, for many commentators, the Reformation's signal achievement was to make the mundane routines of everyday life, the following of one's *Beruf*, or calling, if performed dutifully and in a spirit of good will toward others, every bit as pleasing to God as saintly sacrifice and withdrawal from the world. Calvin may have gone one step further in his attempt to separate altogether the fulfilling of one's duty from the assurance of heavenly reward, but the underlying Lutheran emphasis on dedicating oneself soberly to the mundane task one has been given remained intact. In this sense, the world of Novilla is not just the world of Stoic Greece, modern refugee camps, or communism—it is also, perhaps unsurprisingly, the world of Calvin's "utopian" Geneva. And yet here too there is a crucial difference, for behind Calvin's unforgiving Puritanism, which is a Christian stoicism in its own right, lurks the ineradicable presence of Simón's "idea"—of history, of justice, of ultimate salvation—in ways that are unthinkable in Novilla.

At the Institute, the students are perfectly well aware that some realm of "ideal forms" exists—this is, after all, what they are taught in their philosophy class. It is simply that they have no worldly access to those ideals: perfect chairs and tables exist, but not for the Novillans. Perfect beauty exists too, but it is not attainable by earthly example. This sharp distinction between what exists in this world and what exists in the ideal can never finally be transcended—in fact, it seems that it cannot even be approached by approximation—and in the face of what is certain to be bitter disappointment, the Novillans have chosen something closer to a Schopenhauerian quieting of the will, a stoic avoidance of both the joys and the sufferings of passion in favor of an emotionless serenity. Passion—and the relation in the word to Jesus's suffering is inescapable—is meaningless if there is indeed no possible link between the real and the ideal, the mundane and the transcendent, humans and divinities. This is, after all, precisely the link that an incarnate child of God has been theologically designed to provide.

The possibility of a link between material reality and ideal forms is just what occupies a conversation between Simón and Eugenio, another stevedore, on a bus back from work, though in good Coetzeean fashion, it begins with a debate about Novilla's brothels, "recreation" centers, which (to Simón's further frustration) turn out to be more like sex-therapy clinics. Speaking of the Institute's teaching about "urges of the body," Eugenio argues these are always directed to some abstract ideal of female beauty and that, in going to recreation centers, we merely "traduce the urge," since what we will find there can only be inferior copies, and we will only leave, as a good Stoic might have warned him, "saddened and disappointed." But Simón responds that, after all, since "it is of the nature of desire to reach for what lies beyond our grasp, should we be surprised if it is not satisfied?" (Coetzee, *Childhood*, 141). Clearly referring to Plato's *Phaedrus*—a side of Plato concerning the relationship between physical love and wisdom that seems to be sorely neglected at the Institute—Simón asks, "Did your teacher at the Institute not tell you that embracing inferior copies may be a necessary step in the ascent towards the good and the true and the beautiful?" Seeing that Eugenio is silent, Simón continues, "Think about it. Ask yourself where we would be if there were no such things as ladders" (Coetzee, *Childhood*, 142). The point is double-edged, whether or not Eugenio grasps it. For on the one hand, the simple ladder is the essential tool of the stevedores in their efforts to supply the grain that makes the bread that feeds Novilla (the "bread of life" against which Simón, in his meat-deprived early days, has argued "man does not live by bread alone"). Having no cranes, each stevedore must bear, cross-like, eighty-pound sacks of grain on his shoulders, up a ladder, out of the ship's hold, across a gangplank, and over to a horse-drawn cart. For Simón, the ladder becomes an analogy for the link between the real and the ideal, between a frequently disappointing human existence and a realm of transcendent perfection.

On the one hand, ladders have long been a metaphor in Platonic and Neoplatonic philosophy for making the transition between mere worldly appearance and true reality, matter and form, or what we today (like those in Novilla) would call the real and the ideal. It is a philosophical device, as Simón suggests, evidently not taught at the Institute. The classical ladder derives from Plato's *Symposium*, Socrates' extended explication of the nature of love and beauty (both real and ideal, and decidedly male and homosexual), and perhaps the dialogue in all of Plato that would be most out of place in Novilla.

> And so, when his prescribed devotion to boyish beauties has carried our candidate so far that the universal beauty dawns upon his inward sight, he is almost within reach of the final revelation. And this is the way, the only way, he must approach, or be led toward, that sanctuary of Love. Starting from the individual beauties, the quest for the universal beauty must find him ever mounting the heavenly ladder, stepping from rung to rung—that is, from one to two, from two to *every* lovely body, from bodily beauty to the beauty of institutions, from institutions to learning, and from learning in general to the special lore that pertains to nothing but the beautiful itself—until at last he comes to know what beauty is.[34]

Plato's ladder of beauty became a commonplace in the Neoplatonic dialogues and courtly literature of the Renaissance; Dante's own account of the way mere love poetry can be refigured as a vehicle of philosophy depends upon it. But this ladder is a metaphor in Plato, a trope, and this is precisely the sort of rhetoric that is not (or at least is no longer) understood in Novilla.

On the other hand, there is Jacob's ladder, a ladder that in a sense both prefigures and postdates Plato's, especially in the way the Gospels interpret Hebrew Scripture as prefiguring what is for *The Childhood of Jesus* the incarnate ladder of the New Testament Jesus/David. It is the ladder that appears in a dream to the decidedly less than perfect Jacob while on his way into exile. Jacob has extorted his twin (but firstborn) brother Esau out of his birthright and then deceived his father Isaac by pretending, with his mother's help, to be Esau, so that Isaac bestows the spiritual and material benefits of Esau's inheritance on Jacob instead. Jacob is told to leave after his deception is exposed. The ladder about which he dreams on his journey reaches from earth up to heaven, and on it angels descend and ascend. At the top of the ladder, the Lord stands and promises Jacob (as he had promised Abraham and Isaac before him) not only the land on which he lies, but also the right in that land of first insemination, in all senses of the word, along with His divine protection (see Gen. 28:11–15). (Here, one might say, is the true beginning of Calvin's sense of unearned election.) But this is the same ladder to which Jesus alludes as a metaphor for his own person near the start of the Gospel of John, when Nathanael, impressed that Christ seems to know him in advance, acknowledges him as Son of God and King of Israel. "Thou shalt see greater things than these. / And he saith unto him, Verily, verily, I say unto you, Hereafter ye shall see heaven open, and the angels of God ascending and descending upon the Son of man" (John 1:50–51). It is thus with both Plato's and Jacob's ladders that we will take our fourth and final hermeneutic step into the anagogical, or cosmic, significance of the novel.

That David desperately wants brothers, to be conceived by Inés, is very much in keeping with his unacknowledged Abrahamic lineage, for Abraham, Isaac, and Jacob, not unlike Cain and Abel at the start of Genesis, and Moses and Aaron later, all have brothers with whom they must compete to be the primary bearer of their father's seed before they become bearers of the Lord's covenant. Influenced by a bedtime story that Inés likes to tell him about three brothers who are sent to find a cure for their mother's deathly pain—the first two fail, and the third succeeds in bringing back the curative herb *Escamel* (in Spanish, the long arm of an anvil on which swords are beaten out) only by allowing his heart to be devoured by a bear—David wants to be "the Third Brother" (Coetzee, *Childhood*, 146–48), the sacrificial son who is turned into a star after his quest. That star reappears at the end of the novel. Like Jesus, however, David remains an only and fatherless child, and in that respect he breaks a mold, as if Coetzee were implying that the fraternal bifurcations that repeatedly produce inexplicably chosen and inexplicably abandoned tribes in the Pentateuch according to clan and tribal filiations would be transformed instead into a process of election that is, in its darker Pauline, Augustinian, and Calvinist interpretations, both inscrutable and humbling, if not humiliating. The ladder that Jesus appropriates from Jacob in the Gospel of John is in Coetzee a biblical allusion that, as ladders do, leads both transcendently up and mortally down at the same time.

As we approach the middle of the novel, it becomes clear that there is something odd about Simón's memories. "It is true: I have no memories," he tells Elena, who believes he is foolish to entrust David to Inés. "But images persist, shades of images. How that is I can't explain. Something deeper persists too, which I call the memory of having a memory" (Coetzee, *Childhood*, 98). Plato's theory that all human knowledge is in fact the recovery of knowledge from a time before we were born into this life is the obvious reference, given the stoic context of Novilla and the Institute. *Phaedo*, a dialogue that occurs during Socrates' last hours before his execution, is largely devoted to the question of the life of the soul, both before birth and after death, so that all learning becomes an act of memory, or at least the memory of a memory. "And if it is true," Socrates says, "that we acquired our knowledge before our birth, and lost it at the moment of birth, but afterward, by the exercise of our senses upon sensible objects, recover the knowledge which we had once before, I suppose that what we call learning will be the recovery of our own knowledge, and surely we should be right in calling this recollection" (Plato, *Collected Dialogues*, 59; *Phaedo*, 75e2–7). Still, Coetzee clearly has more in mind than a Platonic theory of knowledge, which would mark Simón as perhaps the only true "philosopher," in a Socratic sense, in all of stoic Novilla. What emerges a bit further on in the novel is that the lives led in Novilla are part of a larger cycle of reincarnation. When Simón tries to explain to David the meaning of the term *dead bodies* while cleaning out Inés's clogged toilet, he tells him, "But we don't have to be troubled about death. After death there is always another life. You have seen that. We human beings are fortunate in that respect. We are not like poo that has to stay behind and be mixed again with the earth." To David's subsequent question, "What are we like?" Simón answers, "We are like ideas. Ideas never die. You will learn that in school" (Coetzee, *Childhood*, 133). As in Socrates' account of the possibility of reincarnation in *Phaedo*, Novilla appears to be a way station, one stop among others in a longer cycle of lived lives, which helps to explain the stoicism of its inhabitants. In a world where death itself is more or less meaningless, where one life follows another with inevitability and regularity and without much in the way of memory (though the inevitable problem then arises of just *how* the inhabitants of Novilla know of their reincarnation once memory itself is erased at birth), the advice of Elena and the stevedores—that is, to accept things the way they are, to banish thoughts of other worlds (which will come of their own accord), and to wash oneself clean of whatever dim memories of previous lives remain (since in a cycle of reincarnation such memories have little value)—all becomes fairly reasonable. The Stoic concept of reincarnation is precisely what makes the concept of history insignificant, even if Simón stubbornly resists the obvious Stoic conclusions.

In *Phaedo*, Socrates suggests that perhaps newly living souls come from those who have died (Plato, *Collected Dialogues*, 53; *Phaedo*, 70c5–d6); that the souls of those who embrace their corporeality are doomed to Hades, to the haunting of graveyards, or to reincarnation in the form of "donkeys and other perverse animals" (Plato, *Collected Dialogues*, 64–65; *Phaedo*, 81c6–e6); that the souls of those who have "cultivated the goodness of an ordinary citizen—what is called self-control and integrity," will return as social and disciplined creatures such as bees and wasps, and perhaps once again as members of the human race (Plato, *Collected Dialogues*, 65; *Phaedo*, 82a10–b5); and that the souls of those who practice philosophy "may attain to the divine nature," which is why philosophers are so willing to abstain from bodily pleasures (Plato, *Collected Dialogues*, 65; *Phaedo*, 82b7–c8). Still, after having worn out a number of bodies, the soul will then itself perish. Plato thus implies, however unsurely, a vision of both reincarnation and the progressive approach to divinity through ever more "philosophical" lives that is no more than half-embraced in Novilla, where reincarnation seems assured, but neither the value of a life of ideas nor any sense of longing for a progression—a ladder—toward divine perfection is to be found.

It is important to recognize that Coetzee seems to have two versions of pre-Christian Greek morality in mind here, one rigorously ruled by a this-worldly rationalism and Stoic utilitarianism, and a second version dominated by an otherworldly imagination and mysticism. Both versions derive from Pythagoras, simultaneously mathematician and mystic of the good life, though to add to the confusion, he quite intentionally, if unfortunately, wrote nothing down (not unlike Socrates). The subsequent Pythagoreans from whom Plato and Aristotle borrowed so much can be divided into, on the one hand, *mathēmatikoi*, who developed the ideas of the master related to mathematics, natural philosophy, and (most important for Coetzee's novel) a theory of numbers; and on the other hand, the *akousmatikoi*, who—tending to believe that they were the authentic inheritors of Pythagoras's teaching—focused instead on matters relating to religion, cosmology, reincarnation, and ritual practice, including abstinence from meat and beans. But Pythagoras may not have made any such distinction, and it seems clear that Coetzee's David does not either. Moreover, the confusion between the two ways of interpreting Pythagoras begins with Aristotle, who provides us with our only account of the influence of Pythagorean thought on Plato as well, and it starts with the theory of ideal numbers.

As Walter Burkert elaborates the problem in his definitive account of "lore and science" in Pythagoreanism, for Aristotle "the Pythagoreans did not differentiate between number and corporeality, between corporeal and incorporeal being"; whereas Plato "separates the numbers, as ideas, from the sensible world and even sets between them the mathematical realm as a realm of its own, for the Pythagoreans, things 'are' numbers, they 'consist of' numbers."[35] In his *Metaphysics*, Aristotle rejected both Plato's dualism and the Pythagoreans' monadic materialism where numbers were concerned, since, in Burkert's terms, "Plato and the Pythagoreans both accepted numbers as the principles (Aristotle, 987b24)—number not as the number of other assumed objects, but as an independent entity, οὐσία" (Burkert,

Lore and Science, 31).[36] In this regard, it is of no small importance that one of David's basic problems at the school to which he is sent—indeed, it has been a problem in Simón's eyes all along—is his refusal to treat numbers "as the number of other assumed objects" rather than as substantive entities in themselves, independent entities that one could, in effect, visit. When David is unable to say what comes after 888—he says, "92"— or to see that 889 is bigger than 888, Simón chides him: "Wrong. 889 is bigger, because 889 comes after 888." David replies to Simón's assertion by asking, "How do you know? You have never *been* there" (Coetzee, *Childhood*, 150). David's sense of things is not that of a uniform, one-dimensional number line, infinitely divisible, as in Aristotle (and in Simón's understanding), and hence packed so tightly with an infinite number of numbers that nothing could fall through it. It is instead three-dimensional, and the holes through which one might fall can open up anywhere, even in the text of *Don Quixote*.

David's insistence on number as οὐσία—as both substantive entity and cosmic principle—derives ultimately from the Pythagoreans' account of the origin of number, since the Pythagoreans' understanding of number (and to some extent Plato's) is also cosmogony. The One, which is a number both even and odd, both male and female, is also the one place where Limit and Unlimited unite. As Burkert observes, "it *is* nothing else than the world before its further evolution" (Burkert, *Lore and Science*, 36) or, in more familiar religious terms, before God introduced difference into the primal chaos. In a process that suggests orphic, gnostic, and kabbalistic thinking, at some point the Unlimited seems to fold in on itself so that it forms an internal difference, a Limit. "The One becomes a Two as the Unlimited penetrates it," Burkert writes. "Here is one of the most widespread cosmogonic themes, 'the separation of Heaven and Earth'" (Burkert, *Lore and Science*, 36–37). Subsequent cosmological growth is like that of an embryo, like the growth of a living being. "The One begins to breathe, and, as the breath flows in, it assumes a more complicated structure" (Burkert, *Lore and Science*, 37). When Simón takes David to fix Inés's clogged toilet, he explains to the boy how water always flows downhill. "But how does the water get into the sky?" he asks

David, dialectically. David's reply is something like a Pythagorean recollection of the initial separation of heaven and earth: "'Because the sky breathes in,' says the child. 'The sky breathes in . . . and the sky breathes out'" (Coetzee, *Childhood*, 131).

Still, it is clear that Plato's fairly inchoate ideas of reincarnation, largely inherited from Pythagoras, will only take us so far, and they are certainly not enough to satisfy Simón. For Elena, "a new life is a new life . . . not an old life all over again in new surroundings" (Coetzee, *Childhood*, 143). What Simón longs for is something far more, something beyond the mere series of reincarnations that one finds in Plato or in Novilla —he wants "the feel of residence in a body with a past, a body soaked in its past" (Coetzee, *Childhood*, 143). He rails against her stoic complacency: "'But what good is a new life,' he interrupts her, 'if we are not transformed by it, transfigured, as I certainly am not?'" (Coetzee, *Childhood*, 143). Elena believes it is enough to be once again like a child, to start over, to begin again with no past—it is the creed, one might say, of the "happy" cosmopolitan who can reinvent a life in a new land, or perhaps of the migrant who either has no use for ideas or has by necessity given up on them altogether. Simón—for better or worse, we might want to add—will have none of this. He craves not only a past in which he is immersed and from which he cannot fully escape, but also a future in which the possibility of transfiguration, a Christological term par excellence, is possible. This is in many ways the Augustine of the *Confessions*, and I believe Coetzee wants us to see the analogy.

I think the appropriate source for the sort of "new life" via transfiguration that Simón longs for is not Plato at all, but the first major Christian theologian, Origen, who is also a heterodox, Neoplatonic philosopher of new lives as successive new worlds, and of final reconciliation or restoration in our original state, which he called *apokatastasis*. Origen Adamantius, whose writings date from the early third century, was a follower of Clement in the school of Alexandria and an inheritor of Pythagorean-Platonic thought. He was also quickly disavowed by the nascent organized Christianity of the era, which declared his ideas anathema in 553 CE (a condemnation alleged to have occurred at the Second Ecumenical Council of Constantinople, though the original Greek records of that meeting have been lost). Origen's importance for Coetzee, I think, is twofold. On the one hand, Origen composes the first sustained Christian refutation of the philosophical critique of Christianity made by a Greek Stoic in his *Contra Celsum*. Second, Origen is situated historically at a moment that reveals precisely what was at stake in the story of Jesus, which is to say that Origen demonstrates just how the Christian message appropriated and transformed Greek stoicism, especially that of Pythagoras and Plato, so that reincarnation becomes something more than an endless series of new lives in which, as in *Phaedo*, the soul eventually exhausts the successive bodies it is given and perishes. In Origen, reincarnation as the Greeks conceived it is rejected in favor of something akin to Jacob's ladder—or rather, akin to the idea of Christ as the fulfillment of Jacob's ladder—so that the succession of new lives the soul is allowed to live is given an eschatological significance. The choices one makes in one life not only determine how one will be incarnated in the next (itself an inheritance from Platonic thought), but there is also now an example of a divine–human "ladder"—the existential fact of Jesus—that one might follow, by moral choice, in the course of migration from one life-world to the one following. It is a process by which, via a potentially endless number of reincarnations, *all* souls—encased finally only in celestial or spiritual (that is, nonmaterial) bodies and hence not subject to physical punishment after their remediation via successive lives—attain a reconciliation, or *apokatastasis*, in God by returning to their uncorrupted being before the fall. But then, part of what made Origen's work heretical was just this notion of *apokatastasis* after numerous, remedial new lives, an epochal, perhaps nearly infinite, drama in which none would ultimately be damned—not even the Devil—and all would be saved. The other offending doctrine was Christological, and it has a particular relevance in *The Childhood of Jesus*: "Origen was charged with teaching that the Son, though generated from the essence of the Father, was nevertheless a creature, bearing the title Son by courtesy and not by right."[37] For Origen, the Son, like the Holy Spirit (or godfather, in Coetzee), is an emanation of the Father, but he is a separate and decidedly lesser creature whose primary distinction is that, in the end, his reunion with God will be purely spiritual. In *The Childhood of Jesus*, Coetzee seems to accentuate David's utter humanness, his lack, as it were, of any obvious connection to divinity, even his arbitrariness, as well as Simón's insistence that David's paternity is somehow irrelevant, as if David himself were no more than some sort of "son" by courtesy, as he is to Inés.

In his *Contra Celsum* (roughly 248 CE), Origen produces the first full-throated rebuttal to the non-Christian Platonists who claimed that Christianity as a whole was nothing more than an incompetent plagiarism of Plato's thought. Origen attempts to refute Celsus point by point, claiming that it is Celsus who has profoundly misunderstood the doctrines of Christianity, largely by seeing in it nothing more than charlatanry and magic based on an inadequate understanding of Plato. But Origen goes a bit further by insisting instead that it is Plato who cribbed from the Hebrews.

> Long ago David showed the profundity and magnitude of the visions of God possessed by those who rise beyond sensible things when he said in the book of Psalms: "Praise God, ye heavens of heavens, and the water that is above the heavens; let them praise the name of the Lord." I do not doubt that Plato learned the words of the *Phaedrus* from some Hebrews and that, as some writers have said, it was after studying the sayings of the prophets that he wrote the passage where he says *"No earthly poet either has sung or will sing of the region above the heavens as it deserves. . . ."*[38]

Even Celsus's account of reincarnation, supposedly derived only from Plato, Origen reinterprets as instead a borrowing from Moses, in Genesis—that is, Jacob's dream of the celestial ladder. "Celsus also follows Plato in saying that *the way for the souls to and from the earth passes through the planets.* But Moses, our most ancient prophet, says that in a divine dream our forefather Jacob had a vision in which he saw a ladder reaching to heaven and angels of God ascending and descending upon it, and the Lord standing at its top" (Origen, *Contra Celsum*, 333). Celsus instead traces Plato's cosmogony back to ancient Mithraic (Persian) conceptions of the soul's ascent through the planets, which function as gates or doors of a sort, symbolized by various metals of increasing rarity and connected by a ladder: lead, tin, bronze, iron, alloy, silver, and gold, at the top of which is an eighth and final gate. (It is a trope that perhaps had also informed Coetzee's title for *Age of Iron*, which seems derived most obviously from Hesiod, for whom it means the present age of decay.) Origen dismisses this derivation since, for him, Christian and Hebrew imagery had little to do with Persian theology, and the Greeks, including Plato, did not consider the "mysteries of Mithras" to have "anything exceptional about them compared with those of Eleusis or with those of Hecate . . ." (Origen, *Contra Celsum*, 335). Origen was probably wrong about the longer, and indeed likely, shadow of Persian thought on the Greeks and Christianity. But the crucial point to be grasped is that it is Origen who reinterprets the Stoic reduction of Platonic philosophy so that, in recovering some of its Pythagorean and Persian mysteries, he is able to link it to the dream of Jacob's ladder, a ladder that occupies a crucial symbolic role in *The Childhood of Jesus.*

In his *On First Principles* (roughly 218 CE), our interpretation of Origen becomes more speculative. We have, along with some fragments in Greek, only the Latin translation composed by Rufinus, who is thought to have actively edited passages in Origen that might have made his work even more offensive to orthodox bishops. Nevertheless, there are several crucial ideas that are clear enough, each of significance for Coetzee's novel. First, like Simón in his resistance to the stoic complacency of the Novillans, Origen refuses to accept what he takes to be the Platonic idea of reincarnation, that is, that "worlds similar to each other and in all respects alike sometimes come into existence," so that, in effect, people will end up living in more or less the same world over and over, whether they know it or not.[39] While *Phaedo* does suggest a scale of rewards and punishments via reincarnation based on how close one comes to adopting the perspective of the philosopher in any given life, it is clear that *Phaedo* projects neither an eschatological vision nor anything like a sense of cumulative history in the course of these cycles, and in any case most souls will eventually not outlive the bodies allocated to them. For Origen, as for

Simón, such a vision lacks weight—it lacks the sense of "a body soaked in its past," which is what Simón tells Elena he longs to have (Coetzee, *Childhood*, 143).

Second, as in Auerbach, the incarnation of God in Christ becomes for Origen the model, the template, on which human history understands the significance of its unfolding. It is, in effect, what gives weight to words, what gives an enduring substance to the past— that is, a past actually *worth* remembering, even if one is ultimately to be washed clean—and finally what gives hope for the future. In Origen, Christ's resurrection is not only what tells rational beings that there is something that can defeat death, but also that rational beings could not exist "unless the Word or reason had existed before them" (Origen, *On First Principles*, 17)—a principle that remains part of Western thought right up to Heidegger's meditations on language as preceding, rather than produced by, human beings. Finally, then, we come to Origen's notion of multiple and successive worlds, which lies at the heart of his rather unique understanding of Christian redemption (a vision so unique it has in fact been banished from Christian theology for fifteen hundred years). What Origen offers to Coetzee, I think, is a way of reconciling the brute yet powerful logic of Calvinist election—in which the grace of forgiveness and salvation can never be earned, or deserved, by either intention or deed, or somehow called upon by means of a confession that in truth only punishes anew through the irreducibility of inauthenticity, endless self-doubt, and thus added guilt—with the possibility that there is, amid the multiple "elections" or "new worlds" that a given soul inhabits, also the opportunity for a gradual approach to truth, a spiritual ladder of sorts that the soul climbs in imitation of Christ.

Origen invokes the idea of multiple worlds at various points, but perhaps the most significant is a section of *On First Principles* in which he responds to the objections of many, especially "from the schools of Marcion, Valentinus and Basilides," who ask why, if God the Creator "lacks neither the will to desire what is good and perfect nor the power to produce it," it should nevertheless turn out to be the case that "souls are in their natures diverse"—by which they mean that God seems arbitrarily to assign habitations to angels and the saved in various hierarchical planes of heaven, and even among rational creatures makes "some of higher rank and others of second and third and many still lower and less worthy degrees" (Origen, *On First Principles*, 133). It is a question perfectly suited to Coetzee's temperament. The question is at the heart of what Leibniz will later call theodicy, which arose in my earlier discussion of Thomas Mann—how should one justify the existence of evil in the light of God's presumed goodness and power? It is a question that has haunted Coetzee's work from *Dusklands* on, and it is a question to which, up to this point, he has only provided narrative responses upon what must be for him, I think, ultimately unsatisfying Calvinist lines. Origen's response to the contradictions raised by Marcion and the others is also the response implied by Coetzee in *The Childhood of Jesus*: while the decision about the nature of our specific "habitation" when arriving on earth is clearly not ours to make, so that we might come into the world in an Australian relocation camp on Christmas Island or in an old-money enclave of elegant residences, the soul's journey through the multiple worlds of Origen's imagination is not simply due to accident or chance.

Indeed, Origen here again refers to the story of Jacob and Esau, the urtext of unearned merit or condemnation, one might say, complete with the dream ladder that promises redemption. On the case of Jacob and Esau, Origen quotes Saint Paul, the source of all Christian notions of election, to make his point, for if anyone could solve the contradiction between "election" and "merit" in the story of Isaac's sons, it would be Paul. "For 'when they were not yet' created 'and had done nothing either good or evil, that the purpose of God according to election might stand,' then, as certain men think, some were made heavenly, others of the earth and others of the lower regions, 'not from works,' as the aforesaid men think, 'but from him who called them.' 'What shall we say,' if this is so? 'Is there then unrighteousness with God? God forbid'" (Origen, *On First Principles*, 135; Origen is quoting here from Rom. 9:11–14). Origen takes his cue from Paul's "God forbid," so that election for him cannot somehow also imply a lack of righteousness in God. But the ingenious solution he provides is his own reworking of Plato's *Phaedo*, the mystical dialogue to be found nowhere in Novilla.

The only way to account for the fact that Jacob "supplanted his brother even in the womb," writes Origen, yet still received God's blessing in his dream, is to assume that "by reason of his merits in some previous life Jacob had deserved to be loved by God to such an extent as to be worthy of being preferred to his brother" (Origen, *On First Principles*, 135). This principle then forms the basis of Origen's larger conception, so long as we note that the diversity of positions of incarnated souls in this world

> is not the original condition of their creation but that for anteced-
> ent causes a different position of service is prepared by the Cre-
> ator for each one in proportion to the degree of his merit, which
> depends on the fact that each, in being created by God as a mind
> or rational spirit, has personally gained for himself, in accordance
> with the movements of his mind and the disposition of his heart,
> a greater or less share of merit, and has rendered himself either
> lovable or it may be hateful to God. We must also note, however,
> that some beings who are of higher merit are ordained to suffer
> with the rest and to perform a duty to those below them, in order
> that by this means they themselves may become sharers in the
> endurance of the Creator, according to the Apostle's own words,
> "The creature was made subject to vanity, not willingly, but by
> reason of him who subjected it, in hope." (Origen, *On First Prin-
> ciples*, 135–36)

Origen preserves a notion of free will within the larger Pauline notion of election by means of a theory of multiple worlds in which what one is born with in this life is whatever one has earned, morally speaking, in the previous one. While it allows Origen to save free will from the gnostic determinists of his time and to justify the seemingly unfair ways of God, it is not hard to see the rather invidious social implications of such a doctrine. It would allow those blessed with the gifts of position to justify their place merely by pointing out that the wretched of the earth must have earned their suffering in a previous life.

In effect, this is to an extent what became of the Puritan tradition after Calvin, with a twist. Instead of imagining, as Max Weber concluded the Puritans did, that the fruits of one's success on earth, in the face of the failure of others, might be taken as the sign of one's divine election, Origen suggests a far more elaborate cosmic scheme: one is subject to a divine election of sorts, but one's incarnation in this life is still earned, except not in this life, but in the previous one. It is a solution worthy of Kafka, and it is also not hard to see why the early Church would have none of it, since if Origen were deemed correct, he would have, long before Luther and Calvin, dealt a fatal blow to the Church itself, which would no longer be able to promise with any assurance that "eternal life" was what would follow this one as long as the precepts of God and the counsel of the Church were obeyed. A doctrine of multiple worlds intervening between this life and eternal life was not nearly so calculable a proposition. There is then a further logical problem here, since Origen must make room for the story of Christ, who doctrinally could not possibly have earned in his previous life the fate that his Father allocated to him. Despite all his ingenuity, Origen is reduced like so many theologians after him to an equivocation over the value of suffering, which even he is forced to admit is often unearned, no matter what the logic of his theory demands. The value of suffering thus emerges in Origen exactly the way it often does in Coetzee—as it does, for example, in the rape of David Lurie's daughter in *Disgrace*, which she accepts even to the point of bearing the child that results—that is, as a duty, a Beckettian *pensum*, performed so that the more privileged in this world become "sharers in the endurance of the Creator" and, by extension, the endurance of the most humble of his creation, in the hope that the vanity instilled by their privilege will thereby be overcome.

This is why, I think, there is also a constant equivocation in *The Childhood of Jesus* with the phrase "new life," which appears in various contexts throughout the novel, since there is finally no way of knowing in Coetzee, as in Origen, whether that new life will be for better or for worse. It means many things: Simón's and David's new life once relocated, like refugees, in Novilla; the possibility of a new life in another town called Estrellita del Norte, which they are told is even worse than Novilla; the new life that Simón longs for where words and history have weight, which must somehow be like one of his old lives, though the memory is dim; the new life (perhaps very much like the one they have now) that the inhabitants of Novilla appear to assume will open up after they have died in this one; and finally the new life that is centered on David as Jesus, that is, the new life offered by Christ, by Christian conversion narratives, by Puritan hope in God's grace, but also by the ingenious Neoplatonic cosmology that Origen constructed around Jacob's ladder and its prefiguration of Christ as the path to redemption. It is perhaps not accidental that Coetzee's most Calvinist novels, from *In the Heart of the Country* to *Age of Iron*, were followed by a Pauline conversion narrative of sorts in *Slow Man* (a title that may also refer to the slowness of Coetzee's own theological evolution), which has now been followed by a novel called *The Childhood of Jesus*. Intentionally or not, what Coetzee has given us in a career of novels is a spiritual autobiography of the first rank.

In the last scene of the novel, Simón drives Inés's car northward, with Inés, David, and Bolívar inside, in a somewhat aimless fashion that David characterizes as that of "gypsies," which appears as yet one more group of Coetzeean outcasts, no matter how much Inés resists David's term (Coetzee, *Childhood*, 262). But the group soon begins to expand. David has already invited Señora Robles, who runs the *cabañas* at which the group stays the night of David's accident, to come with him to a new life, but she politely declines. At David's insistence, they pick up an unwashed hitchhiker named Juan (no Baptist, surely, but the point is made) and somehow find room for him. When Simón later says they cannot keep doing this, because "there is no room in the car," David insists there is (Coetzee, *Childhood*, 277). David also invites Dr. García, who treats him for his injuries, to come along, though he too declines. (Even in Novilla, many are called and few are chosen.) David rejects his name—he tells Juan "I've still got to get my name"—and Juan decides to call him Señor Anónimo, as if to say, "Everyman." Eventually, David also declares he likes neither Simón nor Inés any longer, but wants to have only brothers.

The climax of the novel comes, at least in my reading of it, about three pages before the end. Simón tells Juan, who has also come through Belstar, that his name, like David's, is meaningless—that they could have just as well been assigned numbers, since Simón holds, as he has throughout the novel, that numbers are mere placeholders, merely the means, as in Aristotle, for naming the number of other objects and hence as arbitrary as proper names assigned by a bureaucracy. But Juan disagrees. "Actually, there are no random numbers," he says, because when you try to come up with a random number, you are bound to be remembering a number that once had meaning: "my old telephone number or something like that. There is always a reason behind a number" (Coetzee, *Childhood*, 274). Simón tells Juan he must be a number mystic like David, but then adds, "Of course there are no random numbers *under the eye of God.* But we don't live under the eye of God. In the world we live in there are random numbers and random names and random events, like being picked up at random by a car containing a man and a woman and a child named David. And a dog. What was the secret cause behind that event, do you think?" (Coetzee, *Childhood*, 274–75; Coetzee's emphasis). Simón's comment is both a perfectly serious metaphysical observation and a perfectly outrageous joke on the reader (one must recall Coetzee's fondness for Cervantes here). For, "of course," Simón, Inés, David, Bolívar, and now Juan *do not at all* live in a world of random numbers, names, and events—they live only in the world of Coetzee's novel, over which he is, properly speaking, presiding like God, and within which pretty much nothing has been left to chance. As in all good allegory, especially one with fourfold hermeneutic ambitions, everything would seem to be determined in advance, as in a radically deterministic cosmos, so that Simón's naive insistence that he exists in a reality that is not lived "under the eye of God" turns into farcical self-satire when he asks an itinerant named Juan, or John, what reason there might have been behind his invitation into the car containing someone who might be Jesus. For the reader, it is suddenly Simón the stubborn, if also earnestly loyal, realist who seems out of his depth, for he has unwittingly been living a rigorously predetermined life all along.

The question raised by this exchange is both inevitable and profound. Is Coetzee simply making the same metafictional point that, say, Thackeray makes about his narrative "puppets" at the end of *Vanity Fair* (a novel, I should add, that cannot be reduced to that point), or is Coetzee also implying that the naiveté of Simón is very much our own—that is, not that we are all unwitting participants in a story about the childhood of Jesus, but that, in one way or another, we are inevitably and perhaps unwittingly trapped in allegorical structures—"All is allegory," in Lord Chandos's words—which are clearly not simply of our own making and may not be limited only to questions of God or religion, even if they certainly include such theological questions? If this is the case, we are faced with the problem that, despite Origen's and Coetzee's apparent desire to maintain somehow the efficacy of free will in determining our fates, we are only thrown back upon the Calvinist Puritanism that has haunted Coetzee's work from the start. Given such a perspective, what would it even mean to say that one could compose a narrative of *any* sort that was not somehow always already an allegory? If, as Beckett insists, the voice that narrates is always a voice that comes from somewhere else, is "someone else's affair," to use Geulincx's terms, then every narrative is already in some sense an allegory of the one that came before it, like the successive worlds of Origen's theology. When we take these questions seriously, then *The Childhood of Jesus* also emerges as the latest version of the novel that Coetzee has tried to write in every fictional world he has set into motion, one that emerges, perhaps, as one more stage in a personal evolution. In this sense, Coetzee's entire oeuvre suddenly appears to be an allegory of his own spiritual (though happily not Bunyan-like) quest. As in Beckett, in certain respects, each of Coetzee's novels has also been, perhaps inevitably, an allegory of the ones that preceded it, and *The Childhood of Jesus* may be the most complex and self-referential one of all. There is, in the end, no indication that Coetzee has finally rid himself of the ineradicable shame that permeates all his previous works. But at least this time he has allowed himself a ladder with which he may climb out of his slough of despond, and as Simón asks Eugenio, where would we be if there were no such things as ladders?

Conclusion

Reading in the Afterlife of the Novel

One of the big critical issues raised by my approach to the novel in this book has to do with the question that the Russian formalists, early in the twentieth century, posed explicitly in terms of artistic "motivation."[1] It is also the question raised, implicitly, by Salman Rushdie in his brief but highly critical review of J. M. Coetzee's *Disgrace*, cited in chapter 3. When I write in my introduction that, quite contrary to Lukács's early hopes, the novel after Dostoevsky and Kafka turned (at least in part) to the dark religious comedy of the almost unbearable disgrace that is human existence in a world where grace is no longer available, I am implying that it was quite real (if for Lukács at the time unforeseen) historical events and their imaginative effects—war, violence, inhumanity on a scale previously unimaginable, deracination, moral and political collapse, intellectual "bad faith," and the withering away of religious expectations for some kind of divine justice, if not in this world, then the next—that produced the kind of writing we find in *The Unnamable*, *Doktor Faustus*, and *Age of Iron*. As Viktor Shklovsky argued, however, we might just as easily view such writing as instead responding, in varying degrees, to a set of themes inherited from a literary tradition—and, in the case of my argument, from a religious tradition—themes that can then be embodied by strategies such as realism, romance, or allegory

and that require only that the writer produce adequately "defamiliar-
ized" language and imagery to interest the reader all over again.[2]
Moreover, the problem of aesthetic versus real-world artistic motivation persists even if we assume, as both later Russian formalists and
Theodor Adorno did in different ways, that the historical development of artistic forms actually encoded in its logic the pressures of the
real world *as a whole*—a social, cultural, and political system, with all
its structural contradictions, that perhaps pointed in the modern era,
as Adorno claimed, to a totality that was always in effect bad, false,
administered, and unfree, a totality that could then no longer be represented, as Lukács and later Rushdie claimed it could, as a social
whole that a critical, realistic novel could explain in terms of material
causes and to which such a novel might offer an alternative, redemptive path beyond the impasses it revealed.[3] For writers such as Beckett, Mann, and Coetzee, the latter solution only defers the original
question about artistic motivation. Even if artistic forms somehow
encode the totality of a social system or culture at a given time—the
way one might claim Beckett does, only two years after World War II,
with *Molloy*, the narrator of which tells us at one point, "I am
still obeying orders, if you like, but no longer out of fear. No, I
am still afraid, but simply from force of habit" (Beckett, *Selected
Works*, 2:126)—even then, the attentive reader will want to know
why. Is Molloy, the character, obeying orders out of habit because
that is what a secular, administered, and rationalized modern society
demands in war and in peace? Or is he instead commenting, as Robbe-
Grillet's novels surely did, and as Coetzee's Paul Rayment does in
Slow Man, on the nature of *all* fictional characters in novels, right
from the start—that is, are they not all ultimately puppets in the
hands of their authors, so that the most intractable mode of authority
(as Thackeray understood) is in the end the authority of the author,
who is at all times an allegorical representation of the autocrat?

Such questions rarely allow for clear answers. Most writers, confronted by them, would no doubt decline to respond. Indeed, Coetzee's *Elizabeth Costello* leaves its title character pondering these sorts
of dilemmas at the end. Will she take responsibility for a moral point
of view, or is "point of view" itself, narrative as well as moral, as she

implies at one point, simply a fictional device? Nevertheless, I believe one particular issue needs to be addressed more than others in the authors I discuss, and that is the question of allegory. It is obvious that, in small ways akin to the novels of Dostoevsky, but perhaps much more related to those of Kafka, the literature that concerns me in this book has more than a superficial bias toward the allegorical. Thomas Mann rather cleverly solved the issue of aesthetic motivation by embedding one story—the somewhat eternal story of the Faustian composer Adrian Leverkühn, who responds only to the formal problems of his chosen art—inside another story, that is, the "realistic" narrative of Serenus Zeitblom, a man with two sons fighting for Germany in World War II, who then tells the tale of his friend's life as if it were quite disconnected, in terms of "motivation," from his own, but slowly discovers that it is not. Allegory—as has always been the case, even in Benjamin's book on *Trauerspiel*—depersonalizes both innocence and guilt. (In Benjamin, it is a grand historical process of decay that is at issue.)[4] It makes us, both actual victims and actual victimizers, seem to be remarkably alike, and that is perhaps why those who want to stress the political implications of a literary work tend to be uncomfortable with allegory. This has certainly been true of post-existential responses to Camus, as Edward Said demonstrates in his compelling critique of Camus's embrace of the "absurd" as a technique that obscures the novelist's dismissive, if narratively unexpressed, views of Algerian independence.[5] Worst of all, it makes it seem as if human affairs are not simply human affairs, as if (intolerable as it may sound) we—that is, the good, autonomous, bourgeois individuals who read and write novels, the Serenus Zeitbloms of the literary world—are not really in control of anything. As many readers of Mann and Coetzee have surely felt, and as Rushdie vaguely implies without saying so in his review of Coetzee, this strategy may appear to be all too convenient when one is a scion of the dominant, white, Christian, Eurocentric order. When Thomas Mann decides to turn a book that could well have been about German responsibility for the Holocaust—naming names and counting bodies and providing reasons for it all—into a fantastically detailed and often wildly arcane meditation on the history of composition in German music, and then decides to cram that history into a fusty and largely forgotten story of a medieval German magus named Faust, the correct political response is, for some, obvious. How dare he, as a Christian German, try to evade responsibility by allegorizing genocide as if it were nothing but a story about German musical form and absurd religious myths!

Yet Mann's choices in *Doktor Faustus* are not, in the end, all that different from J. M. Coetzee's in almost everything he has written. In general, I think the discomfort of so many readers with all the allegorizing in Coetzee is also a refusal of everything in Coetzee that points beyond the secular—that is, everything that is not historically concrete, uniquely individual, and, in the end, the consequence of an identifiable responsibility (either blameworthy or praiseworthy) of someone in a specific place and time. And while Beckett's novels have by contrast often escaped the label of allegory per se, his plays have usually not, and those plays controversially have stimulated much religious debate from the beginning. This broader or more abstract sense of religious allegory in the theater has also at times inflected the reading of Beckett's novels. To put the question bluntly: should we see the turn to allegory here, to obviously varying degrees, as a response to unnerving yet lived historical moments (World War II in the case of Beckett and Mann, and South African apartheid in the case of Coetzee) that would be, perhaps, simply unbearable to face, or impossible to represent using the techniques of the secular realism described by Watt, McKeon, Moretti, and others? Is there not something about the nature of world war, atomic weaponry, genocide, and apartheid that is simply not conducive to the use of mindless narrative "fillers"? Or, on the contrary, is the affection for something that at least looks like allegory in Beckett, Mann, and Coetzee primarily a function of an aesthetic reaction to prior novels and novelists, something that Harold Bloom once called the "anxiety of influence": for example, Beckett's minimalist volte-face away from James Joyce's encyclopedic and mythic maximalism; Mann's late immersion in religious legend (*Der Erwählte, Joseph und seine Brüder*) rather than the domestic bourgeois narrative of his earlier realism (*Buddenbrooks*); and what I can only call Coetzee's deep, and finally ethical, discomfort with the professional skill and tastefully crafted descriptive prose of well-trained, university-credentialed "creative writers," powers of description that he has openly claimed not to possess? Is allegory, albeit for different reasons in each case, at heart an aesthetic solution to an aesthetic problem, and not a historical commentary at all? And finally, is allegory as a genre simply a way of avoiding the thornier problems of actual historical responsibility for evil? When Beckett embraces Geulincx, and Mann rewrites the Faust legend, and Coetzee's Elizabeth Curren implies that perhaps behind the sins of apartheid is the far more unavoidable stain of original sin, are not all these members of the dominant Eurocentric culture simply throwing up their hands—just as Rushdie claims Coetzee is doing in *Disgrace*—because sorting out the particulars of moral responsibility would be far too painful for them?

This is not, I think, in the end a solvable set of problems—at least, it is not solvable without exploring something like the Freudian unconscious of entire societies as an explanation, and I am not going to do that here—but I raise it nevertheless because understanding what is at stake in posing the problem of allegory helps to illuminate the discussion at the heart of this book, that is, how to understand the endlessness of the process of secularization that emerges from the novels I discuss. For both good and ill, all allegorical reading tends toward universalizing generalities concerning human existence that can too easily be used to obfuscate or ignore the political specificity of particular historical moments, particular individuals, and particular experiences in our resolutely material world. As Angus Fletcher writes, in what is for me still the best account of allegory we have, "Finally, whether one thinks there is such a thing as pure storytelling, or only degrees of abstract thematic structure (Aristotle's *dianoia*) underlying every fiction, the main point is surely that in discussing literature generally we must be ready to discern in almost any work at least a small degree of allegory. All literature, as Northrop Frye has observed, is from the point of view of commentary more or less allegorical, while no 'pure allegory' will ever be found."[6] Moreover, while Fletcher is certainly alert to the notion—indeed, the oldest idea about allegory— that it is a "human reconstitution of divinely inspired messages . . .

which tries to preserve the remoteness of a properly veiled godhead," he is just as committed to the idea that allegory is at the same time a deeply political act (A. Fletcher, *Allegory*, 21). In times of political oppression, for example, "we may get 'Aesop-language' to avoid censorship of dissident thought" (A. Fletcher, *Allegory*, 22). And even in relatively open societies, allegories are almost always what Fletcher calls a conflict of authorities, so that they "are less often the dull systems that they are reputed to be than they are symbolic power struggles" (A. Fletcher, *Allegory*, 23). In the midst of relentless routinization, he observes, the presentation of human behavior "in a grotesque, abstract caricature" (we may think here of Karel Čapek's brilliant *Válka s mloky* [*War with the Newts*, 1936] or George Orwell's better known *Animal Farm* [1945]) may be the most effective way of arousing reflection and self-criticism. Fletcher's emphasis on allegory as what the Russian formalists would have called the defamiliarization of everyday life has great merit, especially in the case of Coetzee, whose reviewers in the popular press have time and again complained about the strangeness and inexplicable nature of his novels.

It would not be an exaggeration, then, to say that the novel as a genre—perhaps more than the epic of antiquity—is suspended between two aesthetically problematic poles of discourse. On the one hand we find the discourse that we would call pure *reportage*—the discourse, for example, that Truman Capote tried, and I think failed, to fuse with the genre in the form of something called the "nonfiction" novel. The fact that a great deal of newspaper reporting has always had, and been known to have, a fair amount of fictionalizing already built into it did not stop Capote, via *In Cold Blood* (1965), from trying to use the discourse of the *news*—far more than Defoe or any novelist after Defoe had—for the purposes of something that was both "immaculately factual" and yet artistic in style, however ambiguous the effect of his experiment on the genre as a whole.[7] On the other hand, it has long been argued that books such as John Bunyan's *Pilgrim's Progress* do not in fact constitute novels, and it is not simply the complete absence of *news* in Bunyan that supports this claim. It is the fact that characters within a book such as *Pilgrim's Progress* do not seem, in any sense, to be free, autonomous individuals—but then, as Coetzee demonstrates, what fictional character could ever be?—which is precisely the major criterion for "verisimilitude" that lies at the heart of those literary historians, such as Watt, McKeon, and Moretti, who have insisted most on the thoroughly secular nature of the novel as a genre. But it is obvious, right from the start in novels such as *Robinson Crusoe*, that any movement away from the (unattainable) pole of pure *reportage* might lead inexorably toward the (equally unattainable) pole of allegory: the less meaninglessly "real" a tale appears to be, the more meaningfully "allegorical" it threatens to become. The trick of the good realistic novelist, all along, has been to negotiate the treacherous passageway between the Scylla of factual accounting with enough internally generated meaning to be exemplary in some way—it is why Aristotle thought "tragedy" was worth more than "history," since it would tell us not what had happened, but what was likely to happen under given circumstances—while at the same time carefully avoiding the Charybdis of plotting and prose that would lead the reader toward the totalized meaningfulness of allegory where everything seems, dare I say it, *predestined*. What the realistic novelist strives for is just enough reality to make his or her characters seem real (but no more), and not so much abstract meaningfulness as to turn them into the knowing ventriloquists of Beckett, the demonically possessed of Mann, and the self-aware puppets of Coetzee.

▪   ▪   ▪

In a curious way, the theoretical upheaval of the last fifty years, which has been aimed at times at the wholesale dismantling of the autonomous, secular, bourgeois individual of the Enlightenment, for which the autonomous, secular, bourgeois individual of the novel has served as both effect and cause (as Hunt and Nussbaum argue), has actually often had little consequence for our more sophisticated theoretical readings of novels themselves. Like Watt, Goody, McKeon, and Moretti, for example, Derek Attridge is predisposed to the belief that the novel is above all the production site of an extraordinary secularism, individualism, and rationalism, Coetzee included. Instead

of the vulgar, undergraduate readings that tend to discover cheap allegory in Coetzee's works, Attridge favors a kind of reading that he
calls "*literal*" (Attridge's emphasis), by which, oddly, he seems not to
mean *literal* literally but rather, in a very real sense, allegorically.[8]
That is, following closely the theoretical lead of Paul de Man in
Allegories of Reading and J. Hillis Miller in *The Ethics of Reading*,
what Attridge means by reading *literally* is reading in a way that treats
"the experience of reading as an *event*" (Attridge, *Coetzee*, 39; Attridge's emphasis). In short, meaning for Attridge is not something
built into the text by an author to be then "divined" (a significantly
pejorative word choice, I think) by the reader who reads Coetzee, or
any other author for that matter. Instead, the "text," including its "significance," for Attridge "comes into being only in the process of understanding and responding that I, as an individual reader in a specific
time and place, conditioned by a specific history, go through" (Attridge, *Coetzee*, 39). I do not wish to be at all facetious when I say
that, in my estimation, Attridge wants to perform, and to be read as if
he were performing, exactly in the way the putatively autonomous
and unique individual characters perform and are typically understood to perform in realistic fiction, perhaps in something like George
Eliot's *Middlemarch*, which, though it may be full of Morettian "fillers," nevertheless strives to present each character as an individual
who, on the whole (at least, this seems to be Eliot's objective) is in the
"process of understanding and responding . . . as an individual reader
in a specific time and place, conditioned by a specific history." Despite decades of supposedly revolutionary deconstructive and reader-
response criticism, in Attridge's approach to the supposedly unso-
phisticated allegorical propensities of Coetzee's prose we find once
again reproduced precisely the dominant concern for autonomous
and secular events, autonomous and secular persons, and autonomous and secular reading habits that the history of the interpretation
of the novel has told us is exactly what the novel is supposed to produce and reflect.

It is clear that the commitment to the unique *singularity* of the
individual (the individual as determined by a singular time and place,
and even through a singular experience of reading as a singular *event*)

is understood by Attridge as an *ethical* commitment that in part proceeds from our careful reading of novels. This is why Attridge's book is not simply called *How to Read J. M. Coetzee Very Carefully*, though that would be a perfectly accurate title, but rather bears the title *J. M. Coetzee and the Ethics of Reading*. To read *ethically*, according to this critical program, is to read with a rigorous commitment to the idea that we are all profoundly different from one another—above all, there are no notions like "soul" or "grace" or "salvation" to connect anyone to anyone else, even if Coetzee does lapse into the use of such language, so that the essence of ethical action is simultaneously respect for and openness toward "alterity" and empathy for those who represent such "alterity." It is why, Attridge argues, Coetzee reveals (in himself and in the persona of Elizabeth Costello) such a radical disgust for slaughtering animals for food or clothing—what could be more "other" than an animal?

And yet, at least in the person of Elizabeth Costello, the disgust for the slaughterhouse seems to stem from the fact that Costello really *does* regard an animal as having something like a soul. It is only philosophers such as Thomas Nagel who mistakenly claim "a bat is a fundamentally alien creature" (Coetzee, *Elizabeth Costello*, 76), while Costello is quite sure of precisely the opposite: "To be alive is to be a living soul. An animal—and we are all animals—is an embodied soul" (Coetzee, *Elizabeth Costello*, 78). When asked finally whether her vegetarianism "comes out of moral conviction," Costello simply replies, "No, I don't think so. . . . It comes out of a desire to save my soul" (Coetzee, *Elizabeth Costello*, 88–89).[9] All of this implies, quite contrary to what Attridge claims, that neither Costello nor Coetzee himself seems to believe that animals—or any other living creature, for that matter, humans included—are anything like a *singularity*, with singular experiences occurring as singular events, in a "specific time and place" and conditioned by a "specific history." Costello also implies that the entire idea of an "other" as something uniquely foreign with which one must nevertheless somehow find sympathy, as even David Lurie in *Disgrace* seems to imagine at points, is itself a concept foreign to Coetzee's work.

Nevertheless, whatever one may think about the idea of a "singular" reading experience, there is a certain truth to Attridge's approach in that, however inclined toward parable Coetzee may be, his characters retain much of the individuality and uniqueness of characters in traditional realism. That is, Coetzee is in no sense rewriting *Pilgrim's Progress* even in a book such as *Waiting for the Barbarians*, where the protagonist is named only by his occupation, or in *The Master of Petersburg* and *Foe*, both of which are designed to invite the reader to compare Coetzee's central figures with their historical counterparts. Characters such as David Lurie, Michael K, Elizabeth Costello, Paul Rayment, and Elizabeth Curren surely are "singularities" in some sense, and this is perhaps what accounts for the high praise the novels containing these characters have earned in the popular press. Moreover, Coetzee's *The Life of Jesus* appears to confirm Attridge's stress on "singularities" in one other important respect: David, Coetzee's version of Jesus, seems either incapable of or completely opposed to the process of calculation, which is what makes all singularities comprehensible as fitting a formal category of one sort or another. If anyone was a "singular" character in Western culture, many would say, it was Jesus, who not incidentally preached a doctrine that depended on God's interest in each individual in turn as equally singular.

And yet, as Saint Paul's letters make clear, the Christian message was also a message that was universal, and thus if each singular individual, with his or her singular history and abilities, is made "in the image of God," then "singularity" from the God's-eye view is not at all what it might be from Attridge's (as Lady Chandos reminds us at the end of *Elizabeth Costello*). This too Coetzee emphasizes in *The Childhood of Jesus*, when at the end Simón's innocent remark to Juan that they of course do not live in a world "under the eye of God" (Coetzee, *Childhood*, 275), where nothing is random or accidental, is thoroughly undercut by the allegorical nature of the tale, over which the eye of Coetzee has hovered all along. In this sense, Coetzee is taking seriously that very old analogy between divine and human creation, between divine and human authority, that someone like Attridge seems to be at some pains to deny. Adorno's remark about the irreducibly allegorical dimension of all aesthetic *poiesis* is worth recalling. "Form is the law of the transfiguration of the existing, counter to which it represents freedom. Form secularizes the theological model of the world as an image made in God's likeness, though not as an act of creation but as the objectification of the human comportment that imitates creation; not *creation ex nihilo*, but creation out of the created" (Adorno, *Aesthetic Theory*, 143). This is, for me, the allegorical nature of all authorship that Coetzee wrestles with throughout his oeuvre, and I think Adorno's parsing of the issue is just about right: no human author creates from nothing, but he or she cannot be understood as creating anything without imagining at the same time an author who actually does create from nothing. This latter is, in effect, the Barthesian "after-image," the narrative photogene, of all authorship in an endlessly secularizing world.

In *Reflections of a Nonpolitical Man* (1918), Thomas Mann's early, overtly antirepublican and robustly conservative defense of traditional, pre-bourgeois German cultural tradition (and hence implicitly of the Wilhelmian Empire's goals in World War I), Mann's reflections on religion are perhaps among the few opinions that did not change as he moved increasingly to the defense of democracy and the Weimar Republic after 1922:

> But when I say: not politics, but religion, I do not boast of having religion.
>
> Far from it. No, I have none. If, however, one may understand by *religiosity* the freedom that is a path, not a goal; that means openness, tenderness, openness for life, humility; a searching, probing, doubting and erring; a path, as I have said, to God, or, as far as I am concerned, to the Devil as well—but for heaven's sake not the hardened certainty and philistinism of the possession of belief—well, then perhaps I may call some of this freedom and religiosity my own.[10]

Mann's comment is prescient in ways no one could have understood in 1918, when the idea of using the devilish Faust story as a reflection on a war yet to come could not have been possible. But the refusal of what he calls the "hardened certainty and philistinism of the possession of belief," however much the diction here is of the nineteenth century, is a way for Mann to imply a path to religious belief that he at the same time knows he does not, and may never, possess. This paradoxical point of view is not finally what Thomas Huxley and Leslie Stephen knew under the rubric of agnosticism, which is, in their hands, far more about applying the measured skepticism and empiricism that yields scientific insight equally to the religious sphere, even if that leads both of them down a path to measureless doubt in which agnosticism becomes largely a euphemism for atheism, somewhat as their critics claimed. And it is even less something akin to negative theology, in which the ineffable and inscrutable nature of a God beyond human comprehension is in fact what reveals mystical or gnostic avenues of approach external to all language and conception. Instead, I think, Mann is already pointing here to what is perhaps the central impasse in the writers I have addressed in the previous chapters: the idea that the path toward divinity is at the same time, perversely, the path that forbids belief in divinity and hence swerves away from belief precisely because belief has become nothing less than the "hardened certainty" that destroys belief most certainly. It is why Mann's approach to religious belief is almost always proleptic, as it is even in the case of Serenus Zeitblom, or, to borrow from E. M. Forster on the possibility of postcolonial political harmony, it is always something to which one can only respond, "No, not yet," and "No, not there."[11] It is precisely the same obscure prolepsis that the doorkeeper in Kafka's *The Trial* uses in responding to the request for admittance, perhaps in the future, posed by the man from the country: "'It's possible,' says the doorkeeper, 'but not now,'" as if salvation itself were something only possible given a godlike infinity of time, not the finitude of a human life.[12]

Perhaps not surprisingly, this is very close to the path that Coetzee himself seems to envision. In a 1990 interview, David Attwell asks Coetzee whether "grace" might be a good way to describe the state of being attained by Elizabeth Curren at the conclusion of *Age of Iron*—a possibility about which I think Attwell is wrong, as I argued in the previous chapter, on good Calvinist grounds. Coetzee demurs, as we should perhaps expect, saying the ending is more "troubled," but his full response is far more ambiguous than even Attridge later implies, since in paraphrasing the finale of Attwell's interview with Coetzee, Attridge for some reason deletes the last three words: "As for grace," Coetzee actually says, "no, regrettably no: I am not a Christian, or not yet" (Coetzee, *Doubling* 250; see Attridge, *Coetzee*, 178n20). What Coetzee is saying, I think, is a far cry from the pursuit of the doctrinal secularism, the singular individualism, and the view of human life as constituted only by absolutely singular *events* that allow for no generalization, religious or otherwise, which is what Attridge's ethics of reading imply. Rather, Coetzee's statements, taken in context, point toward some far more ambivalent and "troubled" state of mind, embodied by Curren's fate, in which the universality of dying; the persistence of the classics, as in Aeneas's account of crossing over to the land of the dead in Virgil's afterlife—"I am waiting for someone to show me the way across," Curren tells Vercueil (Coetzee, *Age of Iron*, 179); the refusal (rather than the embrace) of the claim to know in the end what constitutes an ethical imperative; and the curious admission that Coetzee is "not a Christian, or not yet" all imply something rather different from the "secular history" of the novel that still shapes our reading practices. It is this relinquishment of the expectation of "grace" as Attwell is using the term in his interview, that is, as a synonym for things such as "absolution" and "redemption," a refusal that one finds in Beckett, Mann, and Coetzee alike, that is the clearest sign of a peripeteia in post-1945 narratives, a curious *Verwindung* or transformation that paradoxically regerminates a set of religious possibilities from the apparently unfertile yet surprisingly well-prepared ground of modern secular consciousness.

As I read Beckett, Mann, and Coetzee, as both realists and allegorists, it is the persistent, deeply skeptical inability to comprehend and explain things such as causal responsibility with any confidence, which is what the seventeenth century called "occasionalism," that becomes a significant characteristic of the novels I discuss, whatever the moral ambiguities of the choice. I have argued that all three writers have been driven, for a variety of reasons, toward radically secular representations of human experience—there is no grace, no absolution, and no redemption that we can possibly hope to achieve by our actions; grace either comes, or it does not, and mostly it does not— and these are representations that ultimately lead them by circuitous and unpredictable paths back to some of the most basic and enduring doctrines of the Western religious tradition. In his essay on Proust, Samuel Beckett refers to the possibility of "accidental and fugitive salvation." It is a bit of Calvin that I think Beckett has smuggled into Proust's Bergsonian vision of intuitive and irrepressible aesthetic creation as itself a redemptive act, and that seems as good a thumbnail description as any for what I am trying to get at (see Beckett, *Selected Works*, 4:524).[13] The profound and often comic levels of disgrace, shame, and guilt that propel the narratives I have examined elaborate a world that is on the one hand bereft of the grace that would provide redemption for fallen, secular existence, and on the other disturbed constantly, rather as Proudhon insisted it should be, by the always already foreclosed human desire (as Coetzee intimates at the end of his interview) to somehow play a role in determining that redemption. As I noted at the start, these are novels by relatively privileged white men from powerful cultural and religious traditions that after 1945 provided much material to feel ashamed about. By midcentury, the creative (as opposed to destructive) potential of the human imagination, conscious or unconscious, so evident in Proust is just what Beckett, Mann, and Coetzee found so difficult to accept. There is, as a result, not one novel in all the works I have discussed that could be called unambiguous in its politics, or in its view of the social good, or in its attitude toward progressive historical development, or in its regard for the artist and the work of art, though there is also not one that is in the least blind to such issues. Rather, these are books that reveal something perhaps more unexpected about our postmodern, postcolonial predicament: the degree to which remarkably old and supposedly outmoded conceptions of our moral nature and our understanding of innocence and guilt—from original sin to divine election—are somehow produced anew, reinvented, in and because of the decidedly secular prose of a most secular age.

Introduction

1. See Nussbaum, *Love's Knowledge.*

2. Hunt, *Inventing Human Rights.*

3. Wallace, *Pale King*, 233.

4. Several recent books have addressed the question of religion and secularization in roughly the same period as that covered by this book, but their focus has been on American literature. See especially John A. McClure, *Partial Faiths: Postsecular Fiction in the Age of Pynchon and Morrison* (2007); and Amy Hungerford, *Postmodern Belief: American Literature and Religion since 1960* (2010). In *Fiction beyond Secularism* (2014), Justin Neuman examines a host of postcolonial-postmodern novels, including several by Coetzee (though none by Beckett or Mann), but like most others who invoke the term *postsecular*, Neuman makes no doctrinal or confessional distinctions and hence identifies none of the Calvinist or puritan motifs in Coetzee. While it does not discuss much literature per se and is not focused on the question of secularization, Terry Eagleton's *Culture and the Death of God* (2014), with its interest in how "the Almighty has proved remarkably difficult to dispose of," nevertheless overlaps in certain significant ways with themes in my own work.

5. I. Watt, *Rise of the Novel*, 84; hereafter cited in the text as *Rise.*

6. See McKeon, *Origins of the English Novel*, 200.

7. Goody, "From Oral to Written," 21.

8. Shakespeare, *Julius Caesar*, 1.2.139; hereafter cited in the text as *Julius Caesar.* References are to act, scene, and line. Since Cassius is himself clearly a bit of a villainous snake, however, it is not clear whether Shakespeare intends this expression of faith in human self-determination to be taken with no irony. Cassius, after all, not Brutus himself, is finally the architect of Brutus's "fortune." See also Syme, *Sallust*, appendix 2, 313–51.

9. Moretti, "Serious Century," 381.

10. See Blumenberg, *Legitimacy of the Modern Age*, 69.

11. Lukács, *Theory of the Novel*, 88; hereafter cited in the text as *Theory.*

12. Stendhal, *Scarlet and Black*, 500; hereafter cited in the text as *Scarlet.*

13. Woolf, *To the Lighthouse*, 85.

14. Auerbach, *Mimesis*, 554; hereafter cited in the text as *Mimesis.*

15. See Starr, *Defoe and Spiritual Autobiography*; and Hunter, *Reluctant Pilgrim.*

16. See Frye, *Secular Scripture.*

17. See Doody, *True Story of the Novel.*

18. Eliot, *Middlemarch*, 6.

19. Mann, "Homage," x.

20. See Lukács, *Meaning of Contemporary Realism*, 47–92; and Adorno, "Extorted Reconciliation."

21. The question of shame in postcolonial literature more generally has been insightfully addressed in Timothy Bewes, *The Event of Postcolonial Shame*, though Bewes does not discuss the religious elements of this shame or the difficulties arising from their secularization.

22. Benjamin, "On the Mimetic Faculty," 720–21; hereafter cited in the text as "Mimetic Faculty."

23. Benjamin is quoting here from Hugo von Hofmannsthal's one-act play, *Der Tor und der Tod* (1893), usually translated as *Death and the Fool*, a *Faust*-like drama about a wealthy nobleman who has lived his life as a privileged and sheltered aesthete. As the play opens, he regrets having missed so much of real life, even as the poor shelter in his garden. When Death approaches to usher him into the hereafter he expresses a desire to repent, but it is too late. The final words are spoken by Death:

Der Tod (*in dem er kopfschüttelnd langsam abgeht*):
Wie wundervoll sind diese Wesen,
Die, was nicht deutbar, dennoch deuten,
Was nie geschrieben wurde, lesen,
Verworrenes beherrschend binden
Und Wege noch im Ewig-Dunkeln finden.
    (Hofmannsthal, *Der Tor und der Tod*, 44; emphasis in original)
—

Death (*while he slowly leaves, shaking his head*):
How wonderful are these beings,

Who nevertheless interpret what does not signify,
Who read what has never been written,
Who masterfully tie up what is confused
And still find paths into eternal darkness.

As he so often does with the works on which he comments, Benjamin brushes the play against the grain, taking Death at his word and reversing Death's sarcasm. Reading "what has never been written," finding significance in that which seems to have none, is for Benjamin precisely the path to redemption—not into darkness. This attitude is, one might say, the essence of the religious consciousness.

24. See Tylor, *Primitive Society*, 1:71.

O N E .   *Martin Heidegger, John Calvin, and Samuel Beckett*

1. Habermas's speech, "Faith and Knowledge," was given on the occasion of his receipt of the Peace Prize of the German Publishers and Booksellers Association in Frankfurt on October 14, 2001. It originally appeared in the *Süddeutsche Zeitung* for October 15, 2001. See the English translation by Snelson at http://www.nettime.org/Lists-Archives/nettime-l-0111/msg00100.html.

2. In his 2001 speech, Habermas put it as follows: "In Kant we find the authority of divine command reestablished in the unconditional validity of moral duty. In this we hear an unmistakable resonance."

3. Pecora, *Secularization and Cultural Criticism*, 5.

4. Habermas, "Transcendence," 79. In the original German, Habermas, *Nachmetaphysisches Denken*, 60.

5. See Habermas, "Walter Benjamin."

6. See Blumenberg, *Legitimacy of the Modern Age*; hereafter cited as *Legitimacy.*

7. See Israel, *Radical Enlightenment.*

8. See Hitchens, *God is Not Great*; Dawkins, *God Delusion*; and Harris, *End of Faith.*

9. Heidegger, *Identität und Differenz.* This has been translated as Heidegger, *Identity and Difference* (hereafter cited in the text as *Identity*), a volume that includes the original German text. In this latter volume, the German *Verwindung* appears on page 101.

10. Vattimo, *End of Modernity*, 179.

11. See Heidegger, "Age of the World Picture"; see also S. Weber, *Mass Mediauras*, 76–81.

12. Marquard, *Schwierigkeiten mit der Geschichtsphilosophie*, 52; hereafter cited as *Schwierigkeiten*.

13. "Und für sie ist . . . die idealistische Autonomie-Position statt schlimm nur die vielleicht einzig aussichtsreiche Form der Theodizee. Sollte in dieser These Atheismus stecken: dann allenfalls ein 'methodischer Atheismus ad maiorem gloriam Dei.'"

14. Taylor, *Secular Age*, 5–12.

15. Bair, *Samuel Beckett*, 198.

16. Beckett, *Selected Works of Samuel Beckett*, 4:540; hereafter cited in the text as *Selected Works* with volume number following.

17. *Molloy* is part of a trilogy that includes *Malone Dies* and *The Unnamable*; all three were originally written and published in French, the first translated by Patrick Bowles with the author, the second and third by Beckett alone: *Molloy* (1951); *Malone meurt* (1951); and *L'Innommable* (1953). Given Beckett's control of the translations, I refer to the French text only when the difference from the English text is relevant to my argument. Beckett took nearly fifty pages of notes on Geulincx's *Ethics*, almost all of them careful translations of passages from the original Latin. These notes have now been appended to the first English translation of the *Ethics*; see Geulincx, *Ethics, with Samuel Beckett's Notes*, 311–53; hereafter cited in the text as *Ethics*. The combination of the two texts now available for the first time has already been a significant event in Beckett studies (see, for example, Tucker, *Samuel Beckett and Arnold Geulincx*).

18. In early tenth-century Baghdad, Abu al-Hasan Ali ibn Isma'il al-Ash'ari argued that the appearance of a causal relationship between intention and act was an illusion, and that both events were caused and connected only by God. "No man acts in reality except God alone. He is the agent, and men have the acts ascribed to them only by way of metaphor" (al-Ash'ari, *Maqalat*, 279, cited in W. Watt, *Free Will*, 99). The emphasis on divine determinism played a role in the development of traditional or orthodox Sunni Islam. Watt further makes the entirely convincing suggestion that "there are many points of comparison [of al-Ash'ari] with Saint Augustine of Hippo, not the least of them being the tendency to determinism as a result of the experiences of conversion" (W. Watt, *Free Will*, 148).

19. See Uhlmann's introduction to Beckett's notes in Geulincx, *Ethics*, 306.

20. See Van Ruler's introduction to Geulincx, *Ethics*, xv–xlii.

21. Geulincx, *Ethics*, 227. For a fuller elaboration of the relation of Geulincx's skepticism to Descartes's skepticism, see Uhlmann, *Samuel Beckett and the Philosophical Image*. See also Ackerly, *Demented Particulars*; and Wood, "Murphy, Beckett; Geulincx, God."

22. Pascal, *Pensées and Other Writings*, 67; hereafter cited in the text as *Pensées*.

23. See Augustine, *City of God*, 21:10; hereafter cited in the text as *City of God*.

24. The text of the original French version of *L'Innommable* that Beckett published in 1953 is somewhat different from the one that appeared in his own English translation, *The Unnamable*, first published by Grove Press in 1958. In the earlier French edition, the last phrases of the novel read simply, "il faut continuer, je vais continuer" (Beckett, *L'Innommable*, 262)—"you must go on, I'll go on." When Beckett translated the novel into English, he repeated in the finale a phrase that had appeared just prior in the French text after an earlier iteration of "il faut continuer"—that is, "je ne peux pas continuer" (Becket, *L'Innommable*, 261), or "I can't go on." Beginning with Éditions de Minuit's "nouvelle edition" of 1971, Beckett changed the last words of the French text to match the first English translation: "you must go on, I can't go on, I'll go on" (Beckett, *Selected Works*, 2:407). While serious critical energy has been expended on deciphering the reason for the change, my sense is that Beckett probably wanted—or quickly came to want—a more exact repetition of the earlier phrase "you must go on, I can't go on" in the novel's final words, as we have always had them in his English translation, and did not amend the French until a new edition of the French text was prepared. But we will never know for sure. See Van Hulle, "Figures of Script," 253.

25. Barthes, *Writing Degree Zero*, 16–17; hereafter cited in the text as *Writing Degree Zero*.

26. Knowlson, *Damned to Fame*, 324.

27. Beckett, *Letters of Samuel Beckett*, 1:518; hereafter cited in the text as *Letters*.

28. "On a pour les rangées suivantes: vingt-trois, vingt-et-un, vingt-et-un, vingt-et-un. Vingt-deux, vingt-et-un, vingt, vingt. Vingt-trois, vingt-et-un, vingt, dix-neuf, etc. . . ." (Robbe-Grillet, *La Jalousie*, 52).

29. A splendid exception here is an essay by Ronald Thomas comparing Beckett's novels, via simply remarkable verbal echoes, to John Bunyan's *Pilgrim's Progress*: see Thomas, "The Novel and the Afterlife." See also J. Fletcher, *Samuel Beckett's Art*, 84.

30. See Kenner, *Samuel Beckett*, 79–91.

31. See J. Fletcher, *Samuel Beckett's Art*, 131–35.

32. See Casanova, *Samuel Beckett*, 57–68.

33. For an example of the allusion hunting, see Tucker, *Samuel Beckett and Arnold Geulincx*, 127; hereafter cited in the text as *Samuel Beckett.*

34. See Van den Hemel, "History and the Vertical Canon."

35. See Calvin, *Institutes of the Christian Religion*, 207; 1.16.8; hereafter cited in the text as *Institutes.* References are to book, chapter, and section.

36. See also Barthes, "To Write: An Intransitive Verb?" 141–43.

37. See Ackerly and Gontarski, *Grove Companion to Samuel Beckett*, 50–51; hereafter cited in the text as *Grove Companion.*

38. See *Grove Companion*, 431: "Das Leben ist ein Pensum zum Arbeiten: in diesem Sinne ist *defunctus* ein schöner Ausdruck." The translation I provide is my own, not that of the *Grove Companion.*

39. See Brooks, *Reading for the Plot.*

40. In Beckett's original French, the phrase "fear and trembling"— seemingly a reference to Kierkegaard—does not appear. Instead, we get only the trembling: "Et c'était souvent en tremblant qu'il souffrait et en se disant, Ça va me coûter cher" (Beckett, *Malone meurt*, 124). Beckett does allude to Kierkegaard elsewhere, but rarely.

41. See Agamben, *Homo Sacer*; hereafter cited in the text as *Homo Sacer.* While Agamben's phrase may provide a provocative epithet for Beckett's settings, it would be as much a mistake simply to conflate the attitudes of the two writers as it would be to conflate Agamben's ideas with those of Coetzee later. While Agamben remains fixated (unfortunately, in my view) on a Hobbesian notion of sovereignty as the original social crime that leads eventually to modernity's destruction of seemingly valueless human lives (they can be taken at the whim of the sovereign, but never amount even to sacrifice or victimhood), Beckett, Mann, and Coetzee in my reading are all in pursuit of a deeper, and far less namable, sense of guilt than the relatively superficial one addressed by Agamben.

42. See Baudelaire, "Anywhere Out of the World," in *Baudelaire*, 190. (Baudelaire's original title is in English.)

43. For a description of how Calvin's harsher views were transformed in America into a religious outlook that put more power into the hands of believers to *earn* God's grace, we could do no better than Perry Miller's summary of a "covenant" between God and Man developed in early New England:

The covenant theology was a special way of reading scripture, so that the assembled Bible could be seen as a consistent whole. After Adam failed the Covenant of Works, God voluntarily condescended to treat with man as an equal and to draw up a covenant or contract with His creature, in which He laid down the terms of salvation by which, putting off His arbitrary freedom, He would henceforth abide. This Covenant of Grace did not alter the fact that those only are saved upon whom God sheds His grace, enabling them to believe in Christ; but it made clear why and how certain men are selected, and prescribed the conditions under which they might reach a fair assurance of their own standing. Above all . . . God pledged Himself not to run tyrannically athwart human conceptions of justice. (P. Miller, *American Puritans*, 144)

No such theologically ameliorating "covenant" or "contract" exists in the more rigorous Calvinism with which I am concerned in figures such as Geulincx.

44. Proudhon, *Système des contradictions économiques*, 2:255. In Proudhon's French:

L'homme, en tant qu'homme, ne peut jamais se trouver en contradiction avec lui-même; il ne sent de trouble et de déchirement que par la résistance de Dieu qui est en lui. En l'homme se réunissent toutes les spontanéités de la nature, toutes les instigations de l'Être fatal, tous les dieux et les demons de l'univers. Pour soumettre ces puissances, pour discipliner cette anarchie, l'homme n'a que sa raison, sa pensée progressive: et voilà ce qui constitue le drame sublime dont les péripéties forment, par leur ensemble, la raison dernière de toutes les existences. La destinée de la nature et de l'homme est la metamorphose de Dieu: mais Dieu est inépuisable, et notre lutte éternelle.

With his notion of methodical atheism, Proudhon both borrowed and diverged from Ludwig Feuerbach's anthropology of religion. Proudhon's insistence that some tension between the merely human and the God within us is an ineradicable part of all notions of justice and true (or mutualist) community runs throughout his work, and it is central to his refusal of a more thoroughly materialist communism and socialism—precisely the failure for which Marx famously criticized him. For a thorough elaboration of this tension in Proudhon, see Lubac, *Proudhon et la christianisme*, esp. 294–316. The unresolvable theological dialectic grounding utopian ideals of community did not preclude, unfortunately, Proudhon's virulent anti-Semitism, an issue the good Cardinal Lubac never once raises in his account.

T W O . *Thomas Mann, Augustine, and the "Death of God"*

1. Contemporary claims, such as those of Sam Harris, about the way recent neuroscience has shattered our popular belief in "free will" also tend to imagine that such claims are irrefutable proof against the existence of God. But Geulincx's philosophy—not to say Augustine's theology before him— easily puts the lie to such assumptions. It is as if our current, eighteenth century–like penchant for scientific arguments against the existence of God—for example, that our minds make decisions, at least as measured in milliseconds by MRI scans, before we ever know about those decisions— lacks even the most basic understanding of the numerous ways the history of religion, starting at least with Augustine, argued precisely (without the bene- fit of MRIs) that this fact actually *proved* the existence of God. See Harris, *Free Will.*

2. For good accounts of the issues raised in reading Mann's novel as historical allegory, see Stefan Breuer, "Wie teuflisch ist die 'konservative Revolution'?" in Röcke, *Thomas Mann, Doktor Faustus*, 59–71 and 73–88.

3. Thomas Mann, *Doctor Faustus*, 516 and 527; references to the English edition hereafter cited as *Doctor Faustus* in the text, while the original Ger- man is provided in the notes. "Wachet mit mir!" (Mann, *Doktor Faustus*, 657); "stark dissonantem Akkorde" (Mann, *Doktor Faustus*, 673.)

4. "Welch ein höhnisches Spiel der Natur, so möchte man sagen, daß sie das Bild höchster Vergeistigung erzeugen mag dort, wo der Geist entwichen ist!" (Mann, *Doktor Faustus*, 681).

5. "Abtrünnigkeit ist ein Akt des Glaubens, und alles ist und geschieht in Gott, besonders auch der Abfall von ihm" (Mann, *Doktor Faustus*, 178).

6. "Augustinus war wenigstens so weit gegangen, zu sagen, die Funktion des Schlechten sei, das Gute deutlicher hervortreten zu lassen, das um so mehr gefalle und desto lobenswürdiger sei, wenn es mit dem Schlechten ver- glichen werde" (Mann, *Doktor Faustus*, 140–41).

7. See John Calvin, *Institutes*, 271 and 254; 2.2.12 and 2.1.11).

8. The complexity of Augustine's thinking here, over which much ink has been spilt both by those (often Catholics) who want to preserve Augus- tine's early focus on free will and those (often Protestants) who want to em-

phasize his later embrace of election, is actually not so easily understood in chronological terms. The first passage below has been considered Augustine's final word on the subject (he dies in 430), yet it is clearly the more ambiguous of the two. The theological tension between Zeitblom and Leverkühn is nicely encapsulated here as well.

> Therefore, just as the mortification of the deeds of the flesh, even though it is a gift of God, is nonetheless required of us, with life offered as a reward, so also faith is a gift of God, although when it is said, "If you believe, you will be saved" [Rom 8.14], it also is required of us, with salvation offered as a reward. For these things are both commanded of us and shown to be gifts of God, so that we may understand not only that we do them, but that God brings it about that we do them, as he says very clearly through the prophet Ezekiel. For what could be clearer than when he says, "I will cause you to do" [Ezek. 36.27]? Read with care this passage from Scripture, and you will see that God promises that he will cause them to do those things which he commands to be done. Nor indeed does he here overlook the merits, but rather the evil deeds, of those to whom he shows that he will return good things for evil, by the very fact that he causes them to have good works from that point on, when he causes them to carry out the divine commands. (Augustine, "On the Predestination of the Saints" (427 [429?]), in *Four Anti-Pelagian Writings*, 244)

> Hence, the whole mass of the human race is condemned. For he who first gave admission to sin had been punished together with all those who were in Him as in a root, so that no one may escape this just and deserved punishment unless redeemed by mercy and undeserved grace. But the human race is disposed in such a way that the power of merciful grace is demonstrated in some and that of just vengeance in others. Both could not have been demonstrated in all; for if all were to remain under the penalty of just damnation, the mercy of redeeming grace would appear in no one. On the other hand, if all were to be brought across from darkness into light, the truth of retribution would have appeared in no one. But many more are left under punishment than are redeemed from it, so that what was due to all may in this way be shown. If punishment had indeed been visited upon all men, no one could justly have complained of the justice of Him who avenges; whereas we have reason to give most heartfelt thanks to our Redeemer for His free gift in delivering so many from it. (Augustine, *City of God*, 21.12.1,070)

For Calvin's extensive borrowing from Augustine on predestination and freedom of the will, see Calvin, *Institutes*, 241–340 (book 2, chaps. 1–5) and 920–87 (book 3, chaps. 21–24).

9. "Die polyphone Würde jedes akkordbildenden Tons wäre durch die Konstellation gewährleistet. Die geschichtlichen Ergebnisse, die Emanzipation der Dissonanz von ihrer Auflösung, das Absolutwerden der Dissonanz, wie es sich schon an manchen Stellen des späten Wagner-Satzes findet, würde jeden Zusammenklang rechtfertigen, der sich vor dem System legitimieren kann" (Mann, *Doktor Faustus*, 260–61).

10. "die Konsonanz, Dreiklangharmonik, das Abgenutzte, den verminderten Septimenakkord" (Mann, *Doktor Faustus*, 261).

11. "Gewisse Dinge sind nicht mehr möglich. Der Schein der Gefühle als kompositorisches Kunstwerk, der selbstgenügsame Schein der Musik selbst ist unmöglich geworden und nicht zu halten,—als welcher seit alters darin besteht, daß vorgegebene und formelhaft niedergeschlagene Elemente so eingesetzt werden, als ob sie die unverbrüchliche Notwendigkeit dieses einen Falles wären" (Mann, *Doktor Faustus*, 325).

12. "Die Subsumtion des Ausdrucks unters versöhnlich Allgemeine ist das innerste Prinzip des musikalischen Scheins. Es ist aus damit" (Mann, *Doktor Faustus*, 326).

13. "läuft sie auf eine Art von Komponieren vor dem Komponieren hinaus" (Mann, *Doktor Faustus*, 260).

14. "Eine hochtheologische Angelegenheit, die Musik—wie die Sünde es ist, wie ich es bin" (Mann, *Doktor Faustus*, 326).

15. Weber, *Protestant Ethic*, 80; hereafter cited in text as *Protestant Ethic*.

16. "Er wollte es neu und besser machen und eine Musik ins Werk setzen, die der Einfachheit ihrer Seelen besser entsprach und sie instand setzen würde . . . " (Mann, *Doktor Faustus*, 91 and 92).

17. For an interesting account of the musico-historical "Chiffren" (cyphers or codes) of Mann's novel, involving the work of Richard Strauss and Hans Pfitzner (the first alluded to by Mann, the second not) as heirs of Richard Wagner in the context of Hitler's cultural policies, see Vaget, *Seelenzauber*, 223–37.

18. "Die contritio ohne jede Hoffnung und als völliger Unglaube an die Möglichkeit der Gnade und Verzeihung, als die felsenfeste Überzeugung des Sünders, er habe es zu grob gemacht, und selbst die unendliche Güte reiche nicht aus, siene Sünde zu verzeihen,—erst das ist die wahre Zerknirschung, und ich mache Euch darauf aufmerksam, daß sie der Erlösung am

allernächsten, für die Güte am allerunwiderstehlichsten ist" (Mann, *Doktor Faustus*, 333).

19. I have modified Woods's translation. "Eine Sündhaftigkeit, so heillos, daß sie ihren Mann von Grund aus am Heile verzweifeln läßt, ist der wahrhaft theologische Weg zum Heil" (Mann, *Doktor Faustus*, 333).

20. "Es ist dir nicht klar, daß die bewußte Spekulation auf den Reiz, den große Schuld auf die Güte ausübt, dieser den Gnadenakt nun schon aufs äußerste unmöglich macht?" (Mann, *Doktor Faustus*, 333).

21. "Nicht schlecht. Wahrlich ingeniös. Und nun will ich dir sagen, daß genau Köpfe von deiner Art die Population der Hölle bilden" (Mann, *Doktor Faustus*, 334).

22. For Adorno's by no means straightforward elaboration of this conceit, see Adorno, *Aesthetic Theory*, esp. 100–18, on "Semblance and Expression."

23. "Das Echo, das Zurückgeben des Menschenlautes als Naturlaut und seine Enthüllung *als* Naturlaut, ist wesenlich Klage, das wehmutsvolle 'Ach, ja!' der Natur über den Menschen und die versuchende Kundgebung seiner Einsamkeit . . . " (Mann, *Doktor Faustus*, 650).

24. Durch Sünde niemand lassen soll,
    Er tu doch noch etwelches Wohl.
    Niemandes Guttat wird verloren,
    Er sei zur Höllen denn geboren.
    O wöllten ich und die ich mein' (liebe)
    Zur Seligkeit geschaffen sein! Amen.
        (Mann, *Doktor Faustus*, 631)

25. "die Klage des Höllensohns, die furchtbarste Menschen- und Gottesklage . . . auf Erden je angestimmt worden ist" (Mann, *Doktor Faustus*, 649).

26. "Bedeutet es nicht . . . —die Widergewinnung, ich möchte nicht sagen und sage es um der Genauigkeit willen doch: die Rekonstruktion des Ausdrucks, der höchsten und tiefsten Ansprechung des Gefühls auf einer Stufe der Geistigkeit und der Formenstrenge, die erreicht werden mußte, damit dieses Umschlagen kalkulatorischer Kälte in den expressiven Seelenlaut und kreatürlich sich anvertrauende Herzlichkeit Ereignis werden könne?" (Mann, *Doktor Faustus*, 649).

27. It is also more than significant that whereas Heidegger links his *Ereignis* to the unthinking technological developments that have resulted in atomic warfare, Mann is clear that the "event" that most concerns him is the total moral perversion of precisely those traits that would allow him any

sense of national pride. "War diese Herrschaft nicht nach Worten und Taten nur die verzerrte, verpöbelte, verscheußlichte Wahrwerdung einer Gesinnung und Weltbeurteilung, der man charakterliche Echtheit zuerkennen muß, und die der christlich-humane Mensch nicht ohne Scheu in den Zügen unserer Großen, der an Figur gewaltigsten Verkörperungen des Deutschtums ausgeprägt findet?" (Mann, *Doktor Faustus*, 644–45). "Was not this regime, both in word and deed, merely the distorted, vulgarized, debased realization of a mindset and worldview to which one must attribute a characteristic authenticity and which, not without alarm, a Christianly humane person finds revealed in the traits of our great men, in the figures of the most imposing embodiments of Germanness?" (Mann, *Doctor Faustus*, 506).

28. "mehr Rücksicht nehmen auf die Hauptstimme" (Mann, *Doktor Faustus*, 654).

29. "Aber nicht nur, daß es diese mehr als einmal formal zum Negativen wendet, ins Negative zurücknimmt: es ist darin auch eine Negativität des Religiösen,—womit ich nicht meinen kann: dessen Verneinung. Ein Werk, welches vom Versucher, vom Abfall, von der Verdammnis handelt, was sollte es anderes sein als ein religiöses Werk! Was ich meine, ist eine Umkehrung, eine herbe und stolze Sinnverkehrung, wie wenigstens ich sie zum Beispiel in der 'freundlichen Bitt' des Dr. Faustus an die Gesellen der letzten Stunde finde, sie möchten sich zu Bette begeben, *mit Ruhe schlafen* und sich nichts anfechten lassen. Schwerlich wird man umhinkönnen, im Rahmen der Kantate, diese Weisung als den bewußten und gewollten Revers zu dem 'Wachtet mit mir!' von Gethsemane zu erkennen. . . . Damit aber verbindet sich eine Umkehrung der Versuchungsidee, dergestalt, daß Faust den Gedanken der Rettung als Versuchung zurückweist,—nicht nur aus formeller Treue zum Pakt und weil es 'zu spät' ist, sondern weil er die Positivität der Welt, zu der man ihn retten möchte, die Lüge ihrer Gottseligkeit, von ganzer Seele verachtet" (Mann, *Doktor Faustus*, 655–56).

30. "falsche und matte Gottesbürgerlichkeit" (Mann, *Doktor Faustus*, 656).

31. Geulincx, *Ethics* 89; emphasis Geulincx's.

32. I have modified Woods's translation. "Aber wie, wenn der künstlerischen Paradoxie . . . das religiöse Paradoxon entspräche, daß aus tiefster Heillosigkeit, wenn auch als leiseste Frage nur, die Hoffnung keimte? Es wäre die Hoffnung jenseits der Hoffnungslosigkeit, die Transzendenz der Verzweiflung,—nicht der Verrat an ihr, sondern das Wunder, das über den Glauben geht" (Mann, *Doktor Faustus*, 657). Woods translates Mann's *Heillosigkeit* as "despair," but this is clearly an error. As biblical commentaries in

German, which Mann may have consulted, use the term, it means something like "lacking all moral capacity" (see, e.g., Delitzsch, *Biblischer Commentar*, 2:111). The translation of this term is especially important because the depth of moral corruption, the utter loss of moral capacity, is precisely what Augustine and Calvin ascribed to a humanity that had been damned a priori by the original sin of Adam, and that Zeitblom is ascribing to Leverkühn in turn. Finding "hope" in the face of such corruption would indeed be a miracle, and Woods's use of the word "despair" conveys nothing of the word's crucial theological significance. The issue here is not psychological—hope out of despair—but theological: how to find hope in the face of a complete moral collapse. The allegorical resonance with the Nazi debacle is thus also brought sharply into focus.

33. Mann's relative neglect of the fate of the Jews in *Doktor Faustus* has long been a point of contention, beginning with Alfred Werner's "Thomas Mann's Failure." Werner and others after him decried in particular the portrayals of two Jewish figures in the novel, one the music agent Saul Fitelberg, who wants Leverkühn to be a more public artist, and the other a philosopher named Chaim Breisacher. Mann's wife was Jewish, but even family members cringed at his pleasure in acting out unflattering imitations of his friends, some of them Jews. There seems little doubt that Mann's compulsive irony was often in bad taste. But the charge of anti-Semitism in the novel depends on ignoring the novel's narrative voice, and for most readers today the sentimental Catholic Serenus Zeitblom, whose name alone seems to signal his character, is clearly not (or not merely) Thomas Mann. The complexity of Mann's relationship to Judaism becomes obvious when one considers that the character of Breisacher is based on a real-life Jewish philosopher named Oskar Goldberg, who viewed authentic Judaism (that of the Pentateuch alone) as an ethnic/racial/political cult later ruined by the rabbis who turned it into a religion; see Goldberg, *Die Wirklichkeit der Hebräer* (*The Reality of the Hebrews*). Breisacher/Goldberg is ruthlessly parodied in *Doktor Faustus* as a kind of Jewish Nazi—both the character and the man advocate eugenics in the name of racial hygiene—though this view of Goldberg is one that Zeitblom would have shared with Gershom Scholem, who also found Goldberg repulsive; see especially Scholem, *Walter Benjamin*, 95–98. Mann studied with Goldberg, however, and based much of his treatment of the earliest Jews in the first volume of his *Joseph und seiner Brüder—Die Geschichten Jaakobs* (*The Tales of Jacob*), written 1926 to 1930—on Goldberg's ideas, a point Scholem recognized; see Judith Friedlander, Letter to the editors. Whether the description of Breisacher in *Doktor Faustus* should be considered

anti-Semitic is, I think, largely impossible to answer. For the best and most judicious recent treatment of such questions in Mann's oeuvre, see Todd Kontje, *Thomas Mann's World*, esp. 168–73. See also Wimmer, *Kommentar*, vol. 2 of Mann, *Doktor Faustus*, esp. 155–69.

34. For an excellent summary of issues arising from religious interpretation of Mann's novel, see Bergsten, *Thomas Mann's Doctor Faustus*, 201–18. In particular, Bergsten cites Mann's ambivalence about the novel's ending and his memory of Adorno's objections to the original version, which Mann subsequently revised for publication. "[Mann] says of Adorno's share in the shaping of the end: 'He had no objections to make on musical matters, but took issue with the end, the last forty lines, in which, after all the darkness, a ray of hope, the possibility of grace, appears. Those lines did not then stand as they stand now; they had gone wrong. I had been too optimistic, too kindly, too pat, had kindled too much light, had been too lavish with the consolation'" (Bergsten, *Thomas Mann's Doctor Faustus*, 214 n30).

35. McClain, "Irony and Belief in Thomas Mann's *Der Erwählte*," 323.

36. Mann, *Holy Sinner*, 299; references to the English edition hereafter in the text as *Holy Sinner*, while the German original is provided in the notes. "Selten hat der ganz unrecht, der das Sündige nachweist im Guten, Gott aber sieht gnädig die Guttat an, habe sie auch in der Fleischlichkeit ihre Wurzel" (Mann, *Der Erwählte*, 232).

37. "Habetis Papam. Ein Papst ist euch erwählt" (Mann, *Der Erwählte*, 199).

38. "Glaube nur! Der Erwählte muß auch glauben, so schwer es ihm fallen möge. Denn alle Erwählung ist schwer zu fassen und der Vernunft nicht zugänglich" (Mann, *Der Erwählte*, 199).

39. "Denn er sagte, würdig sei keiner, und er selbst sei von Fleisches wegen seiner Würde am allerunwürdigsten und nur durch eine Erwählung, die an Willkür grenze, zu ihr erhoben worden" (Mann, *Der Erwählte*, 239).

40. "Wir gedachten, Gott eine Unterhaltung damit zu bieten" (Mann, *Der Erwählte*, 257).

41. "Da siehst du, erfürchtig Geliebte, und Gott sei dafür gepriesen, daß Satanas nicht allmächtig ist und es nicht so ins Extreme zu treiben vermochte, daß ich irrtümlich auch noch mit diesen in ein Verhältnis geriet und etwa gar Kinder von ihnen hatte, wodurch die Verwandtschaft ein völliger Abgrund geworden wäre. Alles hat seine Grenzen. Die Welt ist endlich" (Mann, *Der Erwählte*, 259).

42. For a comparison of the ambiguous humor in *Der Erwählte* to Flaubert's in *Trois Contes*, see Mendelssohn's "Editor's Afterword," in Mann, *Der*

Erwählte, 270. For a more complete treatment of Gregory's kinship with Kafka's Gregor Samsa, see Ireton, "Die Transformation zweier Gregors."

43. "denn obenauf stelle die Seele sich an und mache ein Wesen von teuflicher Täuschung, die ihr angetan, tief unten aber, wo still die Wahrheit wohne, da habe es gar keine Täuschung gegeben, vielmehr sei ihr da die Einerleiheit bekannt gewesen gleich auf den ersten Blick, und unwissentlich-wissend habe sie das eigene Kind zum Manne genommen, weil es der einzig Ebenbürtige wieder gewesen" (Mann, *Der Erwählte*, 254).

44. "Der Geist der Erzählung" (Mann, *Der Erwählte*, 8 and 234; the phrase is italicized by Mann in the first instance).

45. See Bonhoeffer, *Letters and Papers from Prison*; Bultmann, "The Idea of God and Modern Man"; and Tillich, *Systematic Theology*. The movement was prefigured in certain ways by Gabriel Vahanian's *The Death of God* (1961) in America and John A. T. Robinson's *Honest to God* (1963) in Great Britain.

46. The stage musical of this name, which appeared on Broadway in 1971, was originally a "rock opera" with music by Andrew Lloyd Webber and lyrics by Tim Rice that appeared as a concept album in 1970.

47. My abstract here of the "secularization thesis" derives from Wallis and Bruce, "Secularization: The Orthodox Model," in Bruce, ed., *Religion and Modernization*, 8–30. For an extended, practically book-length elaboration and critique of the "secularization thesis" of this era, see Dobbelaere, "Secularization." For a good bibliography concerning the secularization thesis, see Davie, *Religion in Modern Europe*.

48. Brod, *Franz Kafka*, 75.

49. Altizer and Hamilton, *Radical Theology*, 38; hereafter cited in the text as *Radical Theology*.

THREE. *The Ambivalent Puritan: J. M. Coetzee*

1. For good accounts of the African National Congress controversy, see McDonald, "Disgrace Effects," and Attwell, "Race in *Disgrace*." For the citation from Rushdie's review, see Rushdie, "May 2000: J. M. Coetzee," 340; hereafter cited in the text as "May."

2. See Lukács, *The Meaning of Contemporary Realism*, esp. the essay "Franz Kafka or Thomas Mann?" 47–92.

3. See Adorno, "Notes on Kafka," esp. 268–71.

4. For a broader treatment of abjection in Coetzee, see Boehmer, "Not Saying Sorry, Not Speaking Pain," though Boehmer's reading of Coetzee's

argument about confession both in his "Confession and Double Thoughts" (see n. 9) and in *Disgrace* differs considerably from my own.

5. Hardy, *Jude the Obscure*, 331.

6. Coetzee, *Elizabeth Costello*, 97; hereafter cited in the text as *Elizabeth Costello*.

7. Coetzee, *Diary of a Bad Year*, 83; hereafter cited in the text as *Diary*.

8. See Coetzee, *Scenes from Provincial Life*, 16; hereafter cited in the text as *Scenes*.

9. Coetzee, "Confession and Double Thoughts," in *Doubling the Point*, 251–93; hereafter cited in the text as *Doubling*.

10. Martin Luther and his immediate followers had acknowledged confession to another Christian along with private confession to one's pastor, though to receive absolution he had reduced the act itself to two parts—"contrition" of the heart and "confession" by mouth—without requiring the "satisfaction" of penitential deeds. Also unlike the Church of Rome, Lutheran thought did not expect one's confession to be complete or the sincerity of one's contrition absolute in order for absolution by God to be granted. In a broad sense, all of Luther's Ninety-Five Theses are devoted to his rejection of the Pope's authority to absolve sins, though two articles speak directly to Calvin's and Coetzee's objections: "30) Nullus est securus de veritate sue contritionis, multominus de consecutione plenarie remissionis." (No one is secure in the truth of his own contrition, much less in the attainment of full remission.) "31) Quam rarus est vere penitens, tam rarus est vere indulgentias redimens, id est rarissimus." (He who buys authentic indulgences is just as rare as he who is truly penitent, that is, he is most rare.) (Luther, *Luthers Werke in Auswahl* 1:5; my translations). See also Article XI of Philip Melanchthon's *Augsburg Confession* (1530; from the Latin text): "Our churches teach that private absolution should be retained in the churches. However, in confession an enumeration of all sins is not necessary, for this is not possible according to the Psalm, 'Who can discern his errors?' (Ps. 19:12)." The psalm quoted here is the same one cited by Calvin to show that the Roman Church has not acknowledged the scruples of King David where confession is concerned. For further elaboration, see Article 25. (Tappert, *Book of Concord*, 34 and 61–63.)

11. Coetzee, *Age of Iron*, 30; hereafter cited in the text as *Age*.

12. See Attwell, "'Dialogue' and 'Fulfillment'," 176.

13. Vercueil's name may also be a sly reference to the unnamable narrator's name for Mahood, or for himself—"Worm"—throughout Beckett's *The Unnamable*.

14. For one of the more complete accounts of Coetzee's writing in the light of his biographical (both familial and political) context, see Robinson, "Writing as Penance," though Robinson curiously avoids any detailed commentary on religion in Coetzee and leaves Calvinism out of the picture altogether.

15. Coetzee's outspoken vegetarianism, as eventually encoded in the fictional lectures of Elizabeth Costello, is I think also connected at heart to this Calvinist sobriety. See esp. Coetzee, *The Lives of Animals*.

16. Alyda Faber sums up Coetzee's ethical (as opposed to formal) debt to Beckett by citing Coetzee's characterization of Beckett as "an artist possessed by a vision of life without consolation or dignity or promise of grace, in the face of which our only duty—inexplicable and futile of attainment, but a duty nonetheless—is not to lie to ourselves." Cited in Faber, "The Post-Secular Poetics and Ethics of Exposure," 303. Faber is here quoting from Coetzee, *Inner Workings*, 172. Faber's perspective emphasizes at several points in her essay Coetzee's complete secularity, his lack of any "belief," as have others, though I think this stems perhaps from a too-narrow reading of Coetzee's oeuvre: she finally only discusses one novel, and that novel is *Disgrace*. But Faber begins to approach my own perspective when she writes, toward the end of her essay, "In what I have been calling his post-secular, dialogical novel, this silence emerges in the tensions between secular legal and religious discourses which do not settle into belief, but which nevertheless acknowledge the 'uncanny insistence' of religious sensibilities" (314). (Faber is here quoting from Santner, *On the Psychotheology of Everyday Life*, 67.) However, unlike Faber and many others who have written on Coetzee's ethics, even from a "post-secular" perspective, I believe we can be fairly specific about the details of the religious sensibility pressing upon Coetzee, and that the specificity here makes all the difference between invoking a vague and terribly empty notion of the "other" (as Faber does in drawing upon Santner and Boehmer, both of whom depend in turn on Levinas) and invoking historically real, powerful, and persistent religious ideas and practices, like those one finds in and following John Calvin, who appears almost nowhere in the criticism so far devoted to Coetzee.

17. Coetzee, *Dusklands*, 12; hereafter cited in the text as *Dusklands*.

18. Coetzee, *In the Heart of the Country*, 62; hereafter cited in the text as *Heart*.

19. Coetzee, *Waiting for the Barbarians*, 154; hereafter cited in the text as *Waiting*.

20. Kafka's "Before the Law," in the original German "Vor dem Gesetz," was first published as a story in 1916, but it was written as part of the

"In the Cathedral" episode of Kafka's novel *Der Prozess* (*The Trial*), first published in 1925 (see Kafka, *The Trial*, 215–23). In Kafka's novel, a (presumably Catholic) priest recites the parable, though the extended commentary on it he then provides for K. is clearly Talmudic in character, filled with a wide variety of conflicting but equally plausible interpretations of the moral lesson to be learned from the text. And yet the parable ends on a distinct reference to the irrationality (evaluated in human terms) of all divine judgment, an irrationality that points to judgment, and hence salvation, as finally a matter of necessity, or perhaps of a logic that remains beyond human comprehension. Faced with the dilemma of sorting through the competing interpretations, K. observes that what the priest has proven is that not everything the doorkeeper says to the man from the country can be considered true. "'No,' said the priest, 'you don't have to consider everything true, you just have to consider it necessary.' 'A depressing opinion,' said K. 'Lies are made into a universal system.'" Kafka tells us that this was not K.'s "final judgment," and that "he was too tired to take in all of the consequences of the story." But the priest's Catholic-Talmudic moral lesson nevertheless points finally to the Augustinian-Calvinist nature of salvation as a matter that remains inscrutable, even apparently unjust, and hence beyond human influence, since it points to "belief" as never anything other than the belief in necessity.

21. Coetzee, *Life and Times of Michael K*, 151; hereafter cited in the text as *Michael K*.

22. For a compelling case against reading any of Coetzee's work *simply* as "allegory," see Attridge's chapter "Against Allegory," in *J. M. Coetzee and the Ethics of Reading*, 32–64. Attridge's interpretation of Coetzee's work up to *Disgrace* does not deny the allegorical quotient of Coetzee's work—he acknowledges, for example, that *Waiting for the Barbarians* is certainly an allegory of imperialism itself, and that Vercueil is, as even Coetzee himself suggests, in some sense an angel of death. His comments on Coetzee's resort, through a range of narrators, to notions of "the soul," "grace," and "salvation," as well as to Augustine and Pelagius on the notion of grace (but not, oddly, Calvin) are for me exemplary and important (see Attridge, *J. M. Coetzee and the Ethics of Reading*, 180–81). But in the end, allegory emerges in Attridge as the primitive intellect's explanation for inexplicable phenomena, among which are Coetzee's odd novels—very much like the old theory that religion is nothing more than the response of uncomprehending primitive man to lightning and thunder. In so resolutely discounting the deeper power of allegory in Coetzee, Attridge also discounts what is for me the central

swerve or *peripeteia* in Coetzee's writing that brings his incessant meditations on shame and disgrace back toward the Calvinism he would seem to disavow—a point I will take up in greater detail in my conclusion. For the sort of allegorical reading Attridge perhaps wants to avoid, see Head, *J. M. Coetzee*, though Head also has little interest in either religion or secularization in Coetzee.

23. Coetzee, *The Master of Petersburg*, 75; hereafter cited in the text as *Master.*

24. Coetzee, *Slow Man*, 33; hereafter cited in the text as *Slow.*

25. Thackeray, *Vanity Fair*, 746.

26. Heidegger, *Poetry, Language, Thought*, 195, 206.

27. Dante's discussions of allegory occur in the *Convivio* (1307–19) and (without any distinction between allegory in scripture and allegory in worldly poetry) in his "Letter to Can Grande" (1317), though Dante's authorship of the latter has been disputed. But it is clear that Dante borrows his understanding of allegory from Aquinas, for whom the literal or historical signification of Scripture is doubled by a spiritual sense that contains three parts: the allegorical per se, in which the Old Law, including people and events in the Hebrew Bible, becomes a figure for the New Law and its protagonists; the moral, "so far as the things done in Christ, or so far as the things which signify Christ, are types of what we ought to do"; and the anagogical, to the extent that the thing signified "relates to eternal glory," that is, to redemption (see Aquinas, *Summa Theologica*, part 1, question 1, article 10). Indeed, Aquinas's claim that allegory's purpose is rooted in humanity's natural affinity with "material things"—"For God provides for everything according to the capacity of its nature," so that "it is natural to man to attain to intellectual truths through sensible objects, because all our knowledge originates from sense" (part 1, question 1, article 9)—comes close to Coetzee's account of his own theological position (cited earlier), in which attributing intelligence or purpose to the universe should not be considered "retrograde . . . even if the purpose in question may for ever be beyond the grasp of the human intellect and indeed beyond the range of our idea of what might constitute purpose" (Coetzee, *Diary*, 84).

28. The failure of early reviewers of the novel, especially Australian reviewers, to recognize that *The Childhood of Jesus* is, at least on one level, an allegory of Australian immigration policies over the last fifty years is, in a sense, a vindication of Coetzee's whole attitude to a generalizable sense of complicity in evil—his writing is filled with references that often hit too close

to home even to be seen, turning all of us into versions of the magistrate in *Waiting for the Barbarians*. I have found only one review, at an online literary blog, which has squarely addressed the connection, and that review is by a recent immigrant to Australia who expresses his astonishment at the neglect of the link. "After trawling through pages of reviews, I was staggered at the lack of writers connecting the novel to Australia's current political and sociological position." See Daniel Rooke, "The Childhood of Jesus," at HTMLGIANT, n.d., http://www.htmlgiant.com/reviews/the-childhood-of-jesus/. No doubt Coetzee expected as much. But his larger point is surely about a general blindness to complicity in the neglect of refugees the world over.

29. Coetzee, *The Childhood of Jesus*, 178; hereafter cited in the text as *Childhood*.

30. See Agamben, *Homo Sacer*.

31. Cervantes, *Don Quixote*, 67; hereafter cited in the text as *Don Quixote*.

32. In her largely uncomprehending review of *The Childhood of Jesus* for the *New York Times Book Review*, a review that is on the whole very much like the European and Australian reviews in its expressions of perplexity, Joyce Carol Oates bizarrely seems not to recognize that the strange, turbaned figure of Benengeli invoked by Coetzee's Simón as the true author of *Don Quixote* is actually a character in Cervantes' novel. He is the Arab historian to whom Cervantes, posing as mere editor, ascribes the tale. The oddity of Oates's mistake in a sense makes Coetzee's further point for him, that in many ways we already inhabit a Novillan universe in which even celebrated writers can no longer recognize irony when they see it. See Oates, "Saving Grace," 15.

33. Coetzee himself focuses on Beckett's letter to Kaun in a review of Beckett's letters published some four years before the appearance of *The Childhood of Jesus*:

On this subject a revealing document is a letter he wrote, in German, to a young man named Axel Kaun whom he had met during his 1936–1937 tour of Germany. In the frankness with which it addresses his own literary ambitions, this letter to a comparative stranger comes as a surprise: even to McGreevy he is not so ready to explain himself. To Kaun he describes language as a veil that the modern writer needs to tear apart if he wants to reach what lies beyond, even if what lies beyond may only be silence and nothingness. In this respect writers have lagged behind painters and musicians (he points to Beethoven and the silences in his scores). Gertrude Stein, with her minimalist verbal style, has the right idea, whereas Joyce is moving in quite the wrong direction, toward "an apotheosis of the word" (Coetzee, "The Making of Samuel Beckett," sec. 4).

34. Plato, *The Collected Dialogues*, 562–63 (*Symposium*, 211b5–c8); hereafter cited in the text as *Collected Dialogues*.

35. Burkert, *Lore and Science in Ancient Pythagoreanism*, 32, 31; hereafter cited in the text as *Lore and Science*.

36. In Aristotle's words: "But [Plato] agreed with the Pythagoreans in saying that the One is substance and not a predicate of something else; and in saying that the numbers are the causes of the substance of other things, he also agreed with them; but positing a dyad and constructing the infinite out of great and small, instead of treating the infinite as one, is peculiar to him; and so is his view that the numbers exist apart from sensible things, while *they* say that the things themselves are numbers, and do not place the objects of mathematics between Forms and sensible things" (Aristotle, *Complete Works*, 987b23–987b29). Aristotle's critique can be summed up as follows. The Pythagoreans, like other pre-Socratics, produced an unreasonable theory in that they made everything proceed from a single, original substance— the One, which underwent self-limitation and self-division on its own, in which process the formal property of "number" is identical with "substance" and through which no dialectic is possible. Plato improved upon this, but in the end his theory was not much more reasonable. Plato assumed a dyad, made up of substance and the Forms, which was mediated by number (that is, simple magnitude, or "great and small," precisely the concept Coetzee's David seems incapable of grasping). This was for Aristotle better, in the sense that an opposition or dialectic was now possible, out of which greater complexity could be generated, but it was still inadequate. In contrast, Aristotle insisted, as in *Physics*, on the necessity of his fourfold notion of causality, by which things "come to be," that is, undergo natural change: first, the matter out of which a thing comes to be, as the bronze of a statue; second, the "form or archetype," that is, "the definition of the essence, and its genera," just as 2:1 is the definition of the musical octave; third, the "primary source of the change or rest," as "the father is cause of the child"; and fourth, "that for the sake of which a thing is done (αὖ ἕνεκα)," as in when we ask "why is he walking about?" and answer, "To be healthy," which is to say the end or final purpose (Aristotle, *Collected Works*, 194b24–194b35).

37. Butterworth, introduction to Origen, *On First Principles*, x.

38. Origen, *Contra Celsum*, 332; hereafter cited in the text as *Contra Celsum*.

39. Origen, *On First Principles*, 87; hereafter cited in the text as *On First Principles*.

Conclusion

1. See Tomashevsky, "Thematics," 78–87.

2. See Shklovsky, "Art as Technique," 15–18.

3. See Adorno, "Cultural Criticism and Society"; and Adorno, *Aesthetic Theory*, 225–61.

4. See Benjamin, *Origin of German Tragic Drama*.

5. See Said, *Culture and Imperialism*, 169–85. To some extent, it is hard to overlook the fact that almost all of Said's political readings themselves produce allegories of the Palestinian–Israeli conflict, so that the Algerian nationalists belittled by Camus as having no nation to defend become a figure for the Palestinian nationalists dismissed by Golda Meir for the same reason. But even if this is true, it would not vitiate Said's critique, for as Angus Fletcher (see n. 6) adroitly shows, no allegory is ever "pure," and the conflict of authorities built into it are deeply enmeshed in its structure. The real question to ask about Camus, I think, is not whether some notion of absurd parable is designed only to deflect the reader's attention away from real-world politics, as Said seems to believe, but whether Camus also intends—as I am convinced Coetzee does—that his allegories be read as devices for revealing a state of shame and guilt that he could not allow himself to approach in any other way. Many more authors than we tend to imagine need a version of what Fletcher calls "Aesop-language" in order to say what might otherwise not be said.

6. A. Fletcher, *Allegory*, 8; hereafter cited in the text as *Allegory*.

7. Capote, *In Cold Blood*, viii.

8. Attridge, *J. M. Coetzee and the Ethics of Reading*, 39; hereafter cited in the text as *Coetzee*.

9. For a rather different take on the appearance of the animal "scapegoat" as "scapegrace" (that is, not an innocent who absorbs human guilt, but rather a sinner who has lost God's grace) in Kafka and Coetzee, see Danta, "'Like a dog . . . like a lamb'." In Danta's reading of *Disgrace*, for example, David Lurie moves from the former trope to the latter in his concluding role euthanizing unwanted dogs. Though Danta's is an interesting juxtaposition,

this transformation in Lurie for me introduces a kind of misplaced certainty into Coetzee's neo-Calvinist ethics. In the end, I think, Lurie inhabits not so much a condition in which he knows he has, through his own choices, lost— or 'scaped—the grace of God, but the potentially more isolating condition in which he understands that God's grace was never his to win or lose in the first place. Lurie is no better off, no more in control of his fate than are the impotent dogs that are to be euthanized, for which, ultimately, he can do nothing.

10. Mann, *Reflections of a Nonpolitical Man*, 394.

11. Forster, *Passage to India*, 306.

12. Kafka, *The Trial*, 215.

13. Proust's remarkable narratives owe much not only to Bergson's notions of duration and unconscious memory, but also to Bergson's understanding of "creative evolution," in which God "is unceasing life, action, freedom" and creation something "we experience in ourselves" (see Bergson, *Creative Evolution*, 248). In all this, Bergson borrows much from Spinoza, and though liberal Catholic modernism found great affinity with Bergson, the Catholic Church itself finally denounced what it took to be the philosopher's Spinozistic pantheism. (That Bergson was a Jew surely did not help his cause in many circles of the Church.) Contrary to Beckett's view, that is, Proust's salvific moments may not really be quite so accidental and fugitive as they at first appear to consciousness. They are, on another level, built into the nature of things, the effects of a vital force that includes the human imagination at its core. This is not, I think, exactly what Beckett imagined his own work to be about.

Ackerly, Chris. *Demented Particulars: The Annotated* Murphy. Tallahassee, FL: Journal of Beckett Studies Books, 1998.

Ackerly, C. J., and S. E. Gontarski, eds. *The Grove Companion to Samuel Beckett.* New York: Grove Press, 2004.

Adorno, Theodor W. *Aesthetic Theory.* Edited by Gretel Adorno and Rolf Tiedemann. Translated by Robert Hullot-Kentor. Minneapolis: University of Minnesota Press, 1997.

———. "Cultural Criticism and Society." In *Prisms*, Studies in Contemporary German Social Thought, translated by Samuel Weber and Shierry Weber, 17–34. Cambridge, MA: MIT Press, 1984.

———. "Extorted Reconciliation: On Georg Lukács' Realism in Our Time." In *Notes to Literature*, edited by Rolf Tiedemann, translated by Shierry Weber Nicholsen, 1:216–40. New York: Columbia University Press, 1991.

———. "Notes on Kafka." In *Prisms*, Studies in Contemporary German Social Thought, translated by Samuel Weber and Shierry Weber, 243–71. Cambridge, MA: MIT Press, 1984.

Agamben, Giorgio. *Homo Sacer: Sovereign Power and Bare Life.* Translated by Daniel Heller-Roazen. Stanford, CA: Stanford University Press, 1998.

Altizer, Thomas J. J., and William Hamilton. *Radical Theology and the Death of God.* Indianapolis: Bobbs-Merrill, 1966.

Aquinas, Thomas. *Summa Theologica.* Translated by Fathers of the English Dominican Province. 3 vols. New York: Benziger Brothers, 1947.

Aristotle. *The Complete Works of Aristotle.* Revised Oxford Translation. Bollingen Series 71:2, edited by Jonathan Barnes. 2 vols. Princeton: Princeton University Press, 1984.

Attridge, Derek. *J. M. Coetzee and the Ethics of Reading.* Chicago: University of Chicago Press, 2004.

Attwell, David. "'Dialogue' and 'Fulfillment' in J. M Coetzee's *Age of Iron.*" In *Writing South Africa: Literature, Apartheid, and Democracy, 1970–1995*, edited by Derek Attridge and Rosemary Jolly, 166–79. Cambridge: Cambridge University Press, 1998.

———. "Race in *Disgrace.*" *Interventions* 4, no. 3 (2002): 331–41.

Auerbach, Erich. *Mimesis: The Representation of Reality in Western Literature.* Translated by Willard R. Trask. Princeton: Princeton University Press, 1974. First published in German, 1946.

Augustine. *The City of God against the Pagans.* Edited and translated by R. W. Dyson. Cambridge: Cambridge University Press, 2011.

———. *Four Anti-Pelagian Writings: On Nature and Grace, On the Proceedings of Pelagius, On the Predestination of the Saints, On the Gift of Perseverance.* Translated by John A. Mourant and William J. Collinge. Washington, DC: Catholic University of America Press, 1992.

Bair, Deirdre. *Samuel Beckett.* New York: Harcourt Brace Jovanovich, 1978.

Barthes, Roland. "To Write: An Intransitive Verb?" In *The Structuralist Controversy: The Languages of Criticism and the Sciences of Man*, edited by Richard Macksey and Eugenio Donato, 134–56. Baltimore: Johns Hopkins University Press, 1979.

———. *Writing Degree Zero.* Translated by Annette Lavers and Colin Smith. New York: Hill and Wang, 1977.

Baudelaire, Charles. *Baudelaire.* Edited by Francis Scarfe. Harmondsworth: Penguin Books, 1961.

Beckett, Samuel. *The Letters of Samuel Beckett.* Vol. 1, *1929–1940.* Edited by Martha Dow Fehsenfeld and Lois More Overbeck. Cambridge: Cambridge University Press, 2009.

———. *L'Innommable.* Paris: Éditions de Minuit, 1953.

———. *L'Innommable.* Nouvelle édition. Paris: Éditions de Minuit, 1971.

———. *Malone meurt.* Paris: Éditions de Minuit, 1951.

———. *Molloy.* Paris: Éditions de Minuit, 1951.

———. *Murphy.* New York: Grove Press, 1970.

———. *The Selected Works of Samuel Beckett.* Edited by Paul Auster. 4 vols. New York: Grove Press, 2010.

Bellah, Robert. *Beyond Belief: Essays on Religion in a Post-Traditional World.* New York: Harper and Row, 1970.

Benjamin, Walter. "On the Mimetic Faculty." In *Selected Writings*, vol. 2, *1927–1934*, edited by Michael W. Jennings, Howard Eiland, and Gary Smith, translated by Edmund Jephcott, 720–22. Cambridge, MA: Belknap Press, 1999.

———. *The Origin of German Tragic Drama.* Translated by John Osborne. London: New Left Books, 1977.

Berger, Peter. *The Sacred Canopy: Elements of a Sociological Theory of Religion.* Garden City, NY: Doubleday, 1967.

Bergson, Henri. *Creative Evolution.* Translated by Arthur Mitchell. Mineola, NY: Dover, 1998.

Bergsten, Gunilla. *Thomas Mann's Doctor Faustus: The Sources and Structure of the Novel.* Translated by Krishna Winston. Chicago: University of Chicago Press, 1969. First published in German, 1963.

Bewes, Timothy. *The Event of Postcolonial Shame.* Princeton: Princeton University Press, 2010.

Blumenberg, Hans. *The Legitimacy of the Modern Age.* Translated by Robert M. Wallace. Cambridge, MA: MIT Press, 1985. First published in German, 1966.

Boehmer, E. "Not Saying Sorry, Not Speaking Pain." *Interventions* 4, no. 3 (2002): 342–51.

Bonhoeffer, Dietrich. *Letters and Papers from Prison.* New York: Macmillan, 1962.

Brod, Max. *Franz Kafka: A Biography.* New York: Schocken Books, 1947.

Brooks, Peter. *Reading for the Plot: Design and Intention in Narrative.* Cambridge, MA: Harvard University Press, 1992.

Bruce, Steve, ed. *Religion and Modernization: Sociologists and Historians Debate the Secularization Thesis.* Oxford: Clarendon Press, 1992.

Bultmann, Rudolf. "The Idea of God and Modern Man." Translated by Robert W. Funk. In *Translating Theology into the Modern Age*, edited by Robert W. Funk, 83–95. New York: Torchbooks, 1965.

Burkert, Walter. *Lore and Science in Ancient Pythagoreanism.* Translated by Edwin L. Minar Jr. Cambridge, MA: Harvard University Press, 1972.

Calvin, John. *Institutes of the Christian Religion.* Edited by John T. McNeill. Translated by Ford Lewis Battles. Library of Christian Classics 20. Philadelphia: Westminster Press, 1960.

Capote, Truman. *In Cold Blood.* New York: Modern Library, 2013.

Casanova, Pascale. *Samuel Beckett: Anatomy of a Literary Revolution.* Translated by Gregory Elliott. London: Verso, 2006. First published in French, 1997.

Cervantes, Miguel de. *Don Quixote.* Edited by Joseph R. Jones and Kenneth Douglas. Translated by John Ormsby. New York: Norton, 1981.

Coetzee, J. M. *Age of Iron.* New York: Penguin Books, 1998. First published 1990.

———. *The Childhood of Jesus.* London: Harvill Secker, 2013.

———. *Diary of a Bad Year.* New York: Penguin Books, 2008. First published 2007.

———. *Disgrace.* New York: Penguin Books, 2000. First published 1999.

———. *Doubling the Point: Essays and Interviews.* Edited by David Attwell. Cambridge, MA: Harvard University Press, 1992.

———. *Dusklands.* New York: Penguin Books, 1996. First published 1974.

———. *Elizabeth Costello.* New York: Penguin Books, 2004. First published 2003.

———. *Foe.* New York: Penguin Books, 1987. First published 1986.

———. *Inner Workings: Literary Essays 2000–2005.* London: Harvill Secker, 2007.

———. *In the Heart of the Country.* New York: Penguin Books, 1982. First published 1977.

———. *Life and Times of Michael K.* New York: Penguin Books, 1985. First published 1983.

———. "The Making of Samuel Beckett," *New York Review of Books* 56, no. 7 (April 30, 2009): 13–16.

———. *The Master of Petersburg.* New York: Penguin Books, 1995. First published 1994.

———. *Scenes from Provincial Life: Boyhood, Youth, Summertime.* New York: Penguin Books, 2012. First published 1997, 2002, and 2009, respectively.

———. *Slow Man.* New York: Penguin Books, 2006. First published 2005.

———. *Waiting for the Barbarians.* New York: Penguin Books, 1982. First published 1980.

Coetzee, J. M., with Marjorie Garber, Peter Singer, Wendy Doniger, and Barbara Smuts. *The Lives of Animals.* Edited by Amy Gutman. Princeton: Princeton University Press, 1999.

Cox, Harvey. *The Secular City.* New York: Macmillan, 1965.

Danta, Chris. "'Like a dog . . . like a lamb': Becoming Sacrificial Animal in Kafka and Coetzee." *New Literary History* 38, no. 4 (2007): 721–37.

Davie, Grace. *Religion in Modern Europe: A Memory Mutates.* Oxford: Oxford University Press, 2000.

Dawkins, Richard. *The God Delusion.* New York: Houghton Mifflin Harcourt, 2006.

Delitzsch, Franz. *Biblischer Commentar über Die Poetischen Bücher des Alten Testaments.* Leipzig: Dörffling und Franke, 1873.

Dobbelaere, Karl. "Secularization: A Multi-Dimensional Concept." *Current Sociology* 29, no. 2 (1981): 1–216.

Doody, Margaret Anne. *The True Story of the Novel*. Rutgers, NJ: Rutgers University Press, 1997.

Eagleton, Terry. *Culture and the Death of God*. New Haven: Yale University Press, 2014.

Eliot, George. *Middlemarch*. Boston: Houghton Mifflin, 1968.

Faber, Alyda. "The Post-Secular Poetics and Ethics of Exposure in J. M. Coetzee's *Disgrace*." *Literature and Theology* 23, no. 3 (2009): 303–16.

Fletcher, Angus. *Allegory: The Theory of a Symbolic Mode*. Ithaca, NY: Cornell University Press, 1986.

Fletcher, John. *Samuel Beckett's Art*. London: Chatto & Windus, 1967.

Forster, E. M. *A Passage to India*. New York: Penguin Books, 2005.

Friedlander, Judith. Letter to the editors. *New York Times Book Review*, December 19, 1982.

Frye, Northrop. *The Secular Scripture: A Study of the Structure of Romance*. Cambridge, MA: Harvard University Press, 1976.

Geulincx, Arnold. *Ethics, with Samuel Beckett's Notes*. Edited by Hans van Ruler, Anthony Uhlmann, and Martin Wilson. Translated by Martin Wilson. Brill's Studies in Intellectual History 146. Leiden: Brill, 2006.

Goldberg, Oskar. *Die Wirklichkeit der Hebräer: Einleitung in das System des Pentateuch*. Berlin: David, 1925.

Goody, Jack. "From Oral to Written: An Anthropological Breakthrough in Storytelling." In *The Novel*, 2 vols., edited by Franco Moretti, 1:3–36. Princeton: Princeton University Press, 2006.

Habermas, Jürgen. "Faith and Knowledge." *Süddeutsche Zeitung*, October 15, 2001. English translation by Kermit Snelson available at http://www.nettime.org/Lists-Archives/nettime-l-0111/msg00100.html.

———. "Modernity: An Unfinished Project." In *Habermas and the Unfinished Project of Modernity: Critical Essays on the Philosophical Discourse of Modernity*, edited by Maurizio Passerin d'Entrèves and Seyla Benhabib, 38–55. Cambridge, MA: MIT Press, 1997.

———. *Nachmetaphysisches Denken*. Frankfurt am Main: Suhrkamp Verlag, 1988.

———. "Transcendence from Within, Transcendence in this World." Translated by Eric Crump and Peter P. Kenny. In *Religion and Rationality: Essays on Reason, God, and Modernity*, edited by Eduardo Mendieta, 67–94. Cambridge, MA: MIT Press, 2002.

———. "Walter Benjamin: Consciousness-Raising or Rescuing Critique?" In *Philosophical-Political Profiles*, translated by Frederick G. Lawrence, 129–63. Cambridge, MA: MIT Press, 1983.

Hardy, Thomas. *Jude the Obscure*. New York: NAL Penguin, 1961.

Harris, Sam. *The End of Faith: Religion, Terror, and the Future of Reason*. New York: W. W. Norton, 2005.

———. *Free Will*. New York: Free Press, 2012.

Head, Dominic. *J. M. Coetzee*. Cambridge Studies in African and Caribbean Literature. Cambridge: Cambridge University Press, 1997.

Heidegger, Martin. "The Age of the World Picture." In *The Question Concerning Technology and Other Essays*, translated by William Lovitt, 115–54. New York: Harper and Row, 1977.

———. *Identität und Differenz*. Pfullingen: Verlag Günther Neske, 1957.

———. *Identity and Difference*. Translated by Joan Stambaugh. Incl. German text. Chicago: University of Chicago Press, 1969.

———. *Poetry, Language, Thought*. Translated by Albert Hofstadter. New York: Perennial Classics, 2001.

Hitchens, Christopher. *God is Not Great: How Religion Poisons Everything*. New York: Twelve, 2007.

Hofmannsthal, Hugo von. "A Letter" (The Lord Chandos Letter). *The Lord Chandos Letter and Other Writings*, 117–18. Selected and translated by Joel Rotenberg. New York: New York Review of Books, 2005.

———. *Der Tor und der Tod*. Leipzig: Insel, 1906.

Hungerford, Amy. *Postmodern Belief: American Literature and Religion since 1960*. Princeton: Princeton University Press, 2010.

Hunt, Lynn. *Inventing Human Rights: A History*. New York: W. W. Norton, 2008.

Hunter, J. Paul. *The Reluctant Pilgrim*. Baltimore: Johns Hopkins University Press, 1966.

Ireton, Sean. "Die Transformation zweier Gregors: Thomas Manns *Der Erwählte* und Kafkas *Die Verwandlung*." *Monatshefte* 90, no. 1 (1998): 34–48.

Israel, Jonathan I. *Radical Enlightenment: Philosophy and the Making of Modernity, 1650–1750*. Oxford: Oxford University Press, 2002.

Joyce, James. *A Portrait of the Artist as a Young Man*. Edited by Chester Anderson. New York: Penguin Books, 1977.

Kafka, Franz. *Der Prozess*. Frankfurt am Main: S. Fischer Verlag, 1990.

———. *The Trial: A New Translation Based on the Restored Text*. Translated by Breon Mitchell. New York: Schocken Books, 1998.

Kazantzakis, Nikos. *The Last Temptation of Christ.* Translated by Peter A. Bien. New York: Simon and Schuster, 1960.

Kenner, Hugh. *Samuel Beckett: A Critical Study.* Berkeley: University of California Press, 1973.

Knowlson, James. *Damned to Fame: The Life of Samuel Beckett.* New York: Simon and Schuster, 1966.

Kontje, Todd. *Thomas Mann's World: Empire, Race, and the Jewish Question.* Ann Arbor: University of Michigan Press, 2011.

Lubac, Henri de. *Proudhon et la christianisme.* Paris: Éditions du Seuil, 1945.

Lübbe, Hermann. *Säkularisierung: Geschichte einen ideenpolitischen Begriffs.* Freiburg: Alber, 1965.

Luckmann, Thomas. *The Invisible Religion.* New York: Macmillan, 1967.

Lukács, Georg. *The Meaning of Contemporary Realism.* Translated by John Mander and Necke Mander. London: Merlin Press, 1979. First published in German, 1957.

———. *The Theory of the Novel.* Translated by Anna Bostock. Cambridge, MA: MIT Press, 1971.

Luther, Martin. *Luthers Werke in Auswahl.* Edited by Otto Clemen. 8 vols. Berlin: Walter de Gruyter, 1966.

Mann, Thomas. *Doctor Faustus: The Life of the Composer Adrian Leverkühn as told by a Friend.* Translated by John E. Woods. New York: Vintage Books, 1999.

———. *Doktor Faustus: Das Leben des deutschen Tonsetzers Adrian Leverkühn von einem Freunde.* Frankfurt am Main: S. Fischer Verlag, 1980.

———. *Der Erwählte.* Frankfurt am Main: S. Fischer Verlag, 1980.

———. *The Holy Sinner.* Translated by H. T. Lowe-Porter. Berkeley: University of California Press, 1992.

———. "Homage." In Franz Kafka, *The Castle,* translated by Willa Muir and Edwin Muir, ix– xvii. New York: Schocken Books, 1974.

———. *Joseph and His Brothers.* Translated by John E. Woods. New York: Knopf, 2005.

———. *Joseph und seiner Brüder.* Published as:
　Die Geschichten Jaakobs. Berlin: S. Fischer, 1933.
　Der Junge Joseph. Berlin: S. Fischer, 1934.
　Joseph in Ägypten. Vienna: Berman-Fischer, 1936.
　Joseph, der Ernährer. Stockholm: Berman-Fischer, 1943.

———. *Reflections of a Nonpolitical Man.* Translated by Walter D. Morris. New York: Ungar, 1987.

Marquard, Odo. *Schwierigkeiten mit der Geschichtsphilosophie: Aufsätze.* Frankfurt am Main: Suhrkamp Verlag, 1982.

McClain, William H. "Irony and Belief in Thomas Mann's *Der Erwählte*." *Monatshefte* 43, no. 7 (1951): 319–23.

McClure, John A. *Partial Faiths: Postsecular Fiction in the Age of Pynchon and Morrison.* Athens: University of Georgia Press, 2007.

McDonald, Peter D. "Disgrace Effects." *Interventions* 4, no. 3 (2002): 321–30.

McKeon, Michael. *The Origins of the English Novel, 1600–1740.* Baltimore: Johns Hopkins University Press, 1987.

Miller, J. Hillis. *The Ethics of Reading: Kant, de Man, Eliot, Trollope, James, and Benjamin.* Wellek Lectures at the University of California, Irvine. New York: Columbia University Press, 1987.

Miller, Perry, ed. *The American Puritans: Their Prose and Poetry.* Garden City, NY: Doubleday Anchor Books, 1956.

Moretti, Franco. "Serious Century." In *The Novel*, 2 vols., edited by Franco Moretti, 1:364–400. Princeton: Princeton University Press, 2006.

Neuman, Justin. *Fiction beyond Secularism.* Evanston, IL: Northwestern University Press, 2014.

Nussbaum, Martha. *Love's Knowledge: Essays on Philosophy and Literature.* New York: Oxford University Press, 1992.

Oates, Joyce Carol. "Saving Grace." *New York Times*, September 1, 2013, Sunday Book Review, BR1, 14–15.

Origen. *Contra Celsum.* Translated by Henry Chadwick. Cambridge: Cambridge University Press, 1980.

———. *On First Principles.* Translated by G. W. Butterworth, from the text prepared by Paul Koetschau. Eugene, OR: Wipf and Stock, 2012; reprint of SPCK Publishers, 1936.

Pascal, Blaise. *Pensées and Other Writings.* Edited by Anthony Levi. Translated by Honor Levi. Oxford: Oxford University Press, 2008.

Pecora, Vincent P. *Secularization and Cultural Criticism: Religion, Nation, and Modernity.* Chicago: University of Chicago Press, 2006.

Plato. *The Collected Dialogues.* Edited by Edith Hamilton and Huntington Cairns. Translated by Lane Cooper et al. Bollingen Series 71. Princeton: Princeton University Press, 1989.

Proudhon, Pierre-Joseph. *Système des contradictions économiques: ou, Philosophie de la Misère.* 2 vols. Paris: Libre Internationale, 1867.

Robbe-Grillet, Alain. *La Jalousie.* Paris: Les Éditions de Minuit, 1957.

Robinson, Forrest G. "Writing as Penance: National Guilt and J. M. Coetzee." *Arizona Quarterly* 68, no. 1 (2012): 1–54.

Robinson, John A. T. *Honest to God.* London: SCM Press, 1963.

Röcke, Werner, ed. *Thomas Mann, Doktor Faustus, 1947–1997.* Bern: Peter Lang, 2001.

Rushdie, Salman. "May 2000: J. M. Coetzee." In *Step Across This Line: Collected Non-Fiction 1992–2002*, 338–40. London: Vintage, 2003.

Said, Edward. *Culture and Imperialism*. New York: Alfred A. Knopf, 1993.

Santner, E. L. *On the Psychotheology of Everyday Life: Reflections on Freud and Rosenzweig*. Chicago: University of Chicago Press, 2001.

Scholem, Gershom. *Walter Benjamin: The Story of a Friendship*. Translated by Harry Zohn. New York: Schocken, 1981.

Shakespeare, William. "The Tragedy of Julius Caesar." In *The Riverside Shakespeare*, edited by G. Blakemore Evans, 1105–132. Boston: Houghton Mifflin, 1974.

Shklovsky, Victor. "Art as Technique." In *Russian Formalist Criticism: Four Essays*, translated by Lee T. Lemon and Marion Reis, 3–24. Lincoln: University of Nebraska Press, 1965.

Starr, G. A. *Defoe and Spiritual Autobiography*. Princeton: Princeton University Press, 1965.

Stendhal (Henri Marie Beyle). *Scarlet and Black*. Translated by Margaret R. B. Shaw. Harmondsworth: Penguin Books, 1979.

Syme, Ronald. *Sallust*. Berkeley: University of California Press, 2002. First published 1964.

Tappert, Theodore G., ed. *The Book of Concord: The Confessions of the Evangelical Lutheran Church*. Translated by Theodore G. Tappert, in collaboration with Jaroslav Pelikan, Robert H. Fischer, and Arthur C. Piepkorn. Philadelphia: Fortress Press, 1959.

Taylor, Charles. *A Secular Age*. Cambridge, MA: Belknap Press, 2007.

Thackeray, William Makepeace. *Vanity Fair*. New York: Washington Square Press, 1968.

Thomas, Ronald. "The Novel and the Afterlife: The End of the Line in Bunyan and Beckett." *Modern Philology* 86, no. 4 (1989): 385–97.

Tillich, Paul. *Systematic Theology*. 3 vols. Chicago: University of Chicago Press, 1963.

Tomashevsky, Boris. "Thematics." In *Russian Formalist Criticism: Four Essays*, translated by Lee T. Lemon and Marion Reis, 61–95. Lincoln: University of Nebraska Press, 1965.

Tucker, David. *Samuel Beckett and Arnold Geulincx: Tracing "A Literary Fantasia."* London: Continuum, 2012.

Tylor, E. B. *Primitive Society: Researches into the Development of Mythology, Philosophy, Religion, Language, Art, and Custom*. 2 vols. New York: Henry Holt, 1889.

Uhlmann, Anthony. *Samuel Beckett and the Philosophical Image*. Cambridge: Cambridge University Press, 2006.

Vaget, Hans Rudolf. *Seelenzauber: Thomas Mann und die Musik.* Frankfurt am Main: S. Fischer Verlag, 2006.

Vahanian, Gabriel. *The Death of God: The Culture of Our Post-Christian Era.* New York: Braziller, 1961.

Van den Hemel, Ernest. "History and the Vertical Canon: Calvin's *Institutes* and Beckett." In *How the West was Won: Essays on Literary Imagination, the Canon, and the Christian Middle Ages for Burcht Pranger,* edited by Willemien Otten, Arjo Vanderjagt, and Hent de Vries, 39–54. Leiden: Brill, 2010.

Van Hulle, Dirk. "Figures of Script: The Development of Beckett's Short Prose and the 'Aesthetic of Inaudibilities.'" In *A Companion to Samuel Beckett,* edited by S. E. Gontarski, 244–62. Chichester, UK: Wiley-Blackwell, 2010.

Vattimo, Gianni. *The End of Modernity: Nihilism and Hermeneutics in Post-Modern Culture.* Translated by Jon Snyder. Cambridge: Polity Press, 1988.

Wallace, David Foster. *The Pale King.* New York: Back Bay Books, 2012.

Watt, Ian. *The Rise of the Novel.* Berkeley: University of California Press, 1957.

Watt, W. Montgomery. *Free Will and Predestination in Early Islam.* London: Luzac, 1948.

Weber, Max. *The Protestant Ethic and the Spirit of Capitalism.* Translated by Talcott Parsons. London: Routledge, 2001. First published in German, 1904.

Weber, Samuel. *Mass Mediauras: Form, Technics, Media.* Stanford, CA: Stanford University Press, 1996.

Werner, Alfred. "Thomas Mann's Failure." In *Congress Weekly* 15 (December 13, 1948): 11–14.

Wimmer, Ruprecht. *Kommentar.* Vol. 2 of Thomas Mann, *Doktor Faustus,* Große kommentierte Frankfurter Ausgabe: Werke, Briefe, Tagebücher, 2 vols. (Band 10.1 and 10.2). Edited by Heinrich Detering, Eckhard Heftrich, Hermann Kurzke, Terence J. Reed, Thomas Sprecher, Hans R. Vaget, and Ruprecht Wimmer. Frankfurt am Main: S. Fischer Verlag, 2007.

Wood, Rupert. "Murphy, Beckett; Geulincx, God." *Journal of Beckett Studies* 2, no. 2 (1993): 27–51.

Woolf, Virginia. *To the Lighthouse.* Orlando, FL: Harcourt, 2005.

VINCENT P. PECORA

is the Gordon B. Hinckley Professor of
British Literature and Culture
at the University of Utah.
He is the author of a number of books, including
Secularization and Cultural Criticism:
Religion, Nation, and Modernity.